A TEXTBOOK ON
FOREIGN EXCHANGE

A TEXTBOOK ON FOREIGN EXCHANGE

BY

PAUL EINZIG

SECOND EDITION

MACMILLAN

London · Melbourne · Toronto

ST MARTIN'S PRESS

New York

1969

First edition 1966
Second edition 1969

Published by
MACMILLAN AND CO LTD
Little Essex Street London WC 2
and also at Bombay Calcutta and Madras
Macmillan South Africa (Publishers) Pty Ltd Johannesburg
The Macmillan Company of Australia Pty Ltd Melbourne
The Macmillan Company of Canada Ltd Toronto
St Martin's Press Inc New York
Gill and Macmillan Ltd Dublin

Library of Congress catalog card no 66–13528

Printed in Great Britain by
R. & R. CLARK, LTD
Edinburgh

To

SIR THEODORE GREGORY

CONTENTS

Read

vii

PREFACE TO THE SECOND EDITION

THE two years that passed since the publication of the first edition of this book witnessed many changes, and I took the opportunity of its reprinting for bringing it up to date. The devaluation of sterling made it necessary to make a number of alterations in addition to the obvious need for adjusting the figures relating to parities and exchange rates. The lessons taught by the unsuccessful defence of sterling are duly noted in this edition. It was also necessary to cover some institutional changes, such as the spectacular expansion of the Euro- currency markets and its increasing use by American banks as a secondary money market, the development of a market in dollar certificates of deposits, etc.

After some hesitation I decided to omit from this edition my table of parities and support points The devaluation of sterling, the Danish Krone and the Finnish Mark, which occurred since the publication of the table, would have made it necessary to carry out extensive revision, and it appears highly probable that there will be other devaluations that would make the revised table out of date. When I asked a leading banker whether it would be worth while to take the time and trouble needed for revising it his answer was in the negative. "Those who are interested in the table are familiar with its figures", he told me, "while those who are not familiar with them are not interested in them."

P. E.

120 CLIFFORD'S INN,
  LONDON, E.C.4
October, 1968

ix

PREFACE TO THE FIRST EDITION

I HAVE undertaken to write this book in response to suggestions both from banking and academic quarters. It has been felt for some time that post-War students of foreign exchange are not served adequately by the existing literature on the subject. Before the War there existed some excellent textbooks — among others those of Spalding, Thomas, Evitt and Crump — but, even though some of them were revised as recently as the early 'sixties, it is widely felt that their material has not been brought sufficiently up to date. Their authors deserve credit for the excellent pre-War material they had produced, and their omission to cover the changes that have occurred since the War is understandable. My criticism of their revisions is tempered by my knowledge from personal experience how reluctant authors are, when revising their books, to jettison obsolete but otherwise satisfactory material. There is always a strong temptation, reinforced by the law of inertia, to retain as much as possible. In any case, owing to the high post-War cost of major alterations in the setting, publishers always insist on keeping changes as far as possible within the existing pagination, emulating Procrustes in forcing their victims into a predetermined space.

The best way of breaking away from pre-War material is to try to forget about it altogether and start from scratch instead of trying to patch up a pre-War book. Having regard to the far-reaching changes both in the basic foreign exchange system and its techniques and practices, as well as in the background against which that system operates, it seems that nothing short of a completely new book with a genuinely post-War approach, and written in a post-War mentality, can meet post-War requirements.

This task can best be undertaken by someone who has not written a textbook on foreign exchange before the War and is

x

not, therefore, mentally committed to the pre-War system. While I am the author of a number of pre-War books covering specific aspects of foreign exchange such as forward exchange, gold movements, exchange control, etc., I never attempted until now to produce a comprehensive book on foreign exchange covering the entire subject. Being thus "uncommitted" to the pre-War system I feel justified in making this attempt to fill a genuine gap in post-War financial literature.

To illustrate the imperative need for breaking with the past, let it be sufficient to quote one or two characteristic survivals of pre-War facts in post-War editions of pre-War textbooks. Some authors, in their arithmetical illustrations of post-War practices, continue to quote pre-War exchange rates. This is admittedly a minor matter, but surely students are entitled to something more up to date than calculations based on rates such as $4·86 to the pound or 124 francs to the pound, even if the method of calculation is the same whatever be the rates.

All post-War editions of pre-War textbooks contain lengthy and detailed descriptions of the operation of the gold points mechanism, illustrated with a multitude of examples for calculating gold points. If there were a possibility of an eventual return to that system — as indeed there had appeared to be during the 'thirties — it would be justified to devote some space to it, in spite of the fact that at the time of writing it is of purely historical interest. Since, however, the trend of evolution does not point in that direction — even the so-called gold standard advocated by General de Gaulle only envisages more extensive gold transactions between monetary authorities in which gold point calculations would play no part — it would be useless to burden students, and others interested in the foreign exchange system as it operates today, with a detailed treatment of such obsolete material.

I have also felt justified in excluding material, which occupies a high proportion of the space in pre-War textbooks and even in their post-War editions, dealing with international transfers through transactions in various types of bills of exchange, letters of credit, travellers' cheques, mail transfers, etc. These practices still exist, but their sum total constitutes an infinitesimal proportion of present-day turnover in foreign exchanges. An extreme instance of the survival of obsolete pre-War material in post-War books is that of descriptions of the practice of guaranteed mail transfers, a term which conveys nothing to the post-War generation. Foreign exchange transacted in the form of telegraphic transfers is now of overwhelming importance, and it is with this type of transaction that the book is mainly concerned. There is more than enough material available about the other types of transactions in so far as they are still of some limited interest.

While inclusion of obsolete pre-War material is open to criticism merely because it unnecessarily complicates a subject which is becoming increasingly involved in any case through new developments, the inadequacy of the treatment of these new developments that have occurred since the War is a more substantial ground for complaint. Until quite recently none of the post-War editions of pre-War textbooks attempted to cover the Euro-currency market adequately, and none of them have even mentioned the inter-bank sterling market, even though these two markets form an essential part of the post-War markets. What is even more important, the technique and theory of the support points mechanism has never been described and analysed adequately. Yet it forms the foundations of the post-War system of foreign exchange.

Generally speaking, this book is confined to the description of what we may call the Anglo-Saxon method of foreign exchange — transactions arranged through a network of private telephone lines within the local markets and through long-distance telephone calls and teleprinters between markets in different countries. I only make casual reference to the Continental system of meeting places between foreign exchange dealers, as even in the financial centres where it exists it is of relatively small importance compared with dealings by telephone and telex.

This book is addressed primarily to students of banking who work, or intend to work, in foreign exchange departments. I am aware that most of those with actual experience in dealing rooms must have forgotten more about the techniques described here than anyone without practical experience can possibly know about them. Nevertheless, it may possibly help them to find the rules, which they follow almost instinctively, defined, described and analysed. Moreover, as practices in foreign exchange departments are far from uniform, my survey, which is based on information received from a large number of banks, may be found to be of some use even to practical operators whose experience is confined, after all, to practices in their own banks.

A textbook based on post-War conditions is likely to be found useful also by bankers who have no direct experience in dealers' rooms but take an interest in the practices employed there, being ultimately responsible for the results of their foreign exchange departments. Businessmen of all kinds concerned with foreign exchange transactions also stand to benefit from familiarising themselves with the post-War system.

Last but by no means least, students of economics in general and those specialising in monetary economics in particular may find it advantageous to bring their knowledge of the foreign exchange system up to date. I have kept exchange arithmetic to a minimum. One of the main objects of this book is to try to bridge the gap between the theory and the practice of foreign exchange by making the technique of the post-War system more easily accessible to economists who would fight shy of textbooks which abound in elementary exercises in commercial arithmetic. There are many good books which cover exchange arithmetic very adequately and I had no wish to duplicate their material.

I tried to present the practical material in such a way as to be meaningful also to students of theory. In the sphere of foreign exchange the dividing line between theory and technique is often very indistinct. Many technical points have profound theoretical implications, and in the course of preparing this book I often caught myself on the point of trespassing on the preserves of my next book, *Theories of Exchange Rates*.

I have made extensive use of published material in so far as it is relevant to post-War conditions. A list of them appears in the Bibliography. I am particularly grateful to the authors of two post-War booklets, *The New York Foreign Exchange Market* by Alan R. Holmes, published by the Federal Reserve Bank of New York, and *Foreign Exchange* by G. Pelli, published by the Swiss Bank Corporation. Both contain a great deal of interesting information but are tantalisingly brief. A German textbook, *Devisenhandel* by Helmut Lipfert, is, as far as I know, the only detailed description of post-War practices in any language. But since it is based very largely on conditions in Germany its material, excellent as it is, would be of limited use to English-speaking students, apart altogether from the obstacle of the language. In his Preface the author acknowledged very generously that my pre-War book on forward exchange had influenced his book more than any other non-German publication. (His book appeared before the publication of my post-War *Dynamic Theory of Forward Exchange*). I am happy to repay his compliment with interest by admitting that this book owes more to his book than to any other publication on foreign exchange in any language.

I had to obtain, however, by far the greater part of my material in the hard way, by means of extensive field research in foreign exchange departments. I hardly ever returned from my visits empty-handed. In the course of my numerous long conversations with foreign exchange dealers I almost invariably discovered some new fact or some new interpretation of familiar facts. The few remaining survivors among pre-War dealers gave me the benefit of their comparisons between pre-War and post-War practices. And dealers of the younger generation, with no pre-War experience, enabled me to familiarise myself with the system entirely from a post-War angle.

The more time I spend in foreign exchange departments the more I admire those engaged in the working of that highly involved and sensitive mechanism, the foreign exchange market. Dealers must surely be supermen to be equal to their difficult task. Their familiarity with the complicated techniques, combined with their ability to think of several things at the same moment, and, above all, to take lightning-quick decisions involving deals in amounts of millions of pounds, fills me with awe. It also fills me with apprehension. It is my nightmare that sooner or later some foreign exchange dealer, who is both able and willing to write about his trade and who possesses an analytical mind, might come to acquire the necessary theoretical and historical background enabling him to see his work as part of the economic system. When that occurs I fear I shall become redundant as a channel through which practical information, duly processed, can reach the academic world and through which theoretical material can reach dealing rooms in a suitable form. Meanwhile, I am trying to benefit by my reprieve obtained through the prolonged absence of such a dealer. At the same time I am trying to repay dealers for the generous assistance I received from them over many years, by expressing, comparing and analysing the facts and views received from them, in the hope that my presentation of their material might be of some use to them.

The list of those to whom I owe acknowledgment would indeed be very long, and I feel I owe an explanation why I have decided against giving them here the credit due to them. Interpretations, and even factual information obtained from various equally authoritative sources, are very often contradictory, owing to differences between practices and to the fact that no dealer is in a position to be familiar with the entire market. The experience of each dealer is bound to differ. Having to choose between conflicting facts and views, I had to rely very often on my own judgment. Responsibility for my version of the system as embodied in this book is, therefore, entirely my own. Although the book would gain in authority if I quoted the impressive list of my informants' names, I feel it would be unfair to pass on to them, even by implication, the responsibility for anything contained herein.

The only way in which I could do them full justice without the risk of doing them injustice would be by giving in full detail their respective contributions to the material in this book. Otherwise readers might attribute to them facts and views with which they would not care to be associated. In any case I am sure most of them would not be pleased with such detailed disclosures of the information they had given me since it might be of assistance to their rivals in anticipating their reactions in given situations. I feel that by safeguarding their anonymity I have adhered to the traditions of my profession, at the same time as acting in the best interest of those who have helped me.

I had to make an exception in the case of Mr. William Batt, chief dealer of the Westminster Bank, to whom acknowledgment is due for his kind assistance in going through the typescript of this book. He drew my attention to many mistakes of the kind that those without practical experience in dealing rooms are liable to commit. It is only fair to emphasise, however, that, for reasons indicated in the last paragraph, in many instances I did not follow his suggestions for corrections, so that he is in no way to blame for any inaccuracies that may have survived his scrutiny.

I have dedicated this book to my early teacher, Sir Theodore Gregory. I attended his lectures on foreign exchange during the early 'twenties and I am greatly indebted to him for having initiated me into the mysteries of the London foreign exchange market at the same time as having aroused my interest in it by his excellent exposition in his lectures and his booklet, *Foreign Exchange before, during and after the War*. It greatly assisted me in familiarising myself with the early inter-War operation of the system even before I became more closely acquainted with it in the course of my daily visits to the market over many years.

I am indebted to the Editor of the *Banca Nazionale del Lavoro Quarterly Review* for permission to use some of the material contained in two of my articles, "What Bankers Know, or ought to Know, on Foreign Exchange Theory", and "The Support Points Mechanism", appearing in the September 1964 and September 1965 issues.

My thanks are also due to Mrs. M. H. Hanks, who assisted me with the half-dozen or more drafts of this book as with those of my previous eight books.

P. E.

120 CLIFFORD'S INN,
LONDON, E.C.4

July, 1965

CHAPTER 1

THE POST-WAR SYSTEM OF FOREIGN EXCHANGE

FREE dealings in foreign exchanges, suspended in 1939, were restored in the course of the 'fifties more or less in practically all financially advanced countries of the free world. The foreign exchange system now in operation is not identical with the immediate pre-War system of free dealings, which was based on fluctuating exchange rates. Most countries have again fixed parities, and in most countries exchange dealing is not so free as it had been between the Wars. Nor is the post-War system of fixed exchange parities identical with the one that had existed under the gold standard prior to its suspension in the 'thirties and, further removed, before 1914. Exchange stability is now maintained not by means of private gold arbitrage but by means of systematic official intervention in the foreign exchange market.

The post-War system of foreign exchange differs materially from any previous systems. It may be called the Bretton Woods system, because it is governed by the rules of the International Monetary Fund set up in 1946 under the Bretton Woods Agreement. The currencies of the countries that have adhered to the I.M.F. have fixed parities in terms of both gold and dollars, subject to a number of exceptions. The dollar in turn has not only a fixed parity in terms of gold but is also freely convertible into gold for official holders of dollars — Governments, Central Banks and certain international institutions — at the fixed official selling price of $35 an ounce. The currencies of member countries other than the U.S. are kept stable in terms of dollars and, therefore, in terms of each other, with the aid of official buying and selling of dollars by the Central Banks concerned in order to prevent an appreciation or depreciation of their respective currencies.

Anyone who is entitled to buy dollars in the markets of the member countries under their exchange regulations is in a position to buy them at a price not exceeding the "support point" at which the Central Bank concerned is under obligation to sell dollars against its national currency. Anyone wishing to sell dollars in the market of any of the member countries is in a position to sell them for not less than the support point at which the Central Bank concerned is under obligation to buy dollars against payment in its local currency.

The dollar parities of the member currencies are more important than their gold parities. For while member governments are under no obligation to prevent the price of gold from rising above the parities in their local gold markets, they are under obligation to prevent any deviation of the dollar rate from their dollar parities in their local foreign exchange markets, beyond a maximum of one per cent on either side of these parities.

Under the system that was in operation before 1914, and again in a modified form between the middle 'twenties and the early 'thirties, exchange rates between countries on the gold standard remained in the close vicinity of their gold parities largely as a result of foreign exchange transactions arising from international gold movements carried out by private arbitrage. Such transactions occurred whenever the exchange of a country on the gold standard appreciated or depreciated slightly beyond their gold point — the rate at which it became profitable to import gold withdrawn from a Central Bank abroad, or to export gold for sale to a Central Bank abroad. The immediate effect of the foreign exchange operations connected with the purchase and sale of gold tended to readjust the exchange rate to within gold points. This immediate effect was reinforced by short-range effects of such gold movements on interest rates and, through them, on international movements of funds, and also by long-range effects on the volume of credit and, through it, on prices, on costs, and on the trade balance.

Under the Bretton Woods system gold points have been replaced by "support points" — also called "intervention points" — which are the rates at which Central Banks are under obligation to hold the local exchange against a depreciation or an appreciation in terms of dollars. Although under the rules of the I.M.F. the maximum range of permitted fluctuations is 2 per cent — 1 per cent on each side of the parities, in practice narrower spreads were established between the currencies of the Western European countries under the European Monetary Agreement of 1958. That agreement made it compulsory for member countries to inform each other about the limits they impose on the fluctuations of their currencies in terms of gold, dollars or some other currency. Most member countries found it convenient to fix these limits in relation to the dollar at $\frac{3}{4}$ per cent on each side of their I.M.F. parities, thereby limiting the range of fluctuations in relation to the dollar to $1\frac{1}{2}$ per cent.

The application of this spread was not uniform. For instance the support points of sterling were fixed in 1951 at $2·78 to $2·82, which is ·7 per cent from par. These were retained after 1958. A number of member countries of the I.M.F. followed the example of the majority of the E.M.A. countries, without being under obligation to do so, by fixing the spread between support points at $\frac{3}{4}$ per cent on either side of parity. But several others — for instance, Finland, Honduras and Ecuador — have applied the maximum spread of 1 per cent. On the other hand, Greece has fixed the support points for the drachma at $\frac{1}{2}$ per cent, Kuwait at $\frac{1}{4}$ per cent. In some member countries of the I.M.F. dealings are only permitted at par, though banks are entitled to charge a commission to buyers and sellers of foreign exchanges. In some instances the upper and lower support points are not equidistant from parity, while in other instances the authorities buy foreign exchanges at par and permit transactions at rates between par and 1 per cent premium.

Any member Government is entitled to widen the spread between support points up to the maximum of 1 per cent on either side of its parities, or to narrow it to any fraction of 1 per cent — even to nil, which would mean pegging their exchange rates at par. They are free to fix their support points anywhere between par and 1 per cent premium or discount, without having to ask for the I.M.F.'s consent or even to give

3

notice of their intention to make a change so long as it is kept within the permitted maximum limits. There have in fact been some instances of such changes, apart altogether from those brought about by changes in parities. Thus the Bank of Japan, which fixed originally the spread at ½ per cent from either side of the yen-dollar parity of 360, at 358·20 to 361·80, subsequently changed it by unilateral decision to ¾ per cent on either side of the parity, at 357·30 to 362·70. Although between 1958 and 1967 the Bank of England was unlimited buyer of dollars at 2·82 and unlimited seller at 2·78 — 2·42 and 2·38 since 1967 — it was entitled at any moment to change these limits by unilateral decision and without notice, up to the permitted maximum limits which was 2·7720 to 2·8280 — 2·424 and 2·376 since 1967.

In theory, therefore, support points are subject to limited alterations, but in practice there have been very few such changes, apart from those arising from the infrequent changes made in the parities themselves. Suggestions that the spreads should be widened by all member countries were under consideration from time to time but were rejected. It seems probable, however, that, should any member Government apply to the I.M.F. for authorisation to widen the spread for its own exchange beyond the maximum limit it would not encounter strong opposition. Judging by the fact that on a number of occasions the I.M.F. authorised even major changes in parities, or permitted member Governments to adopt a floating exchange rate, it would not be likely to resist too rigidly less important changes through a widening of the spread between support points of individual currencies. But the I.M.F. and member Government doubtless realise the advantages of firm support points, and they are not likely to give up these advantages without weighty reasons.

As for narrowing the spread, its effects could be achieved by any Central Bank without having to change the official limits, by simply supporting its exchange in practice at rates nearer to its parity. This is done in fact quite frequently. If a Central Bank buys and sells dollars in unlimited amounts at some fixed rate over a period those rates may come to be regarded after a while as the *de facto* support points of

4

its currency. For instance, even though the self-imposed support point of the Swiss franc is 4·2950 actually the Swiss National Bank has been for a long time unlimited buyer of dollars whenever the rate declined to 4·3150. The Bundesbank announces every morning buying and selling rates. The spread between them is wider than between quotations customary in the market, but the Bundesbank often operates between its own rates.

Governments of member countries are under obligation to limit fluctuations of their spot rates by their readiness to buy unlimited amounts of dollars in their local market if the dollar rate depreciates to minimum support point and to sell unlimited amounts of dollars in their local market if the dollar rate appreciates to maximum support point. In practice the necessary operations are often carried out in the New York market, on account of the Central Bank concerned, by Federal Reserve Bank of New York acting as agents for the Central Bank concerned. This is done especially during hours or during holidays when the local markets of the Central Banks concerned are closed while the New York market is open. There is nothing to prevent any member country of the I.M.F. from supporting their exchanges by buying and selling currencies other than the dollar — Denmark and Norway, for instance, intervened mostly in sterling — as long as they prevent the fluctuation of the dollar beyond 1 per cent from parity.

The United States authorities are under no obligation whatsoever to intervene in foreign exchanges on their own account. Their obligation under the Bretton Woods system consists of selling to the authorities of member countries gold at $35·0875 (including handling charge) and to buy from them gold at $34·9125 (allowing for handling charge). In doing so they make a vital contribution towards the maintenance of stable exchanges. In actual practice since 1961 the United States authorities often found it expedient to operate in foreign exchanges on their own account, without being under any obligation under the I.M.F. rules to do so. In given situations they found it more convenient to take the initiative for intervening rather than leave this task to Central Banks of other member countries. They bought or sold foreign exchanges in New York on their own account, or they instructed foreign Central Banks to buy or sell dollars in their own markets on official American account, before the rates at which these Central Banks would have to operate on their own account were actually reached.

As we shall see in Chapter 17, there is close co-operation between the Federal Reserve Bank and other Central Banks in the planning and execution of supporting operations, so as to ensure the maximum of advantage with the minimum of inconvenience for all parties. It is a hard and fast rule that no Central Bank ever intervenes in respect of a currency other than the dollar without the consent of the Central Bank in whose currency it wants to operate. The net result is the same wherever the supporting operations are carried out — net reserves of countries with a weak exchange decline, while those of countries with a firm currency increase.

Whenever the exchange of a member country tends to depreciate against the dollar the Central Bank of the country concerned is under obligation to sell dollars to satisfy excess demand which would otherwise cause the dollar rate to appreciate beyond support point. If it has not sufficient dollars for that purpose it is entitled to sell gold to the U.S. authorities at the official American buying price minus handling charge. If it has not sufficient gold with which it is prepared to part it may obtain additional facilities from the I.M.F. in the form of "drawing rights", supplemented by direct credits from, or reciprocal swap facilities with, the leading Central Banks.

Whenever a currency tends to appreciate in relation to the dollar the Central Bank concerned is under obligation to absorb the excess supply in the market, which would cause otherwise a depreciation of the dollar rate beyond support point. In doing so it accumulates dollar balances which it is entitled to convert into gold in the U.S. at the official American gold selling price plus handling charge. In actual practice many central banks have voluntarily abstained from converting a substantial part of their dollars into gold. What is essential from the point of view of the system is that they are entitled to do so.

The dollar thus occupies the central position in the post-War system of exchange stability. For some time, between 1958 and 1960, member Governments of the E.M.A. were also under obligation to quote their support points in each other's currencies, and were ready, if called upon, to prevent exchange rates between non-dollar member currencies from appreciating or depreciating beyond such support points in terms of each other. Under a rule adopted in 1960, however, they now only quote their support points in relation to the dollar and leave it to private arbitrage to ensure that exchange rates between member currencies other than the dollar also remained within their respective unofficial support points. The only "official" support points under the I.M.F. rules are those in relation to the dollar. The *de facto* limits that exist for fluctuations of rates between non-dollar member currencies have no official status and the monetary authorities have no direct responsibility for their maintenance. Nevertheless, they are very effective limits, as private arbitrage performs its allotted task efficiently. It is not strictly correct to call these limits "support points", and they are usually referred to as "arbitrage support points". More will be said about this subject in Chapter 6. These support points are determined by the spread between the maximum support point of one member currency and the minimum support point of another member currency.

The change of 1960 was of considerable importance, not only because it has further increased the importance of the dollar's role in post-War exchange stability, but also because it has doubled, with a stroke of the pen, the spread that may exist in practice between the unofficial but effective limits of the fluctuations of non-dollar currencies in terms of each other. This is because it is feasible — though it very seldom occurs in practice — that while one currency is at its maximum support point in relation to the dollar, another is at its minimum support point in relation to the dollar. In that extreme situation, if the spread for each exchange in relation to the dollar is $1\frac{1}{2}$ per cent, the maximum spread is 3 per cent.

To illustrate this let us suppose that the dollar is very weak in relation to the D.mark, while the peseta is very weak in relation to the dollar. The dollar parity of the D.mark is 4·00 and its official support points are 3·97 to 4·03, being ¾ per cent on either side of parity. The dollar parity of the peseta is 60·00 and its support points are 59·55 to 6·045, being also ¾ per cent on either side of parity. The Bank of Spain prevents the peseta from depreciating beyond 60·45 pesetas to the dollar by selling, if necessary, unlimited amounts of dollars at that rate. At the same time the Bundesbank is an unlimited buyer of dollars at the rate of 3·97 D.marks to the dollar, in order to prevent the D.mark from appreciating beyond that rate. This means that 3·97 D.marks and 60·45 pesetas are both one dollar and therefore they are equal to each other, so that the D.mark rate in Madrid must be 15·2267 pesetas. Any deviation from that rate would be readjusted by space arbitrage. Its mere anticipation is sufficient to prevent such deviation.

On the other hand, if the D.mark rate depreciated to its support point of 4·03 in relation to the dollar, while the peseta appreciated to its support point of 59·55 in relation to the dollar, the D.mark in Madrid would depreciate to 14·7767 pesetas. The spread between that rate and 15·2267 is ·45 pesetas, or exactly 3 per cent of the D.mark–peseta parity of 15. This is because to the spread of 1½ per cent between D.mark and dollar the spread of 1½ per cent between peseta and dollar is added. It will be seen in Chapter 7 how private arbitrage prevents any appreciation or depreciation of the non-dollar exchange rates beyond their "arbitrage support points".

The spreads between arbitrage support points, and even those between official support points in relation to the dollar, are distinctly wider than the spread between gold points had been under the gold standard. In 1913 the spread between the gold import point and the gold export point of the sterling–dollar rate was $4·8509 to $4·89. In 1925 the spread was between $4·8491 and $4·8949, and in 1930 between $4·8534 and $4·8873.

The mechanism that keeps exchange movements within narrow limits under the Bretton Woods system is technically more efficient than the gold points mechanism under the gold standard. For gold points had not been nearly as rigid and dependable as support points are under the present system. They were affected all the time by fluctuations in interest rates that raised or reduced the loss of interest on the shipments. From time to time they were also affected by some discovery of a quicker or cheaper method of transport, by cessation or temporary unavailability of the cheapest facilities, by changes in insurance or freight rates, by changes in the rules of Central Banks concerning their purchases and sales of gold, etc. On the other hand, even though under the post-War system member Governments are entitled to make changes within the prescribed limit of 1 per cent on either side of the parity, in practice they abstain from doing so. It is not part of their technique to seek to influence exchanges by means of making use of this right systematically, or even occasionally. Foreign exchange dealers and others concerned in exchange rates have come to depend, therefore, on the maintenance of the existing support points so long as the parities themselves are not changed.

In practice the range of fluctuations is kept usually even narrower than the full spread between support points. Under the gold standard the spread between gold points was appreciably narrower than the post-War spread between the arbitrage support points of non-dollar currencies, but seasonal influences were apt to cause exchanges to appreciate or depreciate right to their gold points. Under the post-War system, on the other hand, monetary authorities usually intervene long before support points are actually reached, and this keeps actual arbitrage points also narrow. For one thing the authorities are often willing to allow for foreign exchange broker's commission and usually hold the rates a shade higher than the lower support point and a shade lower than the upper support point. Otherwise the commission would bring the exchange rates paid or received by the banks in the market to a fraction beyond support point. What is much more important, Central Banks often deem it expedient to intervene systematically long before support point is even approached. We saw above that the Bundesbank does this as a matter of routine. Other Central Banks often peg their exchange at some distance from their

9

support points, or they iron out fluctuations within support points by means of official intervention in both directions. More will be said about such tactics in Chapter 17.

It is of course as much a matter of opinion whether support points at their fixed stable figures can be trusted implicitly as it had been whether gold points at their fluctuating approximate levels could be trusted implicitly. The more frequently parities or support points are altered the less they are likely to be depended upon. During the whole period of the operation of the Bretton Woods system changes of most parities have in fact been very few and far between. This is not due to the rigidity of the rules — although in theory the I.M.F. may veto changes in excess of 20 per cent and it may delay changes of between 10 and 20 per cent, reckoned from the original parities, in practice if a Government is determined to make a change it is not likely to be prevented by the I.M.F. from making it. For, if a Government feels strongly about the need for the proposed change and encounters strong resistance, it can always leave the I.M.F. or it may simply disobey its veto, leaving it to the I.M.F. to decide whether to expel the offending member or to seek to discipline it by withholding further facilities. The latter course would not necessarily be an effective deterrent because, once an overvalued currency is devalued the pressure on it relaxes, so that it no longer requires immediate assistance.

As discussions about proposed changes in parities take place within four walls we have no means of knowing how many times the I.M.F. succeeded in preventing intended changes. What we do know is that, apart from the devaluations of sterling in 1949 and in 1967 and of the franc and the lira in the 'forties and the 'fifties, and from the revaluation of the D.mark and the guilder, the parities of most leading currencies were never changed. The post-War foreign exchange market experienced a higher degree of stability than the inter-War period even before the crises of the 'thirties, though not such a degree of stability as during the two decades that preceded the first World War.

Foreign exchange dealers have grown used to this post-War stability of the exchanges. As a result, many dealers of the younger generation have only very limited experience in widely fluctuating exchange rates, and some of them were caught when dealing in Canadian dollars during the period of floating rates.

Whilst most spot exchanges have been stable during most of the post-War period, forward rates in general have experienced considerably wider fluctuations. This is because member Governments of the I.M.F. are under no obligation to maintain forward rates within support points, or indeed within any limits. It is true, the maintenance of spot rates between support points goes a long way towards discouraging a depreciation or appreciation of forward rates beyond these points — at any rate so long as there is confidence in the Government's willingness and ability to prevent movements of spot rates beyond them. But from time to time, whenever the foreign exchange market came to anticipate devaluations or revaluations, forward rates were inclined to lose touch with the support points of spot rates.

All exchanges are not within the Bretton Woods system. Switzerland, because of her neutrality, chose to remain outside the I.M.F. But in practice this makes no material difference, because, as we already pointed out above, the Swiss authorities voluntarily maintain the Swiss franc within self-imposed support points in relation to the dollar. The only difference is that, since the Swiss Franc is linked with gold, its support points are reckoned not from its parity with the dollar, but from its approximate gold import point and export point. This means that they are at about $1\frac{3}{4}$ per cent on either side of parity. Even though in practice the Swiss National Bank intervenes systematically long before the theoretical official support points are reached, the spread between the maximum and minimum support points of the Swiss franc is much wider than that of any other currency.

There are other currencies outside the system of stable exchanges, because no I.M.F. parities have been fixed for them. Some member countries are permitted by the I.M.F. to maintain floating rates. This was the case of the French franc and the lira during much of the post-War period, and also of the

Canadian dollar. In some Latin-American countries floating rates, multiple exchange rates, sales of foreign exchanges by means of auctions, and other similar practices are still in force. Even some European currencies, including sterling, are not entirely free from the survival of War-time multiple currency practices. Currencies of the Communist bloc are outside the system and are maintained stable by extreme exchange restrictions, though in spite of them Yugoslavia is a member of the I.M.F.

A contributory factor towards exchange stability has been the development of currency areas since the War. Although the Sterling Area had existed already before the War, it assumed new significance as a result of the creation of a number of new currencies by former British Colonies. These new independent nations have chosen to remain in the Sterling Area, so that their change of status has not been followed by exchange instability. The same applies to the Franc Area consisting of the remaining French Colonies and a number of former French Colonies, also to the currency arrangements between the Netherlands and the remaining Dutch Colonies, and between Portugal and the Portuguese Colonies.

The European Payments Union and the European Monetary Agreement arising from it played for some time an important part in the post-War foreign exchange system of Western Europe. The European Economic Community has not achieved, up to the time of writing, any advanced degree of monetary integration.

Although exchanges were unstable in the 'thirties, dealings in the principal currencies — with the notable exception of the Reichsmark — were almost entirely free. War-time and early post-War stability of exchanges had been maintained at the cost of suspending free dealings and transfers. The post-War system aims at reconciling the optimum degree of freedom compatible with the optimum degree of stability.

Exchange control was greatly relaxed during the 'fifties. Although, as we shall see in Chapter 18, most countries have still retained some controls, the extent to which they interfere with free dealings in the principal exchanges is relatively moderate. They do not prevent the operation of a free foreign exchange market in which rates are allowed to fluctuate within the limits set by support points. The surviving controls assume mostly the form of restrictions on speculation and on capital transfers, maximum limits to holdings of foreign currencies by banks and banning credits to non-residents. Foreign departments of banks are now burdened with a great deal of paper-work that did not exist before the War. Forms about transactions with clients have to be handled and returns on such transactions have to be submitted. Banks have also to submit returns about their own foreign exchange transactions and about their covered and uncovered commitments in foreign currencies. The proportion of clerks employed in foreign departments has increased considerably compared with the number of dealers. This in spite of the decline in the volume of documentary credits that had required much clerical work.

Another characteristic feature of the post-War system is the increased extent of official intervention in the foreign exchange market. It has now become an integral part of the foreign exchange system, since, as we saw above, under I.M.F. rules it is the duty of Central Banks to intervene in order to keep spot rates within support points. The need for such intervention is liable to arise not only as a result of some sweeping speculative attack or of some persistent disequilibrium but even as a result of routine seasonal tendencies. Moreover, although there is no obligation to intervene in forward exchanges, it is done on many occasions as a matter of expediency.

Official intervention has been greatly assisted by co-operation between Central Banks that has developed since the War on an entirely unprecedented scale. Foreign assistance to monetary authorities — whether by international institutions or by individual Central Banks — has become an integral part of the system and must be reckoned with as an ever-present major influence affecting exchanges. Under the gold standard automatic forces had been relied upon for the correction of any disequilibrium in foreign exchanges, and first-rate currencies were hardly ever defended with the aid of foreign financial assistance. Under the present system official intervention that has taken the place of automatic gold movements is often only possible thanks to such assistance, without which stability might have to be abandoned. Although automatic functioning of private arbitrage is still relied upon for maintaining stability between non-dollar currencies, the reason why this is possible is the maintenance of their stability in terms of the common denominator, the dollar, with the aid of official intervention financed largely by foreign financial assistance.

In the post-War system of foreign exchange the role of automatic self-correcting influences has come to play a relatively subordinate part. While under the gold standard the effect of gold movements on the volume of credit, on interest rates and on prices in both losing countries and receiving countries tended to restore equilibrium, under the post-War system the purely artificial transactions of official intervention and external assistance produce no such effect. This means that the artificial surface stability is liable to conceal and bolster up a considerable degree of disequilibrium which is bound to produce its disturbing effects sooner or later.

CHAPTER 2

ORGANISATION OF THE MARKET

THE foreign exchange market plays the part of a clearing
house through which purchases and sales of foreign exchanges,
whether originating outside the market or within the market
itself, are offset against each other. Foreign exchange business
is transacted on five different planes:

(1) Between banks and customers.
(2) Between banks in the same market.
(3) Between banks in different centres.
(4) Between banks and Central Banks.
(5) Between Central Banks outside the market.

Operations between banks and non-banking customers, or
even between them and other banks which have no direct
access to the market, do not form part of the activity of the
foreign exchange market, though indirectly they give rise to
market transactions. Central Banks may operate in the
market directly, but usually they operate through other banks.
They may also provide foreign exchange facilities outside the
market to banks and others and they influence the market
indirectly through assisting each other by means of swap
arrangements outside the market. In the present chapter we
are only concerned with the post-War mechanism for dealings
between banks within the market, either in the same financial
centre or between different financial centres.

While the organisation of international dealings between
different foreign exchange centres is more or less uniform, local
dealings within the same markets are based on two different
systems. Under the Anglo-American system that is in force
not only in Britain and the United States but also in Canada,
Switzerland and a number of other countries, the local foreign
exchange markets are not "markets" in the concrete sense of

the term. They are not actual meeting places for the participants who, in fact, need never meet face to face. The term "market" is applied in its abstract sense only, meaning a number of buyers and sellers systematically in contact with each other for the purpose of transacting business with each other. Business is transacted locally through a network of private telephone lines linking the banks with the foreign exchange brokers who act as intermediaries. Such informal markets have no officially fixed hours — though in practice the participants may keep identical hours — with no "official" exchange rates.

Foreign exchange markets in the continental sense of the term consist of meeting places where dealers in foreign exchange meet on every business day. Such markets had existed everywhere from the earliest origins of foreign exchange until the early part of this century. They have survived right to our days in a number of countries — in France, West Germany, the Netherlands, Italy among others. In all such countries there is in each financial centre a meeting place — usually it is situated in a secluded section of the *Bourse* but is not connected with activities in stocks and shares — where foreign exchange operators foregather daily, in order to transact business and also in order to fix "official" exchange rates for certain purposes. Business in foreign exchanges at such meeting places is transacted in much the same way as business in commodities is transacted on commodity exchanges, or as business in stocks and shares is transacted on Stock Exchanges.

But even in centres which have such markets the bulk of the local foreign exchange business and all international business is now transacted in the same way as in the centres which have no such markets — by telephone. The surviving meeting places exist for limited purposes only. Usually they only function for a fraction of the business hours during which it is possible to deal in foreign exchanges outside the formal market. The meetings take place at a fixed time, towards noon or in the early afternoon, and they seldom last more than an hour, during which business can be transacted all the time also outside this market. Generally speaking business in formal markets is confined to spot transactions. In Frankfurt the representative of the Bundesbank attends the meetings and intervenes if he deems it necessary to bridge the gap between supply and demand. The "official" spot rates fixed at the meetings need not be applied at subsequent dealings outside such markets but are merely applied for limited specific purposes only — for instance, for transactions between banks and customers. In some countries, such as Italy and Sweden, meetings for the purpose of fixing such "official" rates are held in the Central Bank or in some other bank.

When a formal market still existed in London it assumed the form of bi-weekly meetings of the senior partners of merchant banking firms on mail days — Tuesdays and Thursdays — at the Royal Exchange. Even then the bulk of the business was transacted more and more outside such meetings, through the intermediary of foreign exchange brokers calling on banks, and later by telephone calls between banks and brokers. When the old-style market was discontinued soon after the end of the first World War its disappearance made very little difference in practice because by then only a fraction of the business was transacted at the Royal Exchange. But the continued existence of similar markets on the continent does affect the organisation of the centres concerned to some extent. It provides occasions for operations that differ in some respects from those transacted by telephone, and it gives rise to arbitrage between dealers in such markets and outside them. Relatively speaking, the international importance of these markets is small. The present description of the post-War system of foreign exchange is, therefore, confined largely to the informal Anglo-American system, with only occasional reference to the formal Continental system.

While participation in the formal markets has always been strictly limited to accepted members — this is so even in Paris where any member of the public has access to the other sections of the *bourse* — until the War any bank was entitled to participate in informal markets, provided that their names were acceptable to other participating banks. Since the resumption of dealings in London in 1951 only banks which are "authorised dealers" are entitled to participate. Similar restrictions are

17

applied in most other countries with exchange control. In Britain authorisation is granted by the Treasury on the recommendation of the Bank of England. At the time of writing there are some 150 authorised dealers, but their number is increasing, owing to the opening of new London branches of overseas banks. Needless to say, the fact that a bank is an authorised dealer does not necessarily mean that its name is taken in the market.

The local market in most major centres consists of a network of private telephone lines between the dealing rooms of foreign exchange departments of banks and the dealing rooms of foreign exchange brokers. In Switzerland the private lines are between banks, as there are no brokers. As a general rule, subject to minor exceptions, all local foreign exchange business in the London market is transacted through the intermediary of brokers. Before the War there were between 30 and 40 broker firms. They closed down when exchange control was adopted in 1939 and when the market reopened in 1951 the Bank of England insisted that the number of brokers should be kept down. At the time of writing there are only 9 of them. They have an organisation called Foreign Exchange Brokers' Association (F.E.B.A.) which represents their professional interests and conducts negotiations with the banks and with the authorities, and which endeavours to achieve uniformity of the rules and practices followed in their dealings with banks, even though it has no statutory powers to enforce its rulings.

The banks engaged in foreign exchange transactions in London are represented on the London Foreign Exchange Bankers' Committee. The main object of that organisation is to standardise the rules that govern the practices in the market and to represent the banks' interests in their relationship with the foreign exchange brokers and with the authorities. It does not aim at restricting competition for clients' business by fixing uniform exchange rates but the commission is fixed at $\frac{1}{8}$ per cent, which is applied to transactions with non-banking customers, except for small amounts for which there is a fixed charge. The committee's rulings, like those of the F.E.B.A., have no statutory power and are not binding for its members. Nevertheless, disregard of them is a very rare exception. As we shall see in the next chapter, the standard of professional conduct in the foreign exchange market, whether that of bankers or brokers, is remarkably high.

In order to establish personal relationship between dealers who never meet in the flesh in the course of their professional duties banks and brokers in London have formed the Forex Club which provides regular opportunities for meetings for both social and educational purposes. Similar Forex Clubs exist in some twenty other countries and they are all affiliated with the international Forex Club or *Association Cambiste International* which has its headquarters in Paris. That organisation, besides furthering personal relationships between dealers of various countries, also aims at studying problems that are liable to arise from the operation of the international market.

Not all banks have foreign exchange departments with dealing rooms. Those whose foreign exchange business is not sufficiently large to justify the expense of a dealing room, or which have no authority to deal in foreign exchange or whose name is not taken, may have direct access to a broker or may buy and sell foreign exchanges through some other bank in the same centre or abroad.

Banks whose activities in the market are sufficiently extensive to justify the expense of a dealing room have many private lines to brokers and employ a staff varying from three or four to a score of dealers or even more. The dealing room contains an electric dealing table which, with its rows of lights, is a perplexing and fascinating sight to the layman. All the private telephone lines are to brokers, though in exceptional instances certain banks that are in special relationship with each other may have private lines, not necessarily for direct dealing — except between affiliates and their parent institutions — but for exchanging information. There are also a number of outside lines for communication with non-banking customers and for long-distance calls to banks in foreign centres. In addition there are several telex teleprinters, and also electronic calculating machines which are both faster and more dependable than the corresponding pre-War appliances.

Brokers usually specialise in certain currencies or groups of currencies, though most of them deal also in dollars. Their dealers, besides specialising in currencies, may also specialise in spot or forward exchanges or in Euro-currency operations. Brokers have private lines to banks with active foreign exchange departments. Some firms have as many as a hundred such lines which are installed and maintained at their expense. They also use outside lines for communicating with the less active banking clients.

When the dealer of a bank wants to establish contact with a broker he presses a button and at the other end of the private line a light goes on at the dealer's table in the broker's dealing room. Thereupon the broker presses a button which puts on a light on his dealing table, indicating that contact is established. At the end of the conversation the pressing of a button at either end disconnects the line. This system operates so efficiently that the broker is able to contact a dozen or more bankers in considerably less than a minute. The lines to the same bank are frequently duplicated or even triplicated, so that on either end two or three dealers may listen in to the same conversation. This assists them in being informed about what their colleagues are doing.

Brokers confine their foreign exchange operations to banks in the local market. They have no contacts either with non-banking clients or with foreign banks in foreign centres. But since 1968 they are entitled to deal in Euro-currencies with foreign banks and also with foreign non-banking customers. In some countries, such as France, brokers may have direct contact with business firms. In most countries they are precluded from dealing on their own account but in the U.S.A. they are permitted to do so. Already before the War some brokers combined their functions with those of money brokers, acting as intermediaries for credits to Local Authorities. At present money brokers also deal in credits to hire-purchase finance houses, and in interbank sterling transactions between London banks, which operations are related to foreign exchange operations. They also deal in dollar certificates of deposits.

In a number of countries there are secondary foreign

exchange markets in addition to their main foreign exchange centres. For instance, although Zürich is by far the most important Swiss market, Geneva and Basle are also very important and there are secondary markets in Berne, Lausanne, St. Gallen and Lugano. In Germany, besides the principal market in Frankfurt, there are markets in Berlin, Hamburg, Munich and Düsseldorf. In the United States there are, in addition to New York, markets also in Boston, Chicago, Philadelphia, Detroit and San Francisco. In Italy Milan is the main market, but there are markets in Rome, Turin, Naples and Genoa. In Japan there are markets, besides that of Tokio, in Osaka and Yokohama. Such secondary markets conduct the bulk of their business through the principal markets of their countries, but the banks also have direct connections with foreign centres. Nevertheless, as a general rule the rates in secondary markets seldom depart to any noteworthy extent from those quoted in the principal markets.

In Britain there are no secondary markets, although clearing bank branches in the big provincial cities and Scottish banks in Edinburgh or Glasgow have foreign exchange departments of their own. They transact their business through the foreign exchange departments of their London offices. Clearing banks have a number of regional foreign branches which act as intermediaries between smaller branches in their districts and the foreign exchange department of their head office. Many of the regional foreign branches have telex connections with the dealers' room in London. There is no direct dealing either between foreign branches in the same city or between them and banks abroad.

Foreign exchange business with banks in foreign centres is transacted either by means of long-distance telephones or, to an increasing degree, by means of telex. The improvement of long-distance telephone service since the second World War has greatly facilitated the development of international dealings in foreign exchanges. While before the War there were often exasperating delays, it is now usually possible to obtain connection with overseas centres very quickly and easily. The operation of telex and its growing popularity also makes for speedier transactions of international business. Although telex has to operate through public telephone cables, contact with foreign centres through it is usually almost instantaneous. Charges are made for the actual duration of the contact according to the number of seconds. Large foreign exchange departments have between five and ten telex instruments, so that they can be in contact with several banks at the same time.

Some London branches of large overseas banks have private lines to their head offices abroad. Apart from these, banks have no private lines to overseas centres because, since they usually work with a number of correspondents in each centre and it would not pay to have private lines to all of them, any discrimination in the form of maintaining a private line to one of them would be strongly resented by the others.

Business between banks in different financial centres is transacted direct without the intermediary of foreign exchange brokers. There is a small number of "international brokers" who act as intermediaries for Euro-currency transactions between London and Continental centres, but they do not transact foreign exchange business except insofar as it relates directly to the Euro-currency transactions they arrange. In local transactions the cost of the installation and of current subscriptions of private line is borne by the brokers. In international transactions banks themselves have to bear the cost of communications by telephone or telex, irrespective of whether or not they lead to actual business. The bank that initiates the contact has to pay for it.

It is no exaggeration to say that, thanks to the efficiency of the long-distance telephone and telex system, in post-War markets it is now practically as easy to transact business with banks across the channel or even across the ocean as with banks across the same street. Dealers have developed a language of their own with a multitude of conventional forms of expression, technical terms and abbreviations, in order to reduce to a minimum the cost of long-distance communications, but mainly in order to avoid misunderstanding.

Transactions in bills and in other negotiable instruments now constitute a bare fraction of the total turnover of the market, though such transactions with clients give rise to covering operations in the market. By far the largest proportion of foreign exchange business assumes the form of buying and selling telegraphic transfers, referred to as "T.T." in the jargon of the market. In the old days buyers and sellers of mail transfers had to reckon with the uncertainties of surface mail when arranging "value dates" for such transactions — *i.e.*, the dates on which the currencies bought and sold had to be delivered. More days, and even weeks, were allowed for transactions with more distant centres. In our time spot transactions are due to be executed in two clear days after their conclusion, on the safe assumption that two days are amply sufficient to ensure that cable instructions for arranging the payments in foreign centres in any part of the globe reach their destination in time. The T.T. rates are the basic exchange rates which largely determine the rates quoted for other types of foreign exchange transactions. Although rates for foreign bills of exchange, cheques, mail transfers, letters of credit, traveller's cheques etc. are affected by interest rate, they are based on the T.T. rates. While in the old days the rates quoted for bills usually included interest charges to maturity — such rates were called *tel quel* rates — nowadays the more usual practice with these transactions is to buy and sell bills on the basis of the T.T. rates and to add or deduct interest to maturity on the basis of the local discount rates prevailing in the centre where the bills are sold.

Rates for foreign notes are based on T.T. rates, but are liable to deviate from them, obeying a set of special laws of their own. They have a separate market outside dealers' rooms, though open positions arising from their purchases or sales are usually covered by the foreign exchange department in the ordinary way and are included in the grand total when reckoning the bank's open position. From time to time a very active market develops in certain notes, and on such occasions it is even possible to deal in them for forward delivery.

Mail transfers are now always made by air mail. They are confined almost entirely to transactions for small amounts which are carried out by mail in order to save cable expenses.

Instructions for making or expecting future payments, and confirmations of the execution of instructions arising from forward exchange transactions or Euro-currency deposits, are usually sent to correspondents by air mail, though it is an increasingly popular practice to make such communications by telex. Even though the cost of that method of communication is higher it saves time and clerical work.

The scope of the foreign exchange market has become considerably extended during the late 'fifties and early 'sixties. To its traditional function — the exchange of currencies against each other — the function of borrowing and lending deposits in terms of foreign currencies has been added. It is true such transactions have always existed to some extent. "Swap and deposit" transactions and "swap and investment" transactions formed an essential part of the activities of foreign exchange departments during the inter-War period. But while foreign exchange transactions form an integral part of such operations, the lending and borrowing of deposits in terms of Euro-dollars or other Euro-currencies need not necessarily be linked with foreign exchange transactions. Inter-bank sterling transactions which developed in the early 'sixties need not be concerned directly with foreign exchange at all, but in most banks they are transacted by foreign exchange departments, because very often they provide a preferable alternative to inward arbitrage transactions. They are connected with foreign exchange transactions when such bank deposits are used for outward arbitrage.

Foreign exchange departments undertake borrowing and lending operations in foreign money markets much more systematically than before the War. It may be said that the functions of foreign exchange departments have come to overlap to a very considerable extent with those of the money market departments of banks. Banks and brokers which deal systematically in Euro-currencies or in inter-bank sterling have usually one or more dealers specialising in such transactions. Likewise there are in some dealing rooms dealers specialising in investment dollars.

Transactions in investment currencies constitute yet another branch of post-War activities for foreign exchange departments. When this type of business first developed in London during the late 'forties it was handled almost exclusively by firms of stockbrokers and by stock departments of banks concerned with transactions in dollar securities and in other foreign securities. More recently, however, foreign exchange departments have come to take an increasingly active interest in such transactions.

The dealing room is the centre of the foreign exchange department but its activities have to be supplemented by a great deal of clerical work not directly concerned with dealing but arising from it. Although the contract notes sent by the broker to both parties are sufficient to confirm the deals the buyer and the seller also communicate with each other. Immediately on concluding a deal the dealer writes down its essential particulars on pink sale slips or green purchase slips which are passed on to the instructions department. The buying bank sends instructions to the seller as to the name of the overseas bank to which the currency purchased has to be paid over on the value date. Some banks notify their correspondents to expect that payment, but others rely on the sellers to carry out the contract and simply await the credit advice from the correspondents informing them about the receipt of the money. The selling bank confirms the transactions to the buyer and sends instructions to its correspondent to pay over on the value date the amount of foreign currencies sold to the bank indicated by the buyer for the latter's account.

In the dealing room itself there is a clerk in charge of the position sheet or position book in which all transactions, whether with non-banking customers or with banks, are entered and which the chief dealer has to follow closely all the time so that he is able to know at any moment whether and to what extent the bank has an overall long or short position and whether and to what extent it has a position in any particular currency. In the position sheet spot and forward transactions are entered indiscriminately, but there is a separate book in which maturities are taken into account and which constitutes the record for payments due to be made and received on particular dates. The senior dealer must know after each deal of any substantial size, whether originating within or outside the market, how it affects the bank's open positions. While he may not get the exact figure until after the closing of the market, he must have all the time an approximate idea — within, say, £50,000 on either side of the exact figure — of the bank's position in any currency.

The accounts department handles the bank's accounts with its foreign correspondents in terms of foreign currencies — the so-called *nostro* accounts — the accounts of foreign banks with the bank in terms of the local currency — the so-called *vostro* account — and the accounts of third parties kept in terms of foreign currencies with foreign correspondents on behalf of customers — the so-called *loro* accounts. One of the tasks of the foreign exchange departments is to ensure that there are adequate but not excessive balances on *nostro* accounts, so that payments maturing on various dates are provided for in good time and there is always some balance left over.

Textbooks before the War devoted much space to the difference between "direct" or "indirect" quotations of exchange rates — according to whether it is the foreign currency unit that is quoted in terms of the local unit or vice versa. Direct quotations are also referred to as "fixed" or "certain" quotations, indirect quotations as "variable" or "uncertain" quotations.

The difference between the two methods of quotations, unimportant as it may be both from an arithmetical and from an economic point of view, is liable to give rise to much misunderstanding unless dealers and students of foreign exchange pursue the habit of applying the appropriate terminology when referring to movements of exchange rates. A "rise" or a "fall" in a rate may mean appreciation or depreciation, according to whether the quotation expresses the value of the national unit in terms of foreign units or vice versa. Likewise a "high" or a "low" exchange rate may mean an appreciated or depreciated currency according to the method of quotation. For this reason dealers, brokers, bankers, students, economists, financial editors, administrators, politicians, merchants and whoever else is interested in foreign exchange, are strongly advised to avoid the use of the ambiguous terms "rise" and "fall", or "high" and "low" rates. They should express what they mean to say by using instead the terms "appreciation" – "depreciation" or "firm" – "weak" exchanges. It is, after all, not the form in which an exchange rate is expressed but the nature of the change in the international value of the currency it indicates that matters.

In countries where indirect quotation is practised, such as London, it is particularly important to avoid confusion that is liable to arise from the use of the terms "rise" and "fall" or of "high" and "low", for, when the dollar rate in London rises from, say, $2·39 to $2·39¼ it means that it is sterling that is firm while a fall in the dollar rate from $2·39 to $2·38¾ means that it is sterling that depreciates, notwithstanding appearances to the contrary.

CHAPTER 3

HOW THE MARKET WORKS

THE leisurely pace of intermittent foreign exchange dealings at the quarterly fairs where most foreign exchange business was transacted until the 17th century, and even at the bi-weekly meetings of dealers at the Royal Exchange on mail days that survived until 1919, has now given way to continuous activity in modern foreign exchange markets. While they experience from time to time dull periods, these are but intervals between spells of lively and at times even feverish activity. On some days the turnover reaches astronomic figures, but even on days when the volume of business actually done is relatively small the difficulty of finding the desired counterparts on acceptable terms keeps dealers reasonably active and in frequent contact with the market.

Improvement of communications between foreign exchange markets and growing internationalisation of trade and finance have contributed towards the integration of free foreign exchange markets into one large international market during the 'fifties and 'sixties. The international language of foreign exchange dealing is overwhelmingly English, although Paris and to a less extent Milan and the Spanish markets still prefer to use French when dealing with London or New York. Nevertheless, English terms such as "spot", "forward", "swap", "outright", "hedging", etc., are used universally even when the language of the negotiations is French. The earlier French supremacy in the foreign exchange market survives to some extent in the use of terms such as "arbitrage" etc.

One of the remaining irremovable obstacles that prevent an even more extensive international integration of the foreign exchange market is the differences in business hours due to geographical circumstances. That difference has disappeared

28

between London and Western European markets since British summer time is now in operation throughout the year. It is six hours between London and New York and is reduced to five hours when New York is on summer time. It is six hours all the year round — except during New York summer time — also between New York and Western European markets. There are even longer discrepancies with the markets of Chicago, San Francisco, the Latin-American centres, Tokio, Hong Kong, Manila, etc. During the hours when the European markets are closed the New York market is to a large extent isolated, and any transactions which cannot be deferred until the following morning have to find a counterpart locally, possibly at a relatively unfavourable rate — a reminder of conditions prevailing before the improvement of international communications.

Although there are no officially-fixed market hours, activities in London usually begin at around 9.30 A.M. Continental markets open earlier, because business hours in general begin earlier than in Britain, but there is usually a dealer on early duty in London foreign exchange departments, to receive advices about rates in early dealings on the Continent. Actually there is usually relatively little activity during the first hour or so. In some foreign exchange departments dealers are kept busy with their morning mails which may contain orders from branches, correspondents or non-banking customers. But other departments receive their orders from branches in the late afternoon, after the closing of the market, so that their morning mails do not contain much that would call for early action.

All chief dealers study in the morning foreign exchange articles and news reports in the Press and on agency tapes, looking out for developments that are liable to affect the rates. Closing rates received from New York overnight always receive attention, even though they do not necessarily determine or even influence opening rates in London.

Unless there is something definite in the air business is usually slow in getting into its stride. Many Continental dealers prefer to await the rate-fixing session in their respective "official" markets — in Germany they await the announcement

29

of the Bundesbank's buying and selling rate — before committing themselves too heavily, though the more enterprising amongst them may open positions in anticipation of the fixing. Banks on the Continent are closed during lunch hours, so that they have no market transactions arising from any new transactions with clients. Nevertheless, reactions from foreign exchange dealings on the *bourse,* which usually take place during an hour or so some time between noon and 2 P.M., often reach London. Frequently real lively activity does not begin until after lunch and afternoons are almost invariably busier than mornings. The opening of New York is usually awaited with interest in the European markets and it often influences the trend. Closing time is supposed to be 4 P.M., but it varies according to the degree of activity and occasionally it may be as late as 5 or 5.30 P.M. or even 6 P.M. Thereafter the banks particularly concerned with the dollar — especially London branches of American banks — may leave a dealer in charge till New York closes, not only for keeping in touch with the trend but to a distinctly increasing extent also for actual dealing. Several London banks follow their example, to take advantage of discrepancies between London and New York quotations.

All markets are now closed on Saturdays. In London under a gentlemen's agreement banks confine their foreign exchange dealings with customers on Saturday mornings to buying travellers' cheques and to similar minor transactions.

Many foreign exchange departments pursue the practice of closing their books at 4 P.M. and report their positions to their managements. Any business done after 4 P.M. goes on the record of next day's business.

All dealers naturally prefer the other party to fire the first shot by quoting opening rates. They circle each other, figuratively speaking, like boxers in the ring, awaiting their opportunity to strike. Dealers wanting to buy or sell, whether to initiate the transaction or to undo positions previously entered into, have the choice between awaiting quotations to be communicated by brokers or contacting brokers to inform them at what rates they are prepared to deal. In the majority of instances both banks and brokers make two-way quotations — they quote buying rates and selling rates at the same time. During relatively calm days when rates are steady banks, having quoted their two-way rates, are always prepared to deal either way, but usually they prefer to deal one way or the other. This means that if their quotation is immediately accepted they are prepared to deal in a large amount or in a much smaller amount, according to whether they would prefer to buy or to sell. They feel bound to operate in an unwanted sense up to a small amount once they have quoted their rates.

The margin between the two rates is supposed to be wide enough to make it appear a matter of near-indifference for the bank which way it deals, as it stands a chance of being able to cover profitably within the spread. Nevertheless banks have most of the time a distinct preference either for buying or for selling because they want to cover positions previously created, or because they want to open a new position, or because they want to anticipate buying or selling orders which they expect to receive from customers. The reason why, even though they want to buy only or to sell only, they quote two-way rates is that by quoting buying and selling rates only they would be disclosing their intentions. The required counterpart would then be forthcoming on less favourable terms. On the other hand, by quoting both ways they may have to buy when they wish to sell, or vice versa.

It is an unwritten law of the market that once a firm quotation is made and it is accepted immediately the dealer who has made it must deal on the basis of the rate quoted. This practice involves no undue risk when the rates are steady so long as dealers are in close touch with the market and adjust their quotations to the prevailing trend. But on hectic days rates are liable to move suddenly and in whichever direction they move the bank, having quoted two-way rates, is liable to suffer a loss if the other bank accepts its quotations immediately. It has the following defences against such losses:

(1) Acceptance must be immediate. No excuse for delay (such as faulty telephone line) need be accepted.

(2) The dealer must keep in close touch with fluctuations of

rates so that he does not make or hold out quotations which no longer correspond to the prevailing rates.

(3) On hectic days spreads between buying and selling rates are widened, so that minor changes in the rates do not necessarily cause a loss to the dealer whose quotation is accepted.

(4) A dealer whose quotation is accepted need not buy or sell more than the minimum amount that is customary in the market for individual transactions.

(5) What a dealer may lose through an unwelcome acceptance of his quotation he may recover by accepting in turn other bank's quotations in similar circumstances.

(6) He may safeguard himself by abstaining from making a firm quotation, making it clear that he is merely giving information about prevailing rates. This is often done when the market is all one-way.

It is very much a matter of opinion when an acceptance of a quotation is deemed to have been immediate. When banks deal direct with each other immediate means exactly what it says. Unless the dealer who receives the quotation accepts it without any delay or hesitation whatsoever, the dealer who quotes has every legal and moral right to back out. In actual practice allowance is often made for the need for some delay, usually on a basis of reciprocity. A bank which is prepared to concede a few seconds' delay may depend on being conceded a similar favour by a rival who had benefited by this attitude. But for this even a simple two-point arbitrage would entail a certain amount of speculative risk, for it is not always possible to synchronise two transactions.

On a comparatively quiet day banks which are on friendly relations with each other are usually easy-going about the acceptance of their quotations up to a point, on the basis of give-and-take. What dealers are determined to avoid is that their quotation should be treated as an option that would enable their rivals to make the best of both worlds, by trying to get a better rate if they can and falling back upon the original quotations if they can't. This would mean "heads you win tails I lose" from the point of view of the banker who had made the quotation.

When the rates are quoted to brokers a certain delay before the quotation is accepted is inevitable, unless the broker has already a firm order in hand so that he is in a position to finalise the transaction without having to refer it back for confirmation to the other part. The broker must satisfy himself that the quotation he has been given is indeed a firm quotation. Unless the rates fluctuate too wildly the bank that quotes rates is usually prepared to maintain it for the few seconds needed for the broker to contact some other bank. In this respect, too, the attitude of banks vary, and on hectic days quotations are not held open even for the unavoidable minimum of delay.

A dealer can only be effectively in contact with market fluctuations by engaging in a large number of actual transactions. Although it is usually possible to obtain quotations he cannot always be certain whether these quotations are really effective unless he actually transacts business in them. For this reason in given circumstances he may deem it worth his while to transact business without any profit or even at some slight loss for the sake of being constantly well-informed about changes in rates.

There is no hard and fast rule about the figure of the minimum amount of transactions in the market. It has increased considerably since before the War in sympathy with the all-round rise of all figures. The amount depends to some extent on the importance of the bank concerned, *e.g.* in London a clearing bank or a leading merchant bank is expected to regard £100,000 or $250,000 as the minimum, but for smaller banks the minimum that is considered acceptable in practice is £50,000 or even $100,000. Transactions usually take place in multiples of such round figures, though transactions in broken amounts are not infrequent. When, in response to a quotation of dollars, a dealer says, "I take one" it always means one million dollars.

The broker's chief qualification is his ability to judge whether a quotation he receives can be depended upon as being firm. His familiarity with the attitude of the dealer who quotes the rate helps him in this difficult task. His dilemma is not enviable. Unless he is able and willing to give his client dependable rates his rivals who are able and willing to do so will secure the business. On the other hand if he over-estimates the firmness of the quotation and disappoints the dealer to whom he communicates the rate he is likely to lose goodwill. He has to choose between these two risks and has to rely on his experience with various banks, and with various individual dealers within each bank, to decide which risk is smaller. If he finds he has erred on the side of optimism, because the quotation was not, after all, as hard as he has thought it to be he has to do his utmost to find another counterpart for his client at the rate quoted.

In many instances dealers take brokers into their confidence and instruct them to find a counterpart for a definite buying or selling order. Sometimes on such occasions the bank quotes a rate to a broker and "leaves it with him" to find the counterpart. But if this takes too long the bank may not feel itself bound by its quotation. Moreover, it may have quoted its rates to more than one broker and the one who finds the counterpart first gets the business, so that the quotation made to the other broker lapses. Dealers may or may not inform the unsuccessful broker that their quotation is no longer valid.

As banks can depend on the discretion of brokers to conceal their identity until the deal is completed they need not quote both ways. Nevertheless in currencies in which a bank is "the market" it makes two-way quotations even to brokers, because it is quite willing to operate either way and to job in and out of the market for the sake of the profit made through the spread between its buying and selling rates. Likewise when a bank wants its operation to produce the maximum effect on the rates it wants to publicise its intentions rather than conceal them.

Unless the broker has already a definite quotation in hand he contacts a number of banks at the same time to discover the required counterpart. They have to act absolutely impartially between the banks and their sole preoccupation must be to ensure that a counterpart is forthcoming at the rate quoted by the bank that had taken the initiative. If, however, they

34

receive a definite order they are expected to act to some extent in the interest of the bank which gave them the order.

Time allowed by banks who have quoted rates is shorter for spot transactions than for swap transactions because, owing to the wide range of possible maturities for the latter, it is more difficult to find a counterpart. Even so a quotation is seldom regarded as binding after a minute or two, and very often it is deemed to have lapsed in a matter of seconds.

Business between banks in different financial centres is transacted without the intermediary of brokers. Dealers of two banks contact each other direct through long-distance telephone calls or by means of telex. The spread between buying and selling rates is usually narrower in direct dealings between banks in two centres than in dealings in the same centre, because there is no need to allow for brokerage. It is the standing rule that if a bank takes the trouble and assumes the expense of contacting a bank in a foreign centre, the latter is under some moral obligation to make a quotation. Here again, as in the case of transactions through the intermediary of brokers, such quotations are only binding if they are accepted immediately, or at any rate with a reasonable delay of a few seconds. It is a familiar device, applied by some banks, to ask for quite a number of quotations, both spot and forward, so as to gain time to decide whether to accept one that is made first while awaiting the subsequent quotations. Many banks don't feel committed in such circumstances.

Very often quotations are requested solely for the purpose of keeping in touch with the market trend. Banks may be anxious to ascertain the rates at which their rivals across the sea operate, or are prepared to operate, without themselves intending to do business on such rates. It is sometimes worth their while to that end to do actual business in small amounts at the rate quoted to them, and to test the market by being prepared even to deal in larger amounts than the customary minimum to see whether the other bank is prepared to deal in excess of the minimum. Any refusal to do so implies disclosure of the direction in which the bank in question really wants to operate. For this very reason it may be at times inexpedient for a bank to confine an unwanted transaction to the bare minimum.

Dealing in telex follows the same principles as dealing through telephone. The caller who pays for the call expects the bank which he has contacted to quote rates. Only if acceptance is immediate is the quotation binding. The service operates so smoothly that even from New York it is possible to obtain instantaneous reply.

The foreign exchange market is a strange combination of two fundamentally conflicting attitudes. On the one hand a remarkable spirit of friendship and chivalry exists among a very high proportion of dealers. A great many of them have come to address each other by their Christian names, even though they may have never met. They are prepared to go out of their way to observe strict fair play, and even to go beyond that, in a spirit of *camaraderie*, outbidding each other in their willingness to comply with the opponents' wishes at times even at the cost of some sacrifice to their own banks. On the other hand there is an incessant struggle for the survival of the fittest, in the course of which dealers do their utmost to outwit each other in so far as this is possible without actually offending against the letter of the accepted rules. While the first attitude may be more prominent in the case of a number of dealers and the second attitude in the case of others, most of them combine the two to some extent. In most cases the principle of reciprocity determines their attitude which varies according to whom they deal with.

The foreign exchange market may be compared with a gigantic poker game, with the essential difference that the players do not even see each other's faces, except in the old-fashioned Continental markets where they actually meet. When in direct communication with each other on the telephone, dealers can hear at any rate each other's voices, which may give them some idea about the keenness of their opponents on transacting business at the rates quoted. But if they have to communicate through telex they have to depend on what they know about the resources, turnover, practices and clientèle of the bank which quotes rates or which responds to their quotations, and also on what they know about the character and temperament of the dealer. Above all, familiarity with the nature of their rivals' business is of some help. The knowledge that certain types of clients are in the habit of buying from or selling exchanges to certain banks at a certain period of the year is liable to be of great assistance.

When dealing through brokers dealers have not even such a limited guidance, at any rate to begin with, since they do not know the identity of the counterpart until after the deal is completed. They are thus at a disadvantage which is roughly offset, however, by the advantage derived from the fact that they too can conceal their operations for a few moments or minutes behind the façade of the broker.

The game has to be played according to well-established rules. Dealers, when giving each other information about their intentions, or indeed about anything related to foreign exchange, may feel entitled to mislead their rivals by implication, so long as anything they say is technically true. In this respect again the attitude of dealers differs widely and is largely based on give-and-take. Some dealers may prefer to transact business on the basis of putting all their cards on the table and expecting their rivals to act likewise. Other dealers, however, deem it to be to their advantage to resort to one of the innumerable varieties of bluff. The following are a selection of examples:

(1) When banks quote two-way exchange rates and are called upon to operate in an unwanted sense — to sell even though they would prefer to buy or vice versa — they may be prepared to operate in larger amounts than the bare minimum, so as to convey the impression that they are keen buyers when in fact they merely want to prepare the market in order to be able to sell on more favourable terms, or vice versa.

(2) Such bluff may assume much larger dimensions. A bank may take the initiative in a narrow market to force rates up or down, and when others follow the trend it had initiated it unobtrusively reverses its operations and covers before its original manœuvre has spent its force.

(3) A bank may spread an operation in space and in time as

widely as possible, in order to conceal its true size from the market.

(4) A bank may put a very junior dealer in charge of the first instalment of a major transaction in order to mislead its rival about the true importance of the intended transaction.

(5) If the bank does not want the market to identify a customer's transaction by its amount — which may have been offered before through some other bank — it deals in a round figure instead of the actual amount it wants to cover.

(6) If a ruse is repeated frequently it is apt to be discounted. On the other hand it might work as a double bluff. For instance, it is always possible that, if a bank has acquired the reputation for putting on junior dealers to initiate the first instalment of a major transaction, it might let the same dealer handle a deal representing the sum total of the intended transaction. In that case the rival might be misled into suspecting it, wrongly, that the operation in question would be once more merely the first instalment of a larger transaction and might respond accordingly, adjusting its quotation in a sense that suits the other bank. If a bank wants to buy, say, $10 million and on previous occasions it was known to have initiated similar transactions by buying in the first instance $1 million through a junior dealer, its rival might conceivably suspect a repetition of the tactics and put up its rate in anticipation of the effect of the entire transaction on the market. This would enable the rival bank to follow up the purchase of $1 million by selling $10 million at the more favourable rates. The success of the ruse depends on whether the rival suspects bluff or double-bluff. His reaction is not easy to foresee, although familiarity with the mentality of the dealer concerned may help.

Some of the above devices are apt to be more successful in local dealings than in international dealings, because the identity of the bank concerned remains undisclosed until the deal is completed. This means that if several instalments of a large transaction are offered to the market simultaneously through different brokers the banks providing the counterparts may not know immediately that they come from the same source. On the other hand any information gets round more quickly in the local market than in the international market. In some markets, especially in Germany, the chances of getting away with subtle devices are somewhat better, because occasionally the name of the bank in question is allowed to remain undisclosed until the broker has actually delivered the contract notes. Meanwhile several transactions can be concluded with the same bank before it discovers that they originate from the identical source. Continental *bourses*, on the other hand, are the least suitable for such devices because dealers have a better idea of what is happening around them.

Many dealers go through life without using any of the sophisticated devices described above, indeed without encountering them — or at any rate without discovering that any of them were used against them. They may be highly successful dealers for that. Possibly their reputation for straightforward dealing may have brought them goodwill that is more valuable than any conceivable advantages they could have gained through resorting to smart tricks. The traditional British diplomatic method of telling the truth and relying on the Continental reputation of "perfidious Albion" for being disbelieved by one's opponents often pays dividends in the foreign exchange market.

Business has to be transacted with an amazing speed. Dealers must be able to make up their minds in a split second and take quick decisions. In addition, all the time they have to follow closely what their colleagues in the dealing room are doing, and to that end they have to develop the faculty of listening to telephone conversations other than their own at the same time as proceeding with their own conversation. They must be well-informed about the prevailing trend in the market and must react quickly to any changes. They must always be on the lookout for fractional discrepancies and arbitrage possibilities that would secure them a profit margin. Very often there is no opportunity to refer back their decisions to the chief dealer. Mistakes are easily made and are costly. The extent to which dealers have a free hand to commit their banks to the tune of millions varies according to the bank and also according to the experience of individual dealers. They receive general guidance from the chief dealer about the direction in which he wants them to operate in various currencies and may obtain specific guidance about individual transactions he wants them to carry out. They must be put into the picture about limits in respect of rates and amounts. Even so each one of them is required on many occasions to assume the initiative and take on a high degree of responsibility.

When dealings are conducted by telephone there is no tangible evidence of the terms of the transactions concluded or indeed whether they have been concluded at all, until they are confirmed in contract notes. There is often a possibility for making mistakes, and misunderstandings or misinterpretations about rates and dates are liable to occur. In spite of this, thousands of deals are put through every day without any disagreement about their terms. Disagreements are a very rare occurrence and are invariably settled amicably. If there is disagreement about the rate the two parties usually split the difference, but if one of the parties feels very strongly that it is in the right the other party may prefer to give way rather than endanger its reputation for fair dealing. That reputation constitutes a very valuable goodwill, for bankers prefer to deal with those noted of fair dealing and avoid dealing with those suspected of being too smart. For the sake of that goodwill it is deemed worth while to incur an occasional loss.

Although the standard of integrity in the foreign exchange market is very high there are occasional exceptions. One of the unwritten rules of the market is to abstain from taking advantage of obvious mistakes made by rival dealers, such as mistaken quotations of rates that are quite obviously well outside the range within which rates were apt to move at the time when the deal was concluded. Most rates are quoted nowadays up to four decimals and, except on particular active days, fluctuations are confined most of the time to changes in the last two decimals, *e.g.*, on a particular day the sterling-dollar rate is quoted at say, 2·7978–2·7981. Conceivably through some error a bank may quote by telex 2·7878–2·7881. If the bank receiving this quotation seizes on the opportunity and accepts the buying rate at 2·7881 the party that made the mistaken quotation may be held to it. Since, however, it is considered unfair to exploit such an obvious mistake the bank that is guilty of that offence will find itself ostracised in the market. Other banks will become unwilling to deal with it. They will never contact it for quotations and will not respond to its initiative. The resulting loss of business is liable to wipe out its ill-gotten gain in a matter of days or weeks, and it is likely to take many months, if not years, for that bank to live down that incident and regain the confidence of the market.

It is always banks with a reputation for fair dealing that are approached in the first instance, and they stand to benefit by the resulting high turnover, both directly and indirectly. The large majority of transactions in the market are concluded between banks which have earned a high place on each other's lists of priorities. In this sphere generosity and fair-mindedness are qualities that bring their reward. It pays to individual dealers, too, to build up a reputation for being pleasant to deal with because they attract much business to their bank. Establishment of personal relationship among dealers and brokers in the local market and among dealers between banks in different markets is very helpful for the creation of the right atmosphere of confidence through give-and-take. From this point of view the Forex Clubs perform a highly valuable task by humanising personal relationships in the market.

Genuine mistakes and misunderstandings are at times inevitable, *e.g.*, when deals are negotiated in French *soixante-six* is at times mistaken for *soixante-dix*. Hence the preference of some dealers to use the Swiss terms *septante, octante* and *nonante* in negotiating deals. When such misunderstandings arise the usual practice is to cancel the deal or to split the difference rather than resort to acrimonious correspondence, arbitration or litigation. Most dealers with very long experience have never had a single lawsuit arising from misunderstandings in respect of foreign exchange transactions.

CHAPTER 4

TRANSACTIONS WITH CUSTOMERS

ALTHOUGH foreign exchange dealers are in a position to initiate in the market itself a wide variety of inter-bank operations it is their bank's transactions with customers that constitute the main foundation and the main justification of their activities. This is shown by the fact that banks which have an extensive clientèle are normally the most active operators in the market. The average turnover of large commercial banks far exceeds that of even the largest merchant bank, although some of the latter too have extensive non-banking clientèle. The covering of transactions concluded with non-banking customers is the bread-and-butter of the foreign exchange departments of commercial banks.

From the point of view of the differentiation between transactions outside the market and those within the market, operations with banks which are not themselves in the market may be classified in the category of transactions with customers. This category also includes central banks which usually do not operate in the market directly but through the intermediary of commercial banks or merchant banks.

Non-banking customers proper may be classified under the following headings:

(1) Manufacturers exporting their own goods and importing raw materials, semi-manufactures or equipment against payment in foreign currencies.

(2) Public works contractors operating abroad.

(3) Industrial firms engaged in the construction of plants abroad.

(4) Industrial firms financing the production, transport or distribution of their goods by their foreign subsidiaries.

(5) Merchants exporting goods produced within their country against payment in foreign currencies.

(6) Merchants engaged in re-exporting imported goods against payment in foreign currencies.

(7) Merchants engaged in transactions in goods bought and sold between two foreign countries.

(8) Importers of goods payable in foreign currencies.

(9) Merchants or manufacturers abroad financing their operations in London in Euro-currencies.

(10) Insurance companies transacting business abroad.

(11) Shipping companies and airlines.

(12) Travel bureaux.

(13) Residents acquiring or realising portfolio investments in foreign currencies.

(14) Stock exchange firms dealing in foreign securities.

(15) Industrial or commercial firms engaged in operation of direct investment abroad.

(16) Residents travelling abroad, emigrating or subsidising residents in foreign countries.

(17) Foreign residents paying visits to this country, immigrating or subsidising residents in this country.

(18) Residents having to service debts in terms of foreign currencies.

(19) Lawyers and executors concerned with foreign legacies or with proceeds of legal claims abroad.

(20) Buyers and sellers of real property abroad.

(21) Recipients of royalties from abroad, payments for patents or copyrights from abroad.

(22) Payments in foreign currencies by Governments insofar as they are not made through central banks.

A very large proportion of the various types of transactions with customers listed above reach the foreign exchange departments through the intermediary of branches or banks which have no direct access to the foreign exchange market. The relationship between bank branches and the foreign exchange department of their head office in respect of transactions with customers vary widely from bank to bank. In Switzerland many branches are to a very large degree independent of their head offices and their foreign exchange departments have a free hand to operate both with customers and in the market with very little reference back to their head offices. This practice is made possible by the arrangement under which rates are fixed in advance every day for transactions with customers. The spread between buying and selling rates is wide enough to safeguard banks against losses through minor fluctuations in the course of a day. Similar arrangements operate in Italy and some other countries. No such rates are fixed in Britain or in the United States, and banks are free to compete with each other by accepting low profit margins over market rates in their transactions with customers. Every morning the branches receive from their head offices the rates which are to apply to small transactions during the day. Indeed it has always been the practice in respect of very small transactions for customers to rely on their banks simply to credit or debit their account with the sterling equivalent based on the current exchange rates without any previous agreement. A small fixed commission is charged on such transactions, and in case of telegraphic transfers they are debited with cable expenses.

Each bank has a different rule about the maximum figure above which transactions with customers must be referred to the head office concerning the rate to be quoted to the customer. In some instances that limit is as high as £1000, in other instances it is as low as £100. When branches have to contact their head office about the rates they are to quote to customers for transactions above that maximum the usual practice is that a reasonable time is allowed to them during which the rate quoted is to remain in force. While in the market itself that interval is expressed in seconds and seldom exceeds a minute or two in the relationship between foreign exchange departments of head offices and branch offices it may be as long as 10–15 minutes. Large branches with a considerable commercial turnover have foreign exchange departments of their own, which are in frequent communication with foreign exchange dealers in London. The banks have regional foreign exchange departments and smaller branches of the same district deal through those departments. What banks are anxious to avoid is that customers should treat quotations as amounting to a free option enabling them to try to improve on it elsewhere.

Banks in their relationship with non-banking customers are not agents but principals. They quote firm rates and it is up to them to ensure that a transaction is covered in the market at a rate which secures them a profit. The ideal state of affairs is that banks, when quoting to customers, quote rates which leaves them a profit margin even on the assumption that they have to cover at the least favourable rate obtainable in the market at that moment. If they sell exchanges to customers they have to envisage the possibility of having to cover at the market's selling rate and if they buy exchanges from customers they have to envisage the possibility of being only able to cover at the market's buying rate. Even this assumption does not absolutely safeguard them, because rates are liable to move against them before they have covered. Indeed if the covering operation is of substantial size it is liable to move the rate against them. Nevertheless in post-War conditions, owing to keen competition, banks can ill afford to play for a hundred per cent safety. In any case their risk of an adverse movement is offset by the possibility of a favourable movement.

There is also the possibility of "marrying". But in quoting rates to customers the dealer, however non-speculative he may be, has to speculate on the prospect of the rates during the brief interval between his quotation and the covering transaction that has to await the acceptance of the quotation by the customer.

Towards the middle 'sixties the post-War tendency for customers to drive hard bargains with their bankers by playing up rivals against each other appears to have relented somewhat. A large and apparently increasing number of customers, having realised the value of their banks' services in providing for their foreign exchange requirements, have come to adopt the practice of instructing them to buy or sell "at best" without haggling about the rate. This does not mean that the banks become their agents and execute their orders in the market on their account, but they allow their customers the rate at which they have been able to cover. It is to the interest of the banks to secure the best rate for good customers. Indeed, in many instances, if the rate moved against the customer during the interval between the receipt of his order and its execution, the bank may deem it worth its while to bear the resulting loss, for the sake of maintaining the goodwill of the customer who might resent it if his bank's "best" rate is unfavourable to him.

Instructions to buy or sell "at best" have to be given in respect of the purchase or sale of exchanges which have not a good market. Banks may also receive such orders in their morning mail when their customers are anxious that orders decided upon on the previous day too late for execution on the same day should be executed first thing in the morning. Such orders are also received by cable from New York and other centres which are open while London is closed.

Transactions with customers may be classified as follows:

(1) Covering current requirements or selling current receipts of foreign currencies.

(2) Covering future requirements or selling future receipts.

(3) Hedging against a possible depreciation of assets in foreign currencies or a possible appreciation of liabilities in foreign currencies.

(4) Borrowing or lending in foreign currencies.

(5) Investment or disinvestment in terms of foreign currencies.

(6) Speculation and arbitrage.

Most transactions with commercial customers assume the form of spot or forward outright transactions. Bankers always advise their commercial customers to cover the exchange risk on all their transactions in foreign currencies, but this advice is seldom followed consistently. During periods of stable exchanges, when fluctuations are within a narrow range, it is difficult to persuade business firms to cover unless they can do so on advantageous terms. Importers stand to gain by buying forward exchanges instead of spot if forward rates are at a discount, while exporters stand to gain by selling forward exchanges which are at a premium. Intermediaries working with narrow profit margins and merchants dealing in staple commodities may feel advisable always to cover, because even moderate fluctuations within support points are liable to convert their profit into a loss. On the other hand the cost of covering might wipe out the profit margin, so that the deal is only profitable if the merchant is willing to assume the exchange risk. From this point of view it is convenient for the trade that the banks of countries such as Australia, New Zealand and South Africa, whose foreign trade consists largely of staple products, provide forward exchange facilities in their currencies against sterling at a nominal cost.

The argument in favour of covering exchange risks becomes powerfully reinforced if there is a possibility of a change in parities. If the currency in terms of which exports are sold is devaluation-prone, or if the currency in terms of which imports are bought is revaluation-prone, it is a matter of elementary commonsense for merchants to cover. On the other hand, if the currency in terms of which exports are invoiced is revaluation-prone or the currency of which imports are invoiced is devaluation-prone merchants may find it expedient to leave the exchange uncovered.

Much depends on the anticipated degree of the expected devaluation or revaluation, on the cost of covering, and on the possibilities of an adverse movement of the spot rate within support points. It is not for banks to try to dissuade their customers from taking a moderate calculated risk. On the other hand they are right in trying to dissuade their customers from having uncovered claims in a devaluation-prone currency or uncovered liabilities in a revaluation-prone currency. Above all, they are right in advising their customers against covering and uncovering as and when the prospects — or to be exact, the customers' opinion of the prospects — change. Jobbing in and out of a currency is clearly sheer speculation even when it is connected with some genuine commercial transaction.

It is argued sometimes that importers of staple commodities in a country with a devaluation-prone currency need not cover the exchange risk, for the prices of the goods in terms of the importing country's currency would rise as a result of a devaluation, so that they would be compensated for the less favourable exchange rate they have to pay when buying the foreign currencies. But there is always a possibility that higher prices in terms of the local currency may give rise to consumer-resistance or it may attract increased supplies produced locally, so that prices of imported commodities do not rise in proportion to the devaluation. In particular, as far as the U.K. is concerned, the Sterling Area provides a large proportion of staple products imported. Before 1967 prices of such imports were not affected directly by devaluation, if their supply was sufficiently elastic to meet U.K. demand that was diverted from non-sterling countries by a rise in the sterling prices of their exports, exporters in non-sterling countries had to reduce their prices to meet Sterling Area competition. Much depended also on whether there was a buyer's market or a seller's market in the commodities concerned, and whether devaluation would occur against an inflationary or a deflationary background. Since 1967 stability within the Sterling Area is no longer assumed.

The forecasting of the effect of devaluations or import prices is by no means a matter of simple arithmetic. Importers must therefore be advised to be on the safe side instead of listening to dogmatic over-simplification of a very complex problem and depend on being compensated for the exchange loss by higher prices in terms of their devalued currency.

Covering of the exchange risk on commercial transactions is complicated by the uncertainty of the date when payment for exports is actually received. Delays in production, or in transport, or in the payments by purchasers, or in the granting of transfer permits in countries with exchange control, are liable to upset the calculations of exporters and also those of importers. For this reason forward exchange transactions for optional dates have come to be resorted to increasingly during the post-War period when the degree of uncertainty of delivery dates has increased considerably. They usually assume the form of contracts within the maximum and minimum time limits between which the currency sold is to be delivered or between which delivery of the currency bought is to be taken.

For instance, the delivery date can be made optional for any day during the last month of the three months' contract. The rates charged to customers on such contracts are usually calculated on the assumption that the customer delivers the exchanges, or asks for their delivery, on the day which is the least favourable from the bank's point of view. If the bank sells forward exchanges for optional dates it has to assume that it has to deliver on the earliest day fixed in the contract. If the bank buys forward exchange for optional dates it has to assume that it will not receive the exchanges until the remotest day allowed under the contract, so that it cannot depend on being able to use that currency from an earlier date.

There is an alternative method of option dealing. The bank may sell forward exchanges to the customer, or it may buy forward exchanges from him, for delivery on one of several alternative dates, with different exchange rates fixed for each date. This method is applied in the United States but is unknown in European countries.

Big commercial banks with a large volume of customers' business are not particularly concerned with special ways of covering of forward exchanges with optional dates. Having a well-filled book of graded maturities they have seldom any difficulty in making the necessary adjustment in the eleventh hour according to the way in which the customer exercises his option.

Although owing to the uncertainties of international trade there is some demand for forward exchange contracts under the terms of which the non-banking buyer or seller would be given the option of backing out of the contract altogether, no such facilities are available to them. The nearest thing to such options is an arrangement made occasionally by banks with good customers who would like them to hold open the quotation of exchange rates for half an hour or an hour, to enable him to finalise a pending goods transaction in the certain knowledge of the exchange rate on the basis of which he has to make his calculations before deciding whether at a given price the operation would be profitable. The rates quoted to the customer on such occasion usually allow for the possibility of some slight movement of the rates against the bank during the brief duration of the option. But when exchanges are subject to wide fluctuations and when such options would be more essential than ever they become usually unobtainable. In any event if the dealer finds that the customer takes advantage of the option for making enquiries with other banks in case he could get a better rate he does not repeat the concession on the next occasion.

Firms which would be in particular need of options for longer periods are industrial firms or contractors tendering for contracts that would involve the expenditure or receipt of large amounts of foreign currencies. It would be expedient for them to cover the exchange risk between the submission of their tenders and the receipt of the answer, for any major change in exchange rates would upset their calculations that are based on the existing exchange rates. No such option is available for them, however, and there is nothing they can do to eliminate such a risk except tendering in currencies which are not likely to change materially during the weeks or months while the fate of their tenders is in the balance. This is one of the instances in which the availability of forward exchange facilities does not provide an adequate safeguard against risks arising from fluctuating exchanges.

Bankers abroad are in an awkward position if customers ask for their advice whether to hedge or not. Decisions on covering definite claims and liabilities are a relatively simple matter, even though complications are liable to arise if the date of the payment is uncertain. When it comes to hedging against assets whose realisable value is uncertain, and when the date of their realisation is also uncertain, then the customer and his banker are confronted with a particularly awkward dilemma. Let us take one very frequent instance. A merchant has imported goods from a country with a devaluation-prone currency and leaves the exchange uncovered until he has paid for the goods. If that currency is devalued his profit on the exchange rate would compensate him for the fall in the price of the goods in terms of his own currency that might result from the devaluation. But if no devaluation occurs by the time the payment is completed, and if he has an unsold stock of the imported goods he is exposed to the risk of a fall in their price through a subsequent devaluation or, for that matter, through a subsequent revaluation of his own currency. As a result of such changes his rivals would be able to import the same goods at a lower price in their currency. Importers abroad can hedge against that risk by going short in the currency of the exporting country at the time when he pays for the goods, to the extent of the value of his unsold stock, reducing his short position in that currency as and when he disposes of the imported goods. The operation might appear to be speculative, for the merchant does not expect any payment in the currency which he would sell-forward. Nevertheless he faces a genuine risk. Yet in the U.K. such hedging is not permitted. Importers can cover the risk of a devaluation of their own currency, but not the risk of devaluation of the exporter's currency.

The situation is liable to be even more complicated when it comes to advising customers about hedging against direct investments in a country with a devaluation-prone currency. A devaluation would not reduce the value of these assets in terms of the local currency. On the contrary there is a chance for an increase in its value through the improved competitive capacity of industries in the country concerned, and in the long run the devaluation is liable to be followed by an appreciation of his assets in terms of the local currency in sympathy with the general rise in the local price level. But the immediate effect of the depreciation of the currency is a fall in the value of his assets in terms of the customer's own currency. The value of these assets would have to be written down in his balance sheet, even though their subsequent appreciation might enable him to write them up again later. To avoid a book-keeping loss he feels justified in hedging. But in Britain such hedging is only permitted up to six months before the realisation of the assets abroad.

The foreign exchange market has improved considerably since the War in respect of forward exchange facilities for long periods. While before the War it was difficult to obtain forward cover beyond six months and virtually impossible beyond

twelve months, at the time of writing it is possible to cover the
exchange risk as a matter of routine up to twelve months — for
which period there is a regular market in the principal exchanges
— and arrangements can be negotiated up to very long periods.
Contracts of up to 7 years are known to have been arranged.
These facilities are of great assistance to shipbuilders, aircraft
manufacturers, firms undertaking construction of plants
abroad, and public works contractors operating abroad. The
alternative solution for such firms with long contracts involving
the receipt of foreign currencies in several years' time is to
borrow through their banks in terms of the currency in which
they are to receive payment and then sell the proceeds. Thanks
to the development of Euro-currency markets and the lengthening of maturities of foreign currency deposits which can be
borrowed in these markets, this solution has become feasible in
some currencies, but it is still impossible in most currencies.

Every form of investment and disinvestment abroad by
British residents and investment and disinvestment of foreign
capital in the U.K. or in other Sterling Area countries constitute an important source of foreign exchange business,
though much of it was transacted in foreign markets. Transactions in foreign securities, too, gives rise to large though
fluctuating volume of foreign exchange transactions. Investment and disinvestment in long-term securities quoted in
Stock Exchanges abroad formerly gave rise to spot transactions,
while stock arbitrage transactions which had to be covered
against exchange risk owing to the narrowness of profit margins
gave rise to forward exchange transactions. Since the War such
operations have come to be financed largely through a special
market — the investment dollar market for resident investment in non-sterling securities. Non-resident investment in
sterling securities is now financed with external sterling. A
large though declining proportion of investment dollars, which
are dealt with in Chapter 13, is transacted outside the foreign
exchange market, between stockbrokers and stock departments
of banks.

The extent to which short-term borrowing and short-term
investment by customers gives rise to foreign exchange trans-

actions has increased considerably since the War. While large firms of international standing — such as the big oil companies — have always been familiar with the facilities of the principal financial markets that offer alternative facilities, during the post-War period a number of other big firms in various countries have come to realise the advantages of borrowing or investing in foreign centres or in terms of foreign currencies. The resulting transactions assume mostly the form of swap operations, though uncovered investment or borrowing by non-banking firms is by no means unknown.

Space arbitrage and time arbitrage are entirely between banks, but much interest arbitrage is transacted nowadays by banks on customers' *loro* accounts. As profit margins are usually fractional, only big firms capable of dealing in large amounts find such operations worth their while. More often under the terms of their arrangements with their customers the banks themselves are in a position to use such funds. Apart altogether from considerations of yield, foreign currency balances may be held on *loro* account for a wide variety of reasons. Whatever these reasons may be, their acquisition, disposal, and switching into other currencies give rise to foreign exchange operations.

As already pointed out there is now much less speculation in exchanges on account of non-banking customers than before the War. Nevertheless the practice is apt to revive from time to time when an exchange comes under acute pressure and under the influence of devaluation rumours or revaluation rumours. Some Continental banks are still prepared to operate speculative accounts for customers, and in countries without exchange control there is no need even for disguising them as genuine commercial transactions. London banks have to scrutinise carefully the transactions of their non-banking customers, but they have no means of scrutinising similarly speculative transactions that reach them indirectly through the intermediary of overseas banks who undo in the London market their positions resulting from their customers' speculative operations. In inter-bank transactions no questions are ever asked or information volunteered about the nature or purpose of the transactions. They all reach London in large round amounts which may cover a multitude of speculative sins. The only restrictions U.K. banks may apply to operations by non-banking speculators abroad that reach them through foreign banks is the limits which are applied to forward exchange transactions or Euro-currency transactions with any particular bank. Once those limits are reached foreign banks may find it increasingly difficult to undo in the London market their commitments with speculative non-banking customers.

Movements of "hot money" representing funds that have found their way out of their countries of origin are from time to time a very important source of foreign exchange transactions. Apart from the original acquisition of foreign exchanges, owners of such funds are usually of a nervous disposition and are inclined to switch from one currency into another. Many of them have deposited their funds on management accounts in Switzerland or elsewhere, and the banks in charge of their money have a free hand to transfer the funds from one currency into another if they deem it necessary in order to safeguard the interests of their customers. In many instances it may be inexpedient to communicate with their customers, and for this reason the banks, aware of their responsibility, may be inclined to err on the over-cautious side by realising holdings of any currency which come under suspicion. Because there are many such accounts in Switzerland, the transfers of funds from one currency to another in Zürich and in the other Swiss markets, whether with or without specific instructions from the customers, has earned Swiss banks an undeserved reputation for themselves engaging in speculation in foreign exchanges on a large scale. Actually most Swiss banks are very conservative in this respect and most of the speculative operations originating from Swiss markets are on behalf of their customers.

CHAPTER 5

COVERING AND HEDGING

In the last chapter we dealt with covering and hedging operations between banks and non-banking customers. Such operations, unless they can be "married" outside the market, have to be covered in the market by operations between banks. They affect exchange rates partly because their trend and their amount influence the quotations given or accepted by the dealers of the banks directly concerned — whenever the Great West Road (a term familiar in the foreign exchange market, symbolizing American branch factories or subsidiaries in Britain) begins to hedge against a sterling devaluation dealers envisage heavy pressure — and partly because they affect actual supply and demand in the market. The present chapter deals with covering and hedging operations by the banks themselves on their own account.

The much-quoted textbook rule, according to which every bank is supposed to cover immediately all its transactions with customers, does not correspond to the true facts. Enterprising chief dealers who have the courage of their convictions prefer to choose the moment when to cover instead of feeling impelled to pursue a rule rigidly. They may or may not be able to persuade their managements to give them as free a hand in this respect as they would like to have. The attitude of banks from this point of view varies widely. It depends on the following circumstances:

(1) Traditions of the bank.

(2) Conservatism of the chief dealer.

(3) Conservatism of the management.

(4) Recent experience of the bank, favourable or otherwise.

(5) Ability of the department to earn adequate profits without taking risks.

55

(6) View taken by the bank on prospects of foreign exchanges.

(7) Official attitude towards open positions.

(8) Law-abiding character of the bank.

Certain banks have long-established traditions for avoiding speculative risks as far as possible. They are "arbitrage-minded", that is, they regard arbitrage as the main if not the only function of their foreign exchange departments. Other banks are "speculation-minded" and have a tradition for willingness to take a certain degree of risks. Their attitude is liable to change, however, through the appointment of a new chief dealer or through changes in the executive or in the board. Recent experience of a bank is also liable to change its attitude. If it had bad luck and suffered losses through delay in covering it is likely to err on the safe side for some time, until the painful experience is forgotten. Some banks might even learn through recent experience of other banks. On the other hand, if through excessive conservatism banks recently missed some good opportunities, they might feel inclined to take a less conservative attitude on the next occasion.

Banks which have ample bread-and-butter business with their customers or which have discovered profitable lines of arbitrage may feel that they are able to earn their keep without taking risks. They may be inclined to cover, while those which have no such sources of profit or are not content with their proceeds may be tempted to take more risks by deferring the covering. This is a generalisation which does not necessarily apply in all instances. Some banks with a good clientèle are nevertheless distinctly "speculation-minded".

Prospects of exchange rates — or rather views taken rightly or wrongly on the prospect — are apt to influence banks in their attitude towards covering in two conflicting senses. When there is a likelihood of an appreciation or a depreciation of an exchange the more conservative banks make a point of avoiding any open positions in them, while the more enterprising banks go out of their way to abstain from covering. There is, of course, a difference of degree between awaiting the favourable moment for covering positions resulting from transactions with customers and deliberately creating open positions. Some banks defer covering in the hope of receiving orders that would enable them to "marry" the transactions. Others may await the appearance of a counterpart in the market on favourable terms rather than move the rates against themselves by taking the initiative for covering. Others again may take the initiative for creating open positions instead of drifting into them through the incidence of operations that happen to come their way through the initiative of customers or of other banks.

The official attitude is always in favour of covering. Even in countries where there are no exchange restrictions and where no limits are imposed on the amount of open positions the authorities usually discourage banks from keeping open positions. The degree of the emphasis with which they do so is apt to vary, however, from country to country and from time to time. The degree of the loyalty with which banks observe official or unofficial limitations of their open positions also varies from country to country and even from bank to bank.

Although according to our definition the term "covering" implies the existence of claims or liabilities of a definite amount maturing on a fixed date, in many instances operations relating to claims and liabilities which do not actually mature on any fixed date also constitute covering. Balances or overdrafts on *nostro* accounts, or holdings of foreign notes, have no maturity dates, nor have in practice funds borrowed or lent in the form of money or Euro-currency deposits at call or at short notice. Money is lent, for instance, very often at seven days' notice to British Local Authorities, but both lender and borrower intend to renew it repeatedly. They do not really know after how many renewals they are likely to decide not to renew the loan. Nevertheless if the lender lends the sterling proceeds of a Euro-dollar deposit he is likely to cover his dollar liability. Technically such operations are hedging, but in practice they are covering if the forward exchange is bought or sold for the maturity which the lender considers it to be the most likely date for the termination of the transaction. There is usually nothing to prevent its termination earlier or later than the date chosen by means of a swap transaction undoing the commitments before maturity date or renewing it on maturity date.

It is very often impossible or too costly to cover transactions with customers immediately for the exact date of their maturity. Banks endeavour to cover in the first instance for the nearest convenient date — usually the nearest standard date, though at times a counterpart for some convenient odd date happens to come their way — and adjust the discrepancy between the maturities by means of the necessary swap transaction. They can take their time over such adjustment by means of a short-long swap once the main exchange risk is covered. In any case many banks are not averse to maintaining commitments in graded maturities.

Banks may or may not cover their balances on *nostro* accounts and their funds engaged in interest arbitrage, largely according to the view they take of the prospects of the exchange rates concerned. Likewise when they borrow Euro-currencies and convert the proceeds into their own currencies or into some third currency they may or may not cover according to their view of the prospects and the probable extent of the exchange risk, and according to the nature and extent of the swap margins. They accumulate uncovered balance in revaluation-prone currencies, and they reduce to a minimum their balances in devaluation-prone currencies if the cost of covering is too high.

In Britain and in other countries official limitation on net balances of overall open positions instead of limiting positions in individual currencies tends to induce banks to keep open positions in individual currencies which they would not keep otherwise. Suppose there is strong anticipation of an impending revaluation of, say, the Swiss franc. Banks which have transferred into that currency uncovered funds right to their authorised limits for net uncovered positions, and would like to increase their long position in Swiss francs further, are able to do so without offending against exchange regulations by simply going short in, say, Italian lire, thereby reducing the overall balance of their long positions. If they anticipate a devaluation of, say, the lira they can maintain a short position in it well in excess of the official limit by going long in, say,

D.marks to the amount of the excess. Such operations are only deemed to be expedient if dealers feel strongly about the imminence of changes in parities or of noteworthy changes in exchange rates.

Generally speaking, the existence of limits to open positions tends to induce banks not only to abstain from deliberately creating large open positions but even to cover open positions resulting from transactions with customers sooner than they would otherwise, in order not to exhaust their limits. They often prefer to keep an unused margin, just in case there should arise some favourable opportunity which they would have to forgo if their limits are reached.

The new regulations adopted in Britain in November 1964 under which banks have to submit to the Bank of England the weekly returns giving their open positions in addition to their monthly returns have provided additional inducement for early covering. So long as there were several weeks to go till the next return during which it remained possible to cover unauthorised open positions there was a strong temptation to overstep the limit temporarily, on the assumption that there was ample time for awaiting a favourable opportunity to cover at a profit.

Banks are normally anxious to cover before week-ends, especially since Saturday closing of the market has lengthened the interruption of dealing and the interval during which changes are liable to occur, thereby increasing the possibility of such changes. But strong definite anticipation of some change, as distinct from vague feelings of uncertainty, is liable to produce the opposite effect on other banks. Their dealers may feel tempted to be short in devaluation-prone currencies or long in revaluation-prone currencies over week-ends. For instance, during 1964–67 speculative week-end influences were usually adverse to sterling and it usually depreciated on Fridays or even on Thursdays, recovering on Mondays.

In their routine dealings banks usually hasten to cover their forward transactions with customers or, for that matter, with other banks, by means of spot transactions in the opposite sense. They do not want to delay covering until they find a suitable counterpart in the form of outright forward exchange. The delays may be a mere matter of minutes or even seconds, but even such a short delay is liable to entail some risk. Although most dealers are not averse to taking such risk in given circumstances they may prefer not to drift into it accidentally but to choose their own moment for taking it. If they want to be short in a currency they may deliberately delay the covering of forward sales to customers. If they want to have a long position they may delay covering of forward purchases from customers. If they hold no definite views about the prospects of the exchange rate concerned they may adhere to the textbook rule of covering the spot exchange risk without delay, but even then they may prefer to give themselves a chance to cover on favourable terms rather than forcing the rates against themselves.

Covering by banks presents special problems in the following situations:

(1) When forward exchanges have been bought from, or sold to, customers for very long periods in excess of the limits for maturities which are normally transacted in the market.

(2) When Euro-currency deposits are lent or borrowed for similarly long periods.

(3) When forward contracts for optional dates have been entered into with customers.

(4) When forward contracts for odd dates have been entered into with customers.

(5) When banks are short in spot exchanges that are to be delivered on the same day or on the following day.

(6) When positions in currencies which have no adequate forward markets have to be covered.

Although the post-War period witnessed a remarkable lengthening of the maximum limit for maturities of forward exchange contracts this trend has not been without reverses. Uncertainty of the outlook for the two reserve currencies during 1964-68 made it more difficult to deal in long forward exchange than it was during the early 'sixties. Banks which felt they had to oblige good customers by giving them forward contracts for periods of up to five years and longer were often unable to cover beyond two years and had to bear the risk of an adverse change in the cost of covering for the remaining period. There is, of course, always the possibility of "marrying" long forward transactions with similar transactions in the opposite sense undertaken with some other customer. The two-years' period for which cover is usually obtainable in the market provides a fair chance for finding such counterpart. In any case the banks are safeguarded by their two-year contracts against a change in the spot rate and the risk is confined to having to prolong the forward covering on less favourable terms at the end of the two years. The development of a market in long-term Euro-dollar deposits — and to a much less extent in other Euro-currency deposits — has created additional opportunities for covering long forward contracts. The trend towards longer maturities suffered a setback in the middle 'sixties, but later employment of proceeds of Euro-bonds revived the trend.

During the late 'fifties a limited market developed for undoing involved commitments undertaken for customers in respect of forward contracts for optional dates, the volume of such transactions having greatly increased in the post-War period owing to uncertainty of delivery rates for goods. But the majority of such contracts is covered in the ordinary way on the basis of the assumption that currencies sold by customers would be delivered on the remotest day provided under the option, while in the market currencies bought by them would be claimed by them on the earliest date. Many banks are reluctant to provide a counterpart for such contracts in the market — unless they happen to have commitments in the opposite sense which they want to cover — because in doing so they would help their rivals to assume such commitments in relation to non-banking customers.

The overwhelming majority of forward contracts in the market are for standard dates. It would interfere with speedy dealings if too many transactions were for odd dates, especially on hectic days when dealers have simply no time to look for counterparts for such transactions. But to many customers standard dates are of no use, as their payments are due on odd dates. This presents no major problem to dealers, as they cover for the nearest standard date and adjust if necessary discrepancies in maturities with the aid of a long–short swap transaction. Alternatively they may take a view on the prospects of forward rates and carry long–short commitments for the period between the date of their contract with the customer and the nearest standard date for which they have covered.

For various reasons banks may find themselves short of spot exchanges which they have to deliver in two days and have to cover on the following day or even on value date itself. There is a market in exchanges on "value tomorrow" or "value today" terms, so that dealers are usually in a position to cover one day ahead or even a few hours ahead of the time limit for delivering. But in a one-way market such operations are apt to be costly, and it is often more convenient in such situations to resort to overdrawing *nostro* accounts if possible and if there are no cheaper short-term borrowing facilities.

Covering of forward contracts in currencies which, owing to exchange control or to other reasons, have no forward markets is always a costly and difficult process. But it is not impossible, and British importers from Nigeria would have been able to safeguard themselves against losses on their liabilities in Nigerian pounds in 1967.

The relative extent to which banks are concerned with hedging on their own account is very small compared with the importance and extent of their covering operations on their own account. Nevertheless there are many instances in which banks cannot cover, owing to the uncertainty of the realisable amount of their assets or liabilities in foreign currencies, or to the date when they are realised. British banks are not permitted to hedge, but overseas banks with branches or affiliates in the U.K. are confronted with the same dilemma as other holders of assets outside their country. As a general rule banks do not hedge against such assets because, apart from any other reasons, it would be costly in the case of countries with devaluation-prone currencies, while it would be profitable but risky in the case of countries with revaluation-prone currencies. Banks with branches in a number of foreign countries usually take the view that book-keeping losses through devaluations in some countries are liable to be offset in the long run by book-keeping profits through revaluations in other countries, and that in any case devaluations are apt to be followed by increases of profits and assets values in terms of the devalued currencies. Anyway, the assets concerned represent such a small percentage of the banks' total assets that their book-keeping depreciation would not affect their positions or profits materially. Nevertheless when there is a really acute devaluation-scare some of the banks at any rate might be tempted to play for safety, especially if the devaluation is expected for the immediate future, so that hedging would have to be undertaken for a brief period only, or if the cost of such hedging is kept down artificially by official support of the forward rate.

Hedging against holdings of foreign securities by banks is a much more prevalent practice. Even in the absence of acute devaluation scares banks may want to safeguard themselves against an unpleasant and costly surprise. They may only hold foreign securities for high yield or for capital appreciation prospects if they deem this worth their while in spite of the cost of hedging against the exchange risk. Or they may hold them as securities against which they can borrow. Since they have no means of knowing the amount that the realisation of such securities at some unspecified future date would yield, they either hedge against exchange losses on the purchase price of securities or take a view on the probable amount of the proceeds when realised.

Banks confine their holdings of foreign securities for the most part to short-dated Government securities, in which case they hedge against the full amount to be received on maturity, even though conceivably they might decide to realise their holdings at lower prices before maturity. As the prices of such securities are usually not much below their nominal amount these operations may be regarded as being on the borderline between covering and hedging.

Holdings of foreign notes by banks give rise to such borderline

A Textbook on Foreign Exchange

operations. Discrepancies between exchange rates for such notes and the corresponding telegraphic transfer rates are liable to fluctuate, so that a simple covering operation by means of a forward exchange transaction to the amount of their current market value may not always eliminate the exact exchange risk. Banks have to take a view about the probable proceeds of their note holdings and hedge against them accordingly.

64

CHAPTER 6
ARBITRAGE IN SPACE

FOREIGN exchange transactions are an integral part of international arbitrage of every kind, not only of the three types of exchange arbitrage — space arbitrage, time arbitrage and interest arbitrage — but also of bullion arbitrage, security arbitrage and commodity arbitrage, the description of which lies outside the scope of this book. In the widest sense of the term it includes even decisions by customers whether to cover their exchange risk by forward exchange operations or by the alternative devices of buying or borrowing spot exchanges. In the three chapters dealing with exchange arbitrage we are concerned solely with arbitrage in space and in time and with interest arbitrage — transactions to take advantage of discrepancies between rates quoted at the same moment in different markets, between forward margins for different maturities, and between yields on short-term investments in different currencies.

Thanks to the progressive improvement of communications in the course of the centuries, to the establishment of closer relations between banks in various countries, and to the larger turnover of foreign exchange transactions, discrepancies between quotations at any given moment have become much narrower. This secular trend has continued in our lifetime. Compared even with the inter-War period, normal discrepancies have become distinctly narrower during the 'fifties and the 'sixties, owing to the improvement of long-distance telephone and telex services and to the greatly increased frequency of operations in foreign exchanges amidst relatively stable conditions. The main influences which tend to keep discrepancies narrow are the following:

(1) The all-round decline of profit margins on commercial transactions, interest arbitrage, etc., during the post-War

period has increased the keenness of foreign exchange departments to take advantage of marginal profits on discrepancies in space whenever possible.

(2) With the improvement of communications foreign exchange departments in different centres are now in more frequent touch with each other. Intervals between their contacts, during which discrepancies are liable to develop, are now much shorter.

(3) For considerations of prestige and goodwill, and in order to attract other business through achieving and maintaining the reputation of being a large operator, bankers are now more inclined to operate for a purely nominal profit to cover their overheads by increasing their turnover.

(4) They may operate at times even without a profit, for the sake of being in frequent contact with foreign markets in order to be informed about the latest quotations and changes in tendencies.

(5) As the support points of the dollar and the arbitrage points of the other currencies based on these support points are firmly established, and the market is thoroughly familiar with them, even the slightest deviations of non-dollar exchanges from their arbitrage points are apt to be speedily readjusted.

(6) While interest arbitrage and speculation other than through forward outright transactions ties down financial resources, space arbitrage, involving as it does simultaneous sale and purchase, can be expanded without limits even if the foreign exchange departments have no funds available.

(7) Even before actual arbitrage operations are carried out, the expectation that they are certain to be carried out when discrepancies develop tend to induce banks to adjust their quotations without awaiting the actual operations.

(8) Space arbitrage may assume the simple form of buying or selling exchanges in a foreign market in preference to transacting the same business in the local market. Banks may cover in the market which quotes the most favourable rates, and in doing so they tend to eliminate discrepancies even before it becomes worth while to buy specifically for the sake of selling at a profit.

(9) If discrepancies widen sufficiently for being noticed by large business firms they are liable to give rise to merchant-arbitrage, and to borrower-arbitrage and lender-arbitrage on account of customers.

In spite of all this, fractional discrepancies in space are apt to arise even now and are likely to continue to arise in spite of any further conceivable improvement in communications. The reasons for this may be listed as follows:

(1) Even within the same market fractional discrepancies are apt to occur.

(2) Supply-demand relationship is liable to differ from market to market. Any sudden unilateral increase in the supply or in the demand in one market tends to bring its rates quite temporarily out of line from those in other markets.

(3) Good markets quote narrower spreads between buying and selling rates. There is a scope for arbitrage between these quotations and the wider spreads quoted in other markets.

(4) The existence of brokerage on deals within local markets and its absence on deals between markets may give rise to discrepancies.

(5) On hectic days exchange movements are apt to be sudden and there may be some delays in operations bringing about the adjustment of rates which are out of line.

(6) On such days dealers may be too busy with more profitable operations, executing clients' orders, opening or covering positions etc., to find time for space arbitrage until profit margins have widened sufficiently to make it worth their while.

(7) Even now communications between markets are far from perfect and any brief delays that may occur occasionally are liable to give rise to discrepancies.

(8) Because official intervention is usually confined to dollars passing discrepancies are liable to arise between dollar rates in markets in which they are bought or sold by the authorities and cross rates in other centres.

The simplest form of space arbitrage is the bilateral or two-point arbitrage. When there is a discrepancy between the quotation of a foreign currency in the local market and the quotation of the local currency in the foreign market concerned, the exchange is bought where it is cheaper and resold where it is dearer. If in London the buying quotation of the dollar is 2·3964 while at the same time in New York the buying rate of sterling is 2·3967 arbitrageurs sell dollars against sterling in London and sell sterling against dollars in New York. There is relatively little opportunity nowadays for making a profit on such simple arbitrage in exchanges which have very active markets in both centres directly concerned, because banks in the two centres are in too close touch with both markets to allow such discrepancies to develop.

Triangular or three-point arbitrage operations may be carried out on the basis of cross rates — that is, the ratio between the quotation of two foreign exchanges in relation to each other in a third market. For instance, if the dollar is quoted in London at 2·40 and the guilder at 10, the dollar-guilder cross rate in London is 24 U.S. cents. If the quotation of the dollar in Amsterdam or the quotation of the guilder in New York differs from this cross rate, arbitrageurs in London or in Amsterdam or in New York may take advantage of the discrepancy and carry out a three-point arbitrage operation.

If there is a discrepancy between cross rates in different centres it may give rise to four-point arbitrage operations. Because such operations are more involved and the timing of all the transactions for the same moment is more difficult, discrepancies are liable to be wider than in the case of two-point or three-point arbitrage before banks are tempted to undertake them.

Sterling's part as an intermediary exchange in triangular and multilateral arbitrage has declined since 1964, even though in practically all markets sterling is quoted in terms of the local currency units, while in London, too, it is sterling that is quoted in terms of most foreign exchanges. This greatly simplifies the comparison of sterling's quotation abroad with the London quotation of the foreign exchange concerned. Admittedly, thanks to the use of modern electric calculating machines, it only takes nowadays a second or two to calculate the equivalents between the Paris quotation of the dollar in terms of francs and the New York quotation of the franc in terms of dollars. But every second counts in arbitrage, and the fact that any discrepancy between the London rate of the franc and the Paris rate of sterling is obvious without having to make any calculation to ascertain it is decidedly an advantage. Nevertheless, arbitrage operates increasingly against the dollar cross rate.

A more important reason for the use of sterling and of London is that sterling has a good market in most financial centres and that London is the best market for dollars and for a number of other important exchanges. The better a market the easier it is to operate in it without moving the rates against the operator. Even if the middle rate of the dollar in Paris is the same as the franc-dollar cross rate in London it is usually advantageous for Paris banks to undo large dollar transactions in London rather than in Paris or in New York, and it is usually advantageous for New York banks to undo large franc transactions in London rather than in New York or in Paris. This is because London, being a large market for both dollars and francs, can provide the counterpart more readily, and can absorb the additional buying or selling more easily, than either the Paris market or the New York market.

Given an identical middle rate, it is very often to the advantage of continental banks to buy or sell dollars in London rather than in their own markets. This is the reason why sterling is bound to be affected when there is buying or selling pressure on dollars in Continental centres.

London also acts as intermediary in transactions between Continental centres in each other's currency. It is a better market, for instance, in Belgian francs than Stockholm and in Swedish kroner than Brussels. For this reason, foreign exchange business between Sweden and Belgium is very often transacted through the intermediary of sterling. The fact that a larger number of banks have *nostro* accounts in London than in any other centre — with the obvious exception of New York — also contributes towards the use of sterling as an intermediate currency in triangular and multilateral transactions. Moreover, from the point of view of operations between Western European currencies London has the advantage of lower costs of communications compared with New York, also the identity of business hours. Nevertheless, in recent years the dollar has been gaining ground on sterling as an intermediate currency. This may be due partly to the development of the Euro-dollar market which is more active than the Euro-sterling market, but mainly to the distrust in sterling.

For purposes of arbitrage, as indeed for other foreign exchange transactions, London is a better market for forward transactions than for spot transactions, because the brokerage is twice as much for the latter than for the former, so that the spread between buying and selling rates for spot transactions tends to be wider. This means that arbitrage involving spot transactions is more likely to find a counterpart abroad when it could not be operated profitably in London, while London is generally acknowledged to be the best forward market in existence.

It is not always easy to synchronise the transactions involved in a triangular operation. Any time lag between them, however short, means the risk of an adverse change in exchange rates that might convert a prospective profit into an actual loss. That risk naturally increases in the case of four-point or five-point arbitrage operations. But precisely because of the deterrent effect of such risks discrepancies are more likely to develop than in respect of two-point arbitrage, for it is hardly worth while to assume the risk unless and until there is a profit-margin to justify doing so.

Arbitrage involves an additional minor risk, to be dealt with in Chapter 16, resulting from the discrepancies between the standard amounts of transactions in various currencies. There is an exchange risk on the amount of the discrepancy until transactions in the opposite sense cover it, or until the accumulation of other uncovered amounts in the same sense makes it worth while to carry out another market transaction. Such discrepancies are apt to be higher if more than two currencies are involved. There is also the delivery risk, even if it is quite negligible in dealings between the first-rate banks that are usually engaged in arbitrage.

Space arbitrage is done in forward exchanges as well as in

spot exchanges. The latter is necessarily more difficult, even in two-point arbitrage, because of the necessity to find a counterpart with an identical maturity, unless space arbitrage is combined with time arbitrage. When it comes to three-point arbitrage, the complications increase. Before the War many dealers were reluctant to transact arbitrage on the cross forward rate. "Why complicate a matter which is already complicated?" was the answer I received from a dealer when asking him the reason for his reluctance to take advantage of a noteworthy discrepancy. Since the War the decline of profit possibilities in various directions has induced foreign exchange departments to resort to such involved transactions for the sake of the wider profit margins that are obtainable on them even in post-War conditions. Today transactions on cross forward rates are part of the market's everyday routine, even though it is confined mostly to standard maturities, three months and to a less extent one month. While newspapers quote forward rates and cross spot rates they never quote cross forward rates.

Even quarters in which the foreign exchange market is looked upon as little better than a gambling den are usually prepared to make the grudging admission that space arbitrage does fulfil useful functions. The most obvious practical advantages derived from it may be summarised as follows:

(1) Isolated markets are relatively narrow. Thanks to systematic space arbitrage foreign exchange markets have merged virtually into a much broader international market. While differences between business hours limit space arbitrage across the oceans to certain hours of the day, the Western European foreign exchange markets may be regarded, thanks largely to space arbitrage, as one large integrated market. As pointed out in Chapter 3, there is even a tendency towards closer integration with New York through maintaining contact while London is closed.

(2) Thanks to this integration through arbitrage, merchants and others are in a position to obtain more favourable rates. Arbitrageurs relieve them of the trouble to search for the best market.

(3) Narrow markets are at the mercy of sudden discrepancies between local supply and local demand, causing relatively wide if temporary fluctuations. Thanks to space arbitrage such fluctuations are now kept relatively narrow and are apt to disappear very soon.

(4) Space arbitrage increases what Lipfert calls the "transparency" of the market — that is, the degree of familiarity of the participants with the latest changes in rates and trends.

(5) By increasing the turnover in exchanges, space arbitrage spreads the overheads of foreign exchange departments over a larger volume of transactions. The same telephone or telex inquiry may produce quotations which can be used both for arbitrage and other transactions.

(6) Like other types of foreign exchange transactions, space arbitrage makes for an increase of goodwill between the banks engaged in the resulting transactions.

In matters of arbitrage, as in those of foreign exchange dealing in general, banks with a large turnover are at a considerable advantage. They are in more frequent contact with other centres as well as with their own market and are, therefore, better placed for spotting favourable quotations and discrepancies, before less well-placed banks are able to take advantage of them.

The new system of official intervention has given rise to new arbitrage opportunities of a kind that had not existed either under the gold standard or during the earlier phases of the post-War system. They constitute an important and interesting feature of the post-War system of foreign exchanges.

We saw in Chapter 1 that until 1960 the monetary authorities of each country belonging to the E.M.A. quoted buying and selling rates representing support points for the exchanges of all other member countries, and they were prepared to buy or sell those exchanges if and when they should reach support points, so as to prevent exchange movements beyond support points. Since 1960 all Central Banks have maintained official buying and selling rates for the dollar only, and obligatory official intervention in unlimited amounts has come to be confined to buying and selling dollars at its support points.

As pointed out in Chapter 1, there are exceptions to the rule of confining intervention to official sales and purchases of dollars. So long as the dollar rates are maintained at their support points it does not matter how this end is achieved. The Danish and Norwegian Central Banks found it more convenient to operate mainly in sterling instead of dollars, leaving it to private arbitrage to produce the indirect effect of such operations on the dollar rate in their respective markets.

There is nothing to prevent the Bank of England from intervening in non-dollar exchanges, but it usually does so for purposes not connected with intervention. It has to buy and sell non-dollar currencies from time to time on account of the Government or of some other Central Bank, and such operations are sought to be integrated into the general strategy of control. They are timed so as to reinforce rather than offset the effect of intervention in dollars. But deliberate intervention means mainly operations in dollars. The same is true about most other member countries of the I.M.F. Nevertheless, these operations effectively set limits also to fluctuations between non-dollar currencies.

What happens is that if the D.mark appreciates in London a shade beyond support point arbitrage ers buy dollars from the Bank of England and sell them through the German banks to the Bundesbank in Frankfurt. The Bundesbank is under obligation to buy dollars in the German market in unlimited amounts at Dm. 3·97 per $1. For this reason holders of sterling are in a position to buy D.marks just as freely in unlimited amounts, through the intermediary of the Frankfurt market, as if the Bank of England itself were an unlimited seller.

The only essential difference is that while an appreciation of the dollar against sterling to a premium of 2 cents (just over ¾ per cent), is sufficient to compel the Bank of England to sell unlimited amounts of dollars, the D.mark has to appreciate ¾ per cent in relation to the dollar before the Bundesbank finds itself under obligation to buy unlimited amounts of dollars. This means that the D.mark has to appreciate in terms of sterling to a premium of over 1½ per cent before its appreciation in terms of dollars is sufficient to set the official support

73

point mechanism in motion. So long as the appreciation of the D.mark against the dollar is less than that, London banks who have bought dollars from the Bank of England are able to buy D.marks in the Frankfurt market at rates cheaper than 3·97.

In given situations space arbitrage plays an important part as a result of the one-sided method of confining official intervention to dollars. It is the practice of most Central Banks to intervene in order to prevent an appreciation or depreciation of their exchanges towards support points. When sterling is weak and is supported at, say, $2·39 the result is heavy official selling of dollars. But an inherent weakness of sterling, as distinct from its depreciation through an inherent firmness of the dollar, means that it tends to depreciate in relation to a number of other currencies as well as in relation to the dollar. When such a situation arises the support of sterling against the dollar and the absence of its support against other currencies is liable to cause an appreciation of those currencies in terms of the dollar as well as in terms of sterling. If this movement is initiated in the London market it is liable to bring the dollar rate in continental markets slightly out of line with the London cross rate between their currencies and the dollar, until space arbitrage eliminates the fractional discrepancies.

Such a situation does not arise if the firmness of the dollar in London that necessitates intervention is caused by buying on U.K. residents' account. In that case the authorities simply meet the surplus demand and other exchanges need not be affected. If the increased demand for dollars is on account of Continental buyers the effect depends on (*a*) whether demand is for spot or forward dollars, and (*b*) whether the buyers of spot dollars possess the sterling to pay for the dollars bought. As Continental buyers of forward dollars in London need not find sterling to pay for the dollars until maturity, and even then they can renew their positions, their exchanges remain unaffected by the official selling of forward dollars. The same is true if they buy spot dollars in London and pay for them with the aid of sterling they already hold.

On the other hand, if they have to buy spot sterling in order to pay for the spot dollars their exchanges tend to depreciate in terms of both sterling and the dollar. If their operations are initiated in their own markets — there is still active dealing in sterling against dollars on the Continent — they tend to depreciate sterling against the dollar and space arbitrage takes advantage of the more favourable rate at which it is possible to cover in London thanks to official intervention.

Another situation in which space arbitrage stands to benefit by the one-sided method of supporting sterling is if its weakness is due to demand for some currency other than the dollar. For instance, repatriations of funds held in London by Swiss residents may cause heavy selling of sterling against Swiss francs. The authorities may offset the resulting weakness of sterling by selling dollars, even though the excess demand is not for dollars but for Swiss francs. Such operations may tend to bring the dollar-Swiss franc rate slightly out of line and space arbitrage may have a chance to secure fractional profit in operations that transfer the effects of the official support from the dollar rate to the Swiss franc rate.

Thanks to arbitrageurs who are always on the alert to spot fractional discrepancies, a one-sided method of supporting sterling and of intervening in general does not create anomalies. The effect of official buying or selling of dollars between support points is spread over all currencies concerned. This obviates the necessity for the authorities to concern themselves with rates other than those of the dollar in relation to their currencies.

Possibilities of space arbitrage in forward exchanges are wider than those in spot exchanges because, owing to the diversity of maturities, discrepancies are more likely to develop and persist for a time. Although, as we saw above, Continental buying of forward dollars in London is possible without first having to buy spot sterling, so that it does not affect the spot exchanges of the buying countries, it does tend to depreciate forward sterling against dollars. When this effect was neutralised by official selling of forward dollars to meet the surplus demand, fractional temporary discrepancies tended to develop between forward sterling-dollar rates in London and in Continental markets.

CHAPTER 7

TIME ARBITRAGE

TIME arbitrage aims at taking advantage of discrepancies between forward margins for different maturities by means of holding short positions in certain maturities against long positions in other maturities. Such positions — which leave the overall position in the currency concerned evenly balanced — may arise fortuitously through the incidence of the bank's operations with customers or in the market, which result, on balance, in oversold positions in certain maturities and over-bought positions in other maturities. Or they may arise through deliberate buying or selling of short forward exchanges against long forward exchanges for the purpose of creating such commitments.

Very broadly speaking, the premium or discount on forward exchanges, expressed in actual swap rates, is supposed to widen in exact proportion to the length of their maturities. For instance, it should be three times as wide for three months as for one month. In practice in a good sensitive market swap margins seldom conform to this rule perfectly for any length of time, not even for standard maturities in which the turnover is always active, and to a much less extent for odd dates in which the turnover is very limited. On frequent occasions discrepancies between forward margins for various dates are apt to become abnormally wide.

Relationship between long and short forward margins is liable to be affected by the following factors:

(1) Forward margins tend to adapt themselves to their interest parities which are usually different for various maturities.

(2) Differentials between interest parities for various maturities are liable to change.

(3) Forward margins are liable to deviate from their interest

76

parities for various maturities to a different extent, in accordance with the differences between supply-demand relationships for particular maturities.

(4) Changes in spot rates are apt to react to a different extent on forward margins for different maturities.

(5) Changes in the market's views on the imminence of an anticipated changes in spot rates affect short and long forward margins to widely different degree.

(6) In normal conditions, in the absence of distorting influences, short forward margins tend to be slightly narrower than long forward margins, owing to the higher degree of uncertainty about the more distant outlook.

(7) During periods of vague uncertainty about the prospects of a currency, but in the absence of an acute scare anticipating an immediate change, long forward margins tend to become materially wider than short forward margins.

(8) During periods of acute speculation, when the market expects early changes in parities, short forward margins tend to widen much more than long forward margins.

(9) Short forward margins are subject to wider fluctuations than long forward margins, being more sensitive to distorting influences and to Money Market influences.

(10) Very long forward margins always deviate considerably from long forward margins, and the spread between buyers' and sellers' rates is always very wide.

(11) The relative extent of banks' commitments for particular maturities may affect differentials because it influences their attitude towards increasing their commitments for those maturities.

(12) Above all, operations by arbitrageurs tend to mitigate discrepancies between long and short forward margins and tend to bring distorted forward margins for odd dates more into line with forward margins for standard dates.

Time arbitrage may be active or passive. It is active if banks deliberately undertake operations to take advantage of discrepancies between rates for various maturities. It is passive if banks, having long positions in certain maturities and short positions in others, decide to allow these positions stand instead of covering them. Such long and short positions are bound to arise through fortuitous accumulation of commitments in both directions for various dates. The practice of having graded maturities for a wide variety of dates as a result of a multitude of forward transactions with customers or in the market makes it necessary for banks to decide whether to adjust these commitments and in what sense. Such decisons need not necessarily constitute arbitrage decisions. Possibly banks may want to increase their long or short positions for certain dates in anticipation of customers' requirements rather than for the sake of any fractional profits expected as a result of changes in forward rates.

The relative importance of time arbitrage has increased considerably since the War for the following reasons:

(1) Reduction of profit margins on business with clients, on interest arbitrage and on the more popular types of space arbitrage has made it necessary for foreign exchange departments to pay more attention to what had been a relatively unimportant sideline before the War.

(2) Foreign exchange dealers are now better equipped, both mentally and technically, for undertaking more complicated transactions, and they are more willing to undertake them.

(3) Even the most conservative banks which insist on covering any open positions at the earliest practicable moment authorise their foreign exchange departments to carry commitments involving short positions in short maturities offset by long positions in long maturities or vice versa.

(4) Time arbitrage does not tie down the liquid resources of foreign exchange departments, unless they choose to combine it with interest arbitrage by taking up and retaining the exchanges bought when the short purchase matures instead of swapping it for a further period.

(5) Since the War the maximum period for which it is possible to transact forward exchange in the market has become much longer, and this provides additional scope for discrepancies between long and very long maturities.

(6) Many banks are now prepared to provide for their customers forward exchange facilities for much longer periods

than the maximum up to which it is possible to cover in the market. The resulting discrepancies in maturities lead to time arbitrage.

(7) Since the War the volume of forward transactions for very short maturities has expanded very considerably, and the wide fluctuations of forward margins for very short maturities provide opportunities for profitable time arbitrage.

(9) The possibility of combining time arbitrage with Euro-currency transactions has increased the range and variety of operations.

Dealers are more inclined to await the appearance of counterparts for covering the long-short commitments arising from time arbitrage than they are when they have an open position, because the risk of a change in the spot rates is covered, so that they are only exposed to the risk of a change in the forward margins to their disadvantage. By carrying long-short commitments they stand to benefit by a change of the forward margins in their favour. Assuming that the chances for a movement of forward margins in either direction are assessed as equal, the bank engaged in time arbitrage operations stands to benefit by the discrepancy that exists at the time of the conclusion of the deal in the following circumstances:

(1) If the premium on a forward exchange is narrower for short maturities than for long maturities, or if the discount is wider on short maturities than on long maturities, it *appears* advantageous to buy at a cheaper rate for short periods and to re-sell at a dearer rate for long periods.

(2) If the premium on forward exchanges is wider for short maturities and narrower for long maturities, or if the discount is narrower for short maturities and wider for long maturities, it *appears* advantageous to sell at a dear rate for short periods and re-purchase at the cheaper rate for long periods.

The accent is on the word "appears". Dealers when engaging in time arbitrage operations on the above lines have to rely on their foresight and their luck in assuming that on the maturity of the short commitments forward margins for the uncovered part of the long commitments would not move against them, or at any rate not to an extent that the covering of the remaining part of the long commitment would wipe out the profit that would arise from the transaction on the basis of existing rates.

To take a simple example, let us suppose that the premium on forward dollars is $\frac{1}{4}$c. for one month and $\frac{5}{8}$c. for two months. On the assumption that at the end of the first month the premium for one month would remain $\frac{1}{4}$c. the combined cost of buying short for one month and renewing it for another month will be $\frac{1}{2}$c., which leaves a profit of $\frac{1}{8}$c. on the sale of the dollars for two months at $\frac{5}{8}$c. On the other hand, if the premium on dollars for one month is $\frac{1}{4}$c. for one month and $\frac{3}{8}$c. for two months, on the assumption that at the end of the first month the premium for one month would remain $\frac{1}{4}$c. the combined premium received for one month and for another month would be $\frac{1}{2}$c. while the cost of buying for two months would be $\frac{3}{8}$c. only, so that there would be again a net profit of $\frac{1}{8}$c.

As the above transactions would not mean an overall open position for either party, any change in the spot rate would not affect their profits directly even though, as we saw above, changes in spot rates are among the factors that are liable to affect forward rates. Any widening of the premium on forward dollars during the first month would benefit the seller for short periods and would be detrimental to the buyer for short periods because he would cover at a higher premium at the end of the month. Any narrowing of the premium on forward dollars would benefit the buyer for short maturity and would be to the disadvantage of the seller for short maturity, because at the end of the month he would sell forward on less advantageous terms.

The parties in the long-short transaction need not cover in one transaction the period between the short and long maturity dates. If the transaction is for one month against three months, either of the parties may cover at the end of the first month for another month only — or even for much shorter periods — instead of the entire two months. When the entire remaining period comes to be covered the arbitrageur will know the exact extent of his profit or his loss. But so long as any part of the period of the long maturity remains uncovered there is always some risk of an adverse change in the forward margin for the remaining uncovered period. There is of course also the possibility of additional profit through a favourable change in the forward margin for the remaining uncovered period.

The counterparts to time arbitrage transactions on the above lines may be provided by other arbitrageurs who operate in the opposite sense because they hold the view that, even though on the basis of the rates prevailing at the time of the operation it would not appear to be profitable to them, the rates would move in their favour by the time the short part of the contract matures. The counterparts may also be provided by operations of interest arbitrage, or by dealers who want to adjust their graded maturities. Above all, the counterpart may be forthcoming, or may exist already, in the form of customers' excess buying or selling orders for particular dates.

We shall see in Chapter 13 that forward margins gravitate towards their interest parities. Since interest rates in domestic money markets are not identical for various maturities, there are different interest parities for each maturity. These interest parities, and changes in them, are liable to affect relationship between short and long forward margins. The succession of rates which represent interest parities for various maturities — beginning with money at call and ending with interest rates for twelve months, which is the maximum period for which there is an active market — constitutes what Lipfert calls the "equilibrium line" for the purposes of time arbitrage. Opportunities for time arbitrage arise when forward rates depart from that line to a different degree for different maturities. Deviations from interest parities provide opportunities for combining time arbitrage with interest arbitrage between the time when the foreign exchanges bought for short maturities are delivered and the date of the long maturity.

Discrepancies between forward margins for various maturities are apt at times to fluctuate rather widely. It is the function of time arbitrage to smooth out such fluctuations and to eliminate or reduce exaggerated discrepancies which are apt to develop during hectic days. Such situations are apt to arise when forward margins of devaluation-prone or revaluation-prone currencies are affected by one-sided commercial and speculative pressure to a different degree according to whether the change of parity is expected, rightly or wrongly, to occur immediately or at some more distant date. Arbitrageurs who expect a devaluation scare to pass and, consequently, forward discounts for very short maturities to contract, buy devaluation-prone currencies for short maturities at a cheap price, against sale of longer maturities, in the hope that, once the acute scare has subsided, they would be able to sell the currency forward for the remaining period of the long commitment at a much narrower discount. It is true, outright purchase of short forward exchange would appear in such circumstances to be more profitable. But that would mean a long position in a devaluation-prone currency, and most dealers would be anxious to avoid this, unless they are absolutely convinced that the devaluation-scare would soon pass.

Discrepancies between long and short forward margins are influenced not only by views taken about the prospects of spot rates but also by views taken about prospects of forward margins. To complicate matters further, they are also influenced by views about the prospects of those discrepancies themselves. When in consequence of the widespread anticipation of an early devaluation the discount for one month becomes much wider than the discount for three months this may not necessarily discourage speculators from selling for one month in preference to selling for three months, but it may discourage arbitrageurs who expect the devaluation to take place within a month from selling for 1 month against buying for 3 months, because the discrepancy is certain to become narrower immediately after the devaluation.

Time arbitrage does not necessarily smooth out discrepancies between long and short rates. In given situations it may even accentuate them. If many arbitrageurs take a strong view about prospects of certain changes their one-sided operations are liable to produce an unbalancing effect. But in abnormal conditions the dominant influence on forward rates and on discrepancies between them is not time arbitrage but speculation.

Window-dressing for the end of the year and for less important dates gives rise to swap operations that distort the relationship between long and short forward margins for brief periods in anticipation of the dates concerned. Since the temporary character of such distortions is obvious they are a free gift to arbitrageurs. In the absence of an active time arbitrage banks anxious to repatriate temporarily their liquid funds from abroad might find it difficult and costly to carry out the necessary swap operations, because they would only be able to attract counterparts at very unfavourable rates.

A built-in cause for discrepancies is the narrowing of swap margins whenever spot rates approach support points and the maintenance of spot rates at support points is trusted. This peculiarity of the system causes long forward rates to contract to a much larger extent than short forward rates. So long as spot rates are at a slight distance from support points there is room for the premium or discount on short forward exchanges to be within support points, but longer forward rates reach support points for spot rates already while spot rates are still at some distance from these limits.

The practice of dealings in very long forward exchanges has provided additional opportunities for time arbitrage. Banks are willing to cover the exchange risk for their customers for a number of years ahead, but they are not in a position to cover in the market for the entire period. If they sell to a customer forward dollars for, say, four years and it would not be possible or convenient for them to cover the transaction by buying and holding spot dollars, they cover by buying in the market forward dollars for, say, two years, which is at the time of writing the maximum period for which it is relatively easy to deal in the market. They assume that at the end of two years they would be able to renew the commitment for another two years at rates which would secure them a profit on the whole transaction.

This chapter does not attempt to cover the almost infinite range of complications inherent in time arbitrage. To indicate the range let it be sufficient to refer to the possibilities of combining time arbitrage with space arbitrage or with interest arbitrage. Many dealers are still reluctant to operate long-short transactions on cross forward rates. Another source of complications is the multiplicity of interest parities already referred to above. Time arbitrage is certainly a sphere with possibilities for enterprising dealers.

CHAPTER 8

INTEREST ARBITRAGE

INTEREST arbitrage may be defined as the investment of short-term funds in a liquid form in another currency for the sake of higher yield. Although the operation usually involves the transfer of the funds through the foreign exchange market, this need not be so. When a bank accumulates on its *nostro* account through the incidence of its various transactions a larger balance than is needed for its current requirements it may eliminate the surplus either by means of a swap transaction or by investing it in a liquid form in terms of the currency concerned. All interest arbitrage need not, therefore, be linked with transfers deliberately undertaken for that purpose. Nor is it necessary for the short-term investment to be made in the country whose currency is held. A bank may employ its dollar balance in the Euro-dollar market, that is, to a borrower outside the United States, possibly in the bank's own country.

Transfers of short-term funds into other currencies or other countries may be made for purposes other than that of the higher yield. The following are some of the alternative purposes:

(1) There is a wider variety of short-term investment facilities in sterling and in dollars than in other currencies. They provide better facilities for holding liquid reserves.

(2) Holders of liquid funds may want to spread the credit risk by transferring some of their funds to banks of first-class standing abroad.

(3) The local currency may be distrusted.

(4) Holders may prefer other currencies for fiscal or political considerations.

(5) The authorities may want to discourage the influx of foreign funds by adopting various restrictive measures, thereby inducing their transfer into other countries even if the yield is lower.

85

The development of the Euro-currency market has greatly broadened the scope of interest arbitrage, by providing a convenient variety of investment facilities, not only in sterling and dollars, but also in currencies of several countries which do not themselves possess such facilities. Although the Continental financial centres can only offer a limited choice of short-term investment facilities, thanks to the existence of markets in Euro-marks, Euro-Swiss francs, Euro-guilders etc., it is now possible to employ liquid reserves in these currencies without having to be content with the limited investment facilities or low interest rates obtainable in Frankfurt, Zürich, Amsterdam, etc. In sterling and dollars, too, there is now an even wider range of facilities for money at call or short notice than before the War, and it is now possible to employ funds for longer periods more profitably in the form of time deposits.

The investment facilities provided by the Euro-currency markets are not the only additional facilities that have become available since the War. We saw earlier that, in addition to time deposits, call money, fine bank bills and Treasury bills which were used by arbitrage before the War, there is now commercial paper both in New York and in London, loans to Local Authorities and to hire-purchase finance houses in London, Federal Funds and Certificates of Deposits in New York.

Although most interest arbitrage is transacted by banks on their own account, there is a relatively moderate but increasing proportion transacted on account of customers. Originally only the very largest international firms had been aware of the benefit derived from the employment of their funds in foreign centres or in foreign currencies, but now a wider range of non-banking clients is taking an active part in such operations, even though they have to be fairly large in order to make it worth their while.

Interest arbitrage may be covered or uncovered, according to whether or not the funds engaged in it are safeguarded against the exchange risk. In uncovered interest arbitrage the gross differential between the yields on short-term investments in two different currencies — or between a currency and its Euro-currency variety — constitutes the profit margin. In

covered interest arbitrage the lender has to add the premium
on the forward exchange of the borrowing centre to the interest
differential in his favour, and he has to deduct the discount on
the forward exchange of the borrowing centre from the interest
differential in his favour, in order to arrive at the net profit
margin. Thus if the interest rate in London on the investment
selected by the lender is 1½ per cent above that of New York
and the discount on forward sterling is equal to 1 per cent per
annum there is a net profit of ½ per cent per annum on transferring funds from New York to London with the exchange risk
covered. If the discount on forward sterling is 2 per cent there
is a net profit of ½ per cent on transferring funds from London to
New York.

In theory uncovered interest arbitrage necessarily involves
some exchange risk and contains, therefore, some speculative
element which is, however, in many instance quite negligible in
practice or at any rate it is limited and calculable — assuming
of course that the support points are relied upon. Maximum
support points of devaluation-prone currencies and minimum
support points of revaluation-prone currencies can always be
relied upon absolutely, and they determine the maximum of
risk on uncovered interest arbitrage involving a short position
in a revaluation-prone currency or a long position in a devaluation-prone currency. That risk cannot exceed the spread
between support points, that is, up to 1½ per cent in relation to
the dollar and up to 3 per cent in relation to non-dollar currencies of member countries of the I.M.F. Its actual extent in
individual instances depends on the margin between the actual
exchange rate and the relevant support point.

The lower the interest differential and the shorter the
maturity the nearer the rate has to be to the support point
in order to enable lenders to engage in risk-free uncovered
interest arbitrage. Otherwise a possible exchange movement
within support points towards the "safe" support point is liable
to wipe out, and more than wipe out, the profit-margin.

To take an example, as 1 per cent of $2·80 is 2·8 cents,
assuming that both support points of sterling can be trusted it
may appear safe to transfer uncovered funds from New York to

London for the sake of an interest differential of 1 per cent p.a. for twelve months so long as the exchange rate is above 2·4080, because the maximum depreciation of sterling is 2·4 cents, which is compensated by the profit of 2·4 cents on the uncovered arbitrage. Conversely, it is safe to transfer uncovered funds from London to New York for the sake of an interest differential of 1 per cent p.a. for twelve months so long as the exchange rate is under 2·3920, because the maximum of appreciation of sterling is 2·4 cents, which is compensated by the profit of 2·4 cents on the uncovered interest arbitrage.

The following table shows the rates at or above which uncovered transfers from dollars into sterling may be undertaken without risk:

Interest differential per cent p.a.	Period of investment		
	12 months	6 months	3 months
1	2·4040	2·3920	2·3860
1⅛	2·4070	2·3935	2·3868
1¼	2·4100	2·3950	2·3875
1⅜	2·4130	2·3965	2·3682

The risk on uncovered transfer into money at call or at very short notice is only covered if the exchange rate is in the very close vicinity of its support point. In practice when a rate is at its minimum support point it is usually because it is de-valuation-prone or, when it is at maximum support point, re-valuation-prone, which means that there is a wide discount on the forward exchange of the devaluation-prone currency and a wide premium on the revaluation-prone currency. It is therefore to the advantage of arbitrageurs to cover their funds switched out of the former or into the latter. The risk is limited if uncovered funds are transferred from sterling into dollar when sterling is under pressure, but since on such occasions the dollar is at a premium it may appear to be more profitable to cover the exchange, unless arbitrage is deliberately combined with speculation. There is always a possibility of a recovery of sterling within support points, so that arbitrageurs can only be on the safe side if even the maximum of a possible recovery would not convert their profit on the interest differential into a loss.

Uncovered interest arbitrage is not confined, however, to situations in which the maximum risk is smaller than the net yield. Very often dealers take the view that a movement of the rates against them is unlikely or that they are at any rate not likely to reach support point. Uncovered arbitrage is thus combined with speculation involving limited and calculable risk.

Even a remote risk of a devaluation of the currency into which arbitrage funds are transferred, or of a revaluation of the currency from which they are transferred, makes uncovered interest arbitrage distinctly speculative. But uncovered transfers in the opposite direction may appear attractive on account of prospects of a profit from the change in parities, even if they involve acceptance of lower yields. The risk involved in swimming against the tide of the market's speculative anticipations may appear to outweigh considerably any profit prospects on uncovered interest arbitrage. Most arbitrageurs would not think of transferring funds for uncovered interest arbitrage into devaluation-prone currencies or out of revaluation-prone currencies. Transfers of funds from a revaluation-prone currency into a devaluation-prone currency would involve a double risk. Such transactions are highly speculative and are only undertaken if dealers are very firmly convinced that the parity changes anticipated by the market are utterly unlikely to take place.

Those transferring funds from a devaluation-prone currency into a stable or a revaluation-prone currency have the choice between speculating on an anticipated change in the exchange rate in their favour or taking advantage of the abnormally wide discount on the forward exchange of the devaluation-prone currency. The choice is between the certainty of an attractive though limited yield without taking any risk and a possible substantial profit involving the risk of an improvement of the revaluation-prone currency within its support points. Inward arbitrage into devaluation-prone currency is usually covered, because the high interest rates that are apt to prevail in countries with such currencies do not offer adequate compensations for the devaluation risk. The cost of covering, however, usually offsets and more than offsets the interest differential if the funds are employed in conventional types of short-term investments. But in recent years it has become profitable from time to time to employ such funds in various unconventional types of investment whose yield is often high enough to attract funds into devaluation-prone currencies in spite of the abnormally high cost of covering. For instance, the high yield on loans to British Local Authorities often attracted funds from abroad during the middle 'sixties even during periods when the discount in forward sterling was wide enough to make it profitable to transfer funds from sterling into more conventional short-term dollar investments.

The multiplicity of interest parities makes it feasible to move arbitrage funds simultaneously in both directions. This is because, apart from considerations of yield, the requirements of owners of such funds differ in respect of the choice of various types of investment, and even the same owners may want to spread their funds among various types of liquid investment.

In the United Kingdom banks are authorised to hold covered funds up to a certain limit which is higher than their authorised limit for open positions through holding uncovered funds. Their balances on *nostro* accounts may or may not be covered, according to the view they take of the prospects of the currencies concerned and according to whether the forward exchange concerned is quoted at a premium or a discount. When their views change or when the forward rates change they may cover formerly uncovered balances or uncover formerly covered balances.

The relative importance of interest arbitrage for foreign exchange departments has increased since the War, owing to the narrowing of profit margins from space arbitrage and on commercial business with large clients. While some banks may be willing to take some risks by running open positions, others depend for their bread-and-butter mainly on covered interest arbitrage. Although, as we saw earlier, profit margins now tend to be narrower also on interest arbitrage, the development of a wider variety of interest parities ensures that dealers are seldom without opportunities for profitable interest arbitrage for any length of time. Moreover frequently recurrent selling pressure on various currencies, by causing abnormal discounts on forward exchanges, ensure attractive profit margins to dealers who prefer one safe bird in the hand to two risky birds in the bush.

Official intervention, while reducing profit possibilities on spot or outright forward transactions, opened up regular profit possibilities on swap transactions. The swap facilities provided by the Bundesbank, the Bank of Italy and the Swiss National Bank to the banks in their respective countries at artificially favourable rates were notable instances of such profitable lines of interest arbitrage.

We saw in the last chapter how the one-sided operation of the support points of dollars and the practice of temporary pegging of the dollar rate somewhere between support points without corresponding official transactions in other exchanges, provides opportunities for space arbitrage both in spot and in forward exchanges. This system also provides interest arbitrage opportunities similar to those that had existed under the gold standard only in even more clear-cut circumstances. As we said in Chapter 1, under the Bretton Woods system support points are much more definite and stable than gold points had ever been. If under the gold standard spot rates were approaching gold points swap margins tended to contract but, since there had always been a possibility of changes in the exact whereabouts of gold points many merchants and bankers preferred to cover the exchange rate even when the spot rate was actually at gold points, just in case gold points should move against them. There is no such risk with support points, so that when spot rates reach them and the parities are trusted it is safe to leave exchanges uncovered rather than covering them outside support points. This means that, given the same degree of confidence in the maintenance of the parities, forward margins are apt to contract more under the I.M.F. system than under gold standard when spot rates approach the normal limits of their fluctuation. In particular forward rates for short maturities tend to remain at par with spot rates when the latter are at support point. This may mean that they must deviate from their interest parities and become undervalued or overvalued providing thereby additional opportunities for covered interest arbitrage.

Interest arbitrage operations tend to keep forward rates in the vicinity of their interest parities, in so far as this is practicable in spite of the multiplicity of the parities. The wider the discrepancy between forward rates and some of their interest parities the more funds are apt to be attracted into arbitrage operations. But the supply of funds available for such purposes is by no means unlimited. We saw earlier that it is subject to both official limitation and to allocation by the managements of the banks themselves. The latter limitations are elastic, however, because exceptionally wide profit margins might tempt managements to allocate additional funds to their foreign exchange departments, or to authorise them to borrow more.

The practice of using borrowed funds in interest arbitrage has been greatly assisted by the development of Euro-currency markets. Before the War such borrowing assumed mostly the form of overdrafts on *nostro* accounts which were very costly, so that discrepancies had to reach abnormal dimensions before it became worth while to resort to such transactions. But owing to the very narrow spread between lending and borrowing rates in the Euro-currency market a relatively moderate widening of discrepancies makes it profitable to use borrowed Euro-currency deposits for arbitrage. The new system has placed additional resources at the disposal of interest arbitrage at the same time as creating a wide variety of new arbitrage opportunities by providing the basis of a number of additional interest parities. When swap rates tend to adapt themselves to their Euro-currency interest parities they are bound to deviate from other interest parities. But it is always possible that Euro-currency rates might adapt themselves to swap rates.

Much has been written about profit-margins that make it worth while to engage in interest arbitrage. Before the War the general rule, subject to many exceptions, was that most banks did not deem it worth their while to operate unless there was a profit margin of at least ½ per cent p.a. Since the resumption of arbitrage they have come to consider it worth their while to operate for the sake of much narrower profit margins, for ⅛ per cent or even less. Indeed in many instances dealers anxious to keep the names of their banks in prominence in the market are willing at times to operate even without any profit. Much depends on the state of activity of the market. If there are other opportunities dealers may not be prepared to engage in arbitrage unless they obtain more attractive profit margins. When there is continuous pressure on an exchange the resulting wide profit margins are apt to induce dealers to exhaust their resources, and once that stage is approached profit margins would have to widen considerably in order to induce managements to authorise more funds for such requirements. In any case the normal requirements of regular clients have a prior claim over that of interest arbitrage even if the latter promises a higher yield.

Interest arbitrage in the broader sense of the term includes also decisions taken by borrowers in which currency to borrow. Their decisions depend both on relative interest rates and on forward rates. Euro-currency rates have come to play an important part in influencing such decisions.

Decisions of importers and exporters and also of hedgers whether to operate in forward exchanges or in Euro-currencies also constitutes a form of interest arbitrage. Speculators in gold and silver, too, have the choice between buying for forward delivery or buying spot metals and financing it by borrowing Euro-currencies. Speculators in exchanges combine speculation with arbitrage when they decide whether to operate in forward exchanges or borrow and sell Euro-currencies. Banks can engage in interest arbitrage not only by transferring funds into other currencies but also by abstaining from covering positions for commitments which they would cover otherwise. Such arbitrage may be called passive arbitrage.

Foreign exchange departments are always on the lookout for unexplored interest arbitrage opportunities. Whoever discovers new possibilities stands to benefit by it until others discover them. A typical example was provided by transfers of funds from London and from Continental centres to the market for Federal Funds in New York. It is possible to lend on that market at a high interest rate, from Fridays to Mondays, and lenders have only to pay interest for one day, as a result of the practice of having to deliver spot exchanges two clear days after their purchase. Profit margins on such transactions narrowed down considerably, however, as soon as a large number of banks came to take an active hand. Nevertheless transfers to and from the Federal Funds market constitute an important "technical influence", often referred to in the financial Press when explaining movements of exchange rates before and after weekends.

CHAPTER 9

SPECULATION

SPECULATION in foreign exchanges assumes the form of creating or maintaining an open position in terms of a foreign currency for the sake of benefiting by its anticipated appreciation or depreciation. That end can be pursued mainly by the following methods.

(1) Selling or buying forward exchanges unconnected with any expectation of future receipts or payments in terms of the currencies concerned.

(2) Acquiring balances and other short-term assets in terms of a revaluation-prone currency.

(3) Borrowing in terms of a devaluation-prone currency and selling the proceeds.

(4) Abstaining from covering claims or liabilities in terms of a foreign currency, although it is the normal practice to cover them.

There is no firm dividing line between speculation on the one hand and covering, hedging or arbitrage on the other. Speculation can be undertaken even in connection with genuine commercial transactions, for instance if they are covered well in advance of the normal time for covering. Imports or exports may be undertaken or timed largely for the sake of benefiting by anticipated changes in exchange rates, and payments may be timed with the same object in view. Since the War speculation in exchanges has assumed to a very large degree the form of changing the "leads" and "lags" — putting forward or delaying the payments for imports or exports — rather than that of deliberately creating short or long positions.

If holders of assets in a foreign currency hedge against its depreciation or if those who have liabilities in a foreign currency hedge against its appreciation they may pursue the end of avoiding losses, but in given circumstances they may also

95

pursue the end of making a speculative profit. It depends on whether or not the profit obtainable through the depreciation of the currency concerned would more than offset the losses to which their assets are exposed through their depreciation. If the effect of depreciation is purely temporary then the net exchange profit derived from hedging against it may be regarded in given circumstances as speculative.

The same ruling cannot be applied, however, to the covering of exchange risk on imports. We saw in Chapter 5 that the extent to which a devaluation is liable to cause a rise in prices is incalculable. In the long run it may produce its full effect and holders of assets in countries which have devalued may thus avoid losses if they can defer the realisation of their assets. But importers have to sell their goods more or less immediately, very often long before the devaluation has produced its full effect on prices. Importers cannot be accused, therefore, of speculation if they cover the exchange risk, even though a partial immediate effect of the devaluation on prices may possibly bring them some profits. They would run speculative risk if they failed to cover their claims in a devaluation-prone currency or their liabilities in a revaluation-prone currency. In most situations the chances are that the potential losses through not covering exceed their potential profits, if any, through covering.

For this reason it is a mistake to accuse merchants of speculation if, faced by the possibility of a change in parities, they endeavour to arrange their imports and exports, or the payment for imports and exports, or the covering of the payments, in order to safeguard their interests against that possibility. Apart from any direct losses to which importers expose themselves if they fail to cover, they expose themselves to indirect losses if rivals who had covered are in a position to undersell them. It is a matter of their instinct of self-preservation to cover for as long a period ahead as possible, for fear that their competitors might do so, in which case they might find themselves at a disadvantage.

As for arbitrage, it often carries the possibility of profit through a favourable change in the exchange rate during intervals that are liable to elapse between the conclusion of the two or more transactions involved, even though such profit is not the main object of the exercise, except in the case of time arbitrage or uncovered interest arbitrage, both of which contain a distinct speculative element.

In this chapter we are not concerned with any such speculation but only with open positions created and maintained solely and directly for the purpose of making a profit on the appreciation or the depreciation of the exchanges. Covered forward commitments with discrepancies between maturity dates may entail a certain amount of speculative risk but are not considered speculation in the sense in which we are concerned here.

It is necessary to distinguish between limited and unlimited speculation according to whether it involves calculated or incalculable risk. When support points are trusted implicitly the profit that is liable to arise through exchange movements is limited by these support points, and the risk involved is similarly limited. Once, however, doubt has arisen about parities or support points, open positions carry much wider profit possibilities and much greater risks. The nature and extent of the risk and profit prospects depends not only on the currency which is the object of the speculation but also on the speculator's own currency, or a third currency against which he may buy or sell the currency concerned. For instance, when in 1968 American or Swiss speculators sold French francs against D.marks they were speculating simultaneously on the chances of a revaluation of the D.mark and those of a devaluation of the franc.

Assuming that the speculator's own currency is neither devaluation-prone nor revaluation-prone, the extent of his risk is limited if his operation swims with the prevailing tide — that is, he is long in a revaluation-prone currency or short in a devaluation-prone currency. We saw in the last chapter that in such circumstances losses are limited to those arising from movements within support points. If speculation is by means of forward exchange transactions their cost must be added to the spread between support points when calculating the risk. When spot transactions are involved, since a devaluation-prone currency is apt to be under par, only the possibility of its recovery to a premium right up to maximum support point in relation to the speculator's own currency, must be weighed against the likelihood and probable extent of the profit that would arise if the anticipated devaluation should take place.

Conversely those who swim against the prevailing tide by speculating on the maintenance of the support points of devaluation-prone or revaluation-prone currencies stand to benefit to a limited extent only, either through a movement of spot rates within support points or through a readjustment of forward rates if they have moved beyond support points, but against this they assume an unlimited risk.

A speculator whose own currency is devaluation-prone assumes a limited risk if he is short in another devaluation-prone currency — though the possibility of differences in the degree of devaluations must be allowed for — but assumes an unlimited risk if he is short in a stable or a revaluation-prone currency. He assumes a limited risk if he goes long in any currency, for his maximum loss is limited by the maximum support points of his own currency, plus forward premium, if any.

A speculator whose currency is revaluation-prone assumes a limited risk if he goes long in another revaluation-prone currency — provided that the latter's revaluation is expected to be at least as large as that of his own currency — but assumes an unlimited risk if he goes long in a stable or devaluation-prone currency. He assumes a limited risk if he goes short in a stable or devaluation-prone currency, for his maximum loss on spot transactions is limited by the minimum support point of his own currency which is not likely to be lowered.

Under a system of floating exchange rates the profit possibilities and risk through an appreciation or a depreciation are unlimited and symmetrical, that is, in theory at any rate evenly balanced. In practice there is always bound to be a difference between the probable extent of profits and losses according to whether speculators swim against the tide or with the tide, according to whether they assess the strength of the tide correctly, and according to the premium or discount on the forward exchange which they buy or sell.

Speculation

This brings us to another aspect of the subject. Speculative profit possibilities, when anticipating a devaluation or a revaluation, depend not only on whether the anticipations materialise and on the extent to which they materialise, but also on the cost of the speculative operations. That again depends not only on forward margins and interest differentials that determine the cost of the operation but also on the length of time for which the open position has to be maintained before the expected change takes place. In respect of speculation in exchanges being right after a long delay might well prove to be as expensive as being wrong after a short delay. In matters of foreign exchanges there are such things as being right at the wrong time. If a speculator is firmly convinced that a certain currency is doomed to depreciate sooner or later and is stubborn enough to carry his open position for a period of years, the accumulated cost might more than wipe out the profit derived from the eventual devaluation. Moreover, he risks having incurred all that expense in vain if, after all, the devaluation should not materialise.

Likewise, if a speculator incurs loss of interest by maintaining a large balance in a revaluation-prone currency over several years then a moderate revaluation might leave him out of pocket. This is what actually happened to those who were consistently long in D.marks from 1957 onward and made a bare 5 per cent profit on its eventual revaluation in 1961.

Those who have the courage of their convictions to the extent of creating and maintaining an open position have to decide not only whether to go short or long, and when to go short or long, but also for what initial period to go short or long. When an early devaluation is expected there is a natural inclination to go short for the briefest possible period so as to reduce the cost of the operation to a minimum. On such occasions, however, the discount on short forward exchange is liable to widen to an extent quite out of proportion to the discount for longer periods precisely because a large number of speculators resort to the same tactics. If the expected devaluation does not materialise immediately they might decide to renew their short positions repeatedly in which case the high cost has to be borne for a longer period.

If speculators feel very strongly about the imminence of the change of parities, many of them, instead of selling or buying short forward exchange, may sell or buy spot exchange in the hope that, by the time they are due to be delivered in two days the change would have taken place so that they would be able to cover at a profit in spite of the extra cost of the necessary buying or selling for delivery on the same day. The four days' interval during week-ends that exists, since markets ceased to function on Saturdays, between conclusion and value date of spot transactions concluded on Thursdays and Fridays, favours the use of this method particularly. After all, many things might happen in four days. But if the expected change does not take place by value date the cost of renewing such short positions again and again is apt to become particularly heavy, relatively small as it may have been for the initial period.

There is an alternative way of speculating on an anticipated depreciation of an exchange without resorting to forward operations — by borrowing in terms of the devaluation-prone currency and selling the spot exchange. Whenever there is an acute attack on a currency the discount on its forward exchange tends to increase well in excess of the increase in interest rates in the devaluation-prone country, so that it becomes distinctly cheaper to resort to this alternative method of speculation. Those who are in a position to do so naturally prefer to choose that alternative. But the extent to which borrowing facilities are available for that purpose in the devaluation-prone country is usually limited. Official or unofficial restrictions may be applied against the granting of credits to foreign borrowers. Even in the absence of such restrictions the extent to which banks are able and willing to employ their liquid resources for such purpose is necessarily limited. Monetary authorities are in a position to reduce it further without having to tighten exchange control, by pursuing a restrictive monetary policy. In any case they have good reason for pursuing a deflationary policy when their exchange is under pressure.

The development of the Euro-currency market has placed,

however, considerable additional facilities at the disposal of speculators. They are now able to create short positions by borrowing currencies obtainable in such markets and selling the proceeds. Or their banks who buy from them forward exchanges are in a position to cover by the same method if they do not possess the required amount on balance of their *nostro* account in that currency and are unwilling or unable to overdraw their account — a very costly method of covering owing to the high charges. Neither the authorities of the country concerned nor its banks have any means of preventing or discouraging the use of non-resident deposits in their national currency for speculative purposes. Holders of such deposits are in a position to sell their holdings, or to lend them to borrowers who in turn are at liberty to sell them for speculative purposes.

This is not a new situation, but the existence of a regular market for lending and borrowing such deposits, at rates which are more favourable to both lender and borrower than those at which it is possible to borrow in the country concerned, has greatly increased the extent to which foreign-owned deposits can be used by speculators. Moreover, the amount of such deposits, which are now actually or potentially available for speculation, has increased considerably since the War.

The increased extent to which Euro-currencies are actually used as an alternative device to operating in forward exchanges has reduced discrepancies between the cost of creating open positions by means of the two devices. The knowledge that such an alternative device is available does itself go some way towards reducing the discrepancies. Diversion of speculative pressure from the forward exchanges market to the Euro-currency market tends to moderate the depreciation of forward exchanges. This reduces the self-correcting effect of speculation which begins to operate when forward selling becomes too costly. Speculation by means of forward exchanges is, therefore, not reduced to anything like the full extent to which speculation assumes the form of selling the proceeds of borrowed Euro-currencies.

The existence of Euro-currency markets assists not only in the creation of short positions but also in the creation of long positions, because it greatly reduces the power of the authorities of revaluation-prone countries to prevent the influx of speculative hot moneys. In the absence of Euro-currency facilities speculators anticipating a revaluation may be discouraged by the heavy loss of interest on their deposits in the revaluation-prone currency, because the authorities may ban interest on foreign deposits and may even make it compulsory for their banks to charge a negative interest in the form of a commission. Owing to the existence of Euro-currency markets, however, speculators are now in a position to earn a relatively high interest on their holdings of revaluation-prone currencies. For instance, if a speculator expects a revaluation of the Swiss franc he buys spot francs and deposits with a Swiss bank which charges him $\frac{1}{2}$ per cent "negative interest" in the form of commission. But he can earn interest on his deposit by lending it in the Euro-Swiss franc market. On the other hand, he incurs expenses in the form of loss of interest, for he would probably earn a higher yield by employing his money in some other currency, especially as interest on a revaluation-prone currency is low because many speculators are anxious to lend their deposits. Even so, such operations are likely to be less costly than going short in a devaluation-prone currency.

During the early inter-War period there was a great deal of pure speculation in foreign exchanges. It was possible on the Continent, and to some extent also in London, for almost any would-be speculator to open an account with some bank and engage in speculative forward exchange operations. Provided that he was well-introduced to the bank or was able to give satisfactory references, and deposited an adequate margin to cover any likely exchange differences — usually 10 per cent was required, but additional deposits had to be made if the margin was becoming too narrow — the bank was prepared to go short or long on his account, on the clear understanding that there was no question of expecting him on maturity to deliver the exchange he had sold or to accept delivery of the exchange he had bought. All that happened was that on maturity date the exchange difference, whether in the speculator's favour or against him, was settled or, alternatively, he instructed the bank to renew the position by means of a swap transaction.

He was in a position to close the account before maturity date by settling the differences in a similar way.

Speculation of that kind was not confined to professionals. From time to time the lay public too took a very active hand. During the 'twenties many thousands of amateur gamblers in every country tried their luck in the foreign exchange market as a preferable alternative to gambling on the Stock Exchange or in commodity markets.

The prevalence of speculation in forward exchange had greatly increased the volume of speculative operations. There are natural limits to the extent of speculative selling with the aid of borrowed currencies. On the other hand, even though it would be wrong to assume that the extent of speculation in forward exchanges is unlimited, its limits are much wider and much more elastic. Moreover, the existence of a speculative forward market makes it much simpler to speculate in revaluation-prone currencies through the intermediary of a third currency because it does not require any substantial capital. If an American resident, for instance, wants to buy spot D.marks in London he must first buy spot sterling in order to be able to pay for them. To that end he must first possess or borrow dollars. On the other hand, if he wants to buy forward D.marks in London he can do so without possessing any dollars beyond the amount required for deposit to cover possible exchange differences. If the would-be buyer is a bank or a customer of standing no deposits are required. There is no need for the speculator to buy spot sterling at all until the forward contract matures and even then it is possible for him to liquidate or renew the contract without having to employ any funds.

A limit is set to speculative forward operations by the necessity for banks which buy or sell forward exchanges to cover the positions they create, in the form of borrowing the currencies concerned or accumulating balances in them. Banks are unable or unwilling to do either to an unlimited extent. The only situation in which unlimited facilities for speculation by means of buying or selling forward exchanges become easily available is when a forward exchange is held at a certain rate by means of official intervention. The authorities then are prepared to provide the counterpart to the speculative forward operations to an unlimited extent and at an artificially low cost. Such tactics usually attract a very substantial volume of additional speculative operations because the rate at which the counterpart is provided is artificially favourable to speculators. The only limit to the volume of such operations is set by the unwillingness of banks to take the name of any bank for unlimited amounts of forward operations.

Although pure speculation on account of clients is still carried out to some extent by some banks, its total extent has declined considerably during the post-War period compared with the inter-War period. Today most of the more respectable banks insist on being shown evidence that the foreign exchange operations with non-banking clients serve some genuine and legitimate commercial or financial purpose. In Britain and in other countries with a limited exchange control they are under statutory obligation to do so. Usually they only deal with their own customers with whose business they are sufficiently familiar to be able to judge whether the proposed operation is genuine or not. Most banks nowadays would not think of accepting obviously speculative accounts from casual customers.

This change in the banks' attitude towards speculation is not realised sufficiently outside banking circles. Some post-War writers on foreign exchanges, especially those among theoretical economists, are under the impression that the settlement of forward contracts through the payment or receipt of the margin of profit or loss is still the general rule. Yet the truth is that even in instances of pure speculation both banker and client nowadays seek to keep up a pretence that the deal is connected with some legitimate transaction. It is not a question of settling the difference between exchange rates. A speculator who has bought exchanges for forward delivery and wants to close the account on maturity instructs his bank to sell the exchanges on his account. If he had sold the exchanges for forward delivery he instructs his bank on maturity to buy in the exchanges for his account and deliver them according to contract. Conceivably he may even find some other bank which would quote him a better rate, in which case he accepts delivery from that bank and delivers to the other bank the exchange. Or if he was a seller he acquires the exchange through the other bank and delivers it to the bank to which he had sold it.

Most banks now maintain that, thanks to the expansion of international trade and finance since the War, they have ample genuine foreign exchange business to keep their foreign exchange departments fully occupied and have therefore no need to acquire any speculative clientèle. In fact they say they wish to reserve their facilities to their regular customers. When they sell to their customers foreign currency for forward delivery they cover by buying spot exchange and this is liable to entail a temporary accumulation of their balances on *nostro* accounts. Even though this does not involve an exchange risk it might involve the risk of exchange control in the countries whose currency they hold. For this reason many banks — especially Swiss banks which still remember their War-time experience with blocked accounts in the U.S. — set a limit to the extent to which they are prepared to accumulate balances in certain currencies even temporarily, and this tends to limit the amount of forward exchanges they are prepared to sell at any given moment. In Britain there are official limits to positions.

The extent to which banks are prepared to carry speculative short positions for the sake of their clients is subject to even more effective limitations. Banks buying forward exchange from their customers cover in the first instance by selling spot exchanges. If they have not sufficient balances on their *nostro* accounts, or if they don't want to deplete their balances any further, they have to borrow in terms of the currency concerned. But we saw above that the extent to which they can do so may be limited.

There remains to be dealt with the question of speculative operations by banks on their own account. Before the War hardly any bank ever admitted that they had ever kept open positions for the sake of making profits on the movements of exchange rates in their favour. Yet it had been generally known that a great many of them had been in the habit of doing so regularly and that some of them — their names were generally known in the market — speculated from time to time on a large scale. But this was firmly denied by most banks, and writers of textbooks faithfully repeated and endorsed their emphatic discliamers. Since the resumption of foreign exchange dealings bankers have become much more candid about their attitude on this matter. They now openly admit that the textbook rule according to which their position must be balanced in every currency not later than at the close of each working day is not necessarily applied very strictly — an admission which is, in many instances, an under-statement. The extent to which various banks are prepared to carry open positions differs very widely but few of them, if any, are nearly as strict in enforcing the textbook rule as is suggested by the textbooks.

The fact that in Britain the authorities themselves authorise banks to run open positions up to fairly substantial amounts is an official confirmation of the well-known existence of such positions. It effectively disposes of the myth that all banks balance all their positions every single day. Anyone familiar with the multitude of transactions that go through a foreign exchange department from the opening to the closing of the market is bound to be aware that open positions are bound to develop from time to time and that it would be very awkward if these positions had to be covered without fail by the end of the day.

Open positions need not be the result of deliberate speculation. It is only natural that dealers should prefer to choose the right moment for covering, and they would be exposed to losses if the rule that they must cover either immediately or at any rate before the market closes were to be enforced. We shall see in Chapter 10 that if it were enforced they would often have to cover exactly when the market expects them to do so and rates would be moved against them. This would mean wider fluctuations of exchange rates because they would have to cover regardless of cost. Banks would only be prepared to provide the desperately-needed counterpart on their terms.

Such an enforced rigidity of the market would greatly exaggerate the effect of any temporary discrepancy between supply and demand on exchange rates. It is because banks are prepared to speculate to some extent that a counterpart to an excess of supply or of demand is so easily obtained in normal conditions. Were they to abstain from having open positions the counterpart could only be attracted by offering sufficiently attractive rates to induce non-banking speculators to step into the breach. A flexible application of the textbook rule serves, therefore, the interest of exchange stability in normal circumstances.

Having said all this, it is necessary to add that many dealers are inclined to go further than to the extent implied by the above remarks. They allow from time to time positions to remain open for days and even weeks when they take a strong view of the prospect of the exchanges and have the courage of their convictions. Nor do their open positions necessarily arise fortuitously from their operations and are kept open deliberately in the hope of covering at a better rate. Many of them may deliberately go long or short if they feel justified in doing so for the sake of the anticipated profit, within the limits imposed on them by official regulations. There are no such limits in New York, Frankfurt or Zürich.

We saw in Chapter 5 that the Bank of England does not require authorised dealers in the U.K. to limit their open positions in any particular currency but only to limit their overall open position. This means that a bank is fully entitled to have a long position in some currency or currencies so long as the excess of its total long positions over authorised overall limits is offset by short positions in other currency or currencies. This rule indicates that the purpose of limiting open positions is not to prevent speculation in foreign exchanges altogether but merely to protect the national currency against speculation.

In practice it is essential for the smooth running of foreign exchange business to have a certain degree of latitude in respect of open positions. The larger the turn-over of a bank in exchanges the more likely it will find itself with open positions arising at times through entirely unforeseen fortuitous circumstances. For this reason the authorities are inclined to take a lenient view even if banks exceed occasionally their authorised limits, provided that they give an acceptable explanation. Any attempt to forbid open positions altogether might force many banks into evading the law. There is no reason to believe that French banks, for instance, which are not permitted to have any open positions, observe that rule very strictly.

Even if banks were to balance their positions at the close of every day this would not rule out limited speculation through having temporarily open positions during the course of the day. On days when exchanges have a distinct one-way trend this provides opportunities for speculative profits between opening and closing even if all positions were balanced at the end of the day.

The extent to which dealers are allowed to engage in operations involving open positions is limited not only by official legislation but also by the attitude of their managements. We saw earlier that their attitude varies according to the nature of open positions. In the majority of instances the officially authorised limits of open positions also constitutes the limits authorised by managements but they may have their own rules about positions in individual currencies.

In many instances the whole market wants to speculate in the same sense, in which case the authorities have to provide the counterpart in order to prevent a depreciation or appreciation of their exchange beyond support points. In many other instances, however, different dealers take different views. Some of them want to go short while others want to go long, or to benefit by the favourable forward rate for interest arbitrage, thereby providing the counterpart to short positions. Differences of opinion are bound to arise on the question whether or not a movement that is in progress has gone too far. Some dealers may expect it to continue and renew their position in the hope of bigger profits, while others may prefer to get out of the market and take their profits. Again some dealers who are on the losing side may feel that it is advisable to cut their losses, while others renew their positions in the hope of being able to close them eventually without a loss or even with a profit. A change in the situation or in the prospects is apt to be interpreted differently by various dealers or by their managements.

Speculation

In normal conditions there is, therefore, a two-way market precisely because of such differences of opinion. It is only when a trend becomes self-aggravating that the market becomes "disorderly" because all dealers want to operate one way.

Even if the authorities of a country are able to prevent residents from speculating against their national currency, they have no means to prevent non-residents from speculating against it. When non-resident speculators sell sterling short in New York or in Zürich there is nothing to prevent American or Swiss banks from covering their resulting commitments in the London market.

Taking everything into consideration it seems correct to conclude that during the post-War period the part played by conventional speculation has been relatively small. Although at the time of strong pressure on a currency it is distinctly in evidence, over a long period its relative importance, compared with that of movements of foreign funds, changes in leads and lags and, in some countries, flight and repatriation of national capital, is much smaller than it had been during the inter-War period. The fact that in 1949 sterling was forced into devaluation mainly if not solely through the operation of leads and lags at a time when advanced exchange control made pure speculation very difficult if not impossible speaks for itself.

Over and above all, there is no smoke without fire in the foreign exchange market. Speculation, outflow of funds, longer leads and lags, flight of national capital are in most instances the consequences of an adverse balance of payments.

CHAPTER 10

TECHNICAL EXCHANGE MOVEMENTS

BOTH this chapter and the next are concerned mainly with trends of exchange rates in general, but with special regard to spot rates. Specific influences affecting forward rates alone will be dealt with in Chapter 12. Our immediate task here is to examine the technical causes of exchange movements, as distinct from the more fundamental causes which are covered in the next chapter. There is of course no dividing line between exchange movements according to whether they are due to technical or fundamental causes. In many situations the difference between them is merely one of degree. A purely technical movement is liable to become self-aggravating and develop into a fundamental movement, while the early phases of fundamental movements are often indistinguishable from technical movements. Pressure due to some basic influence may be absorbed by the market without any effect on the rate until some technical influence comes to bring its effect into evidence.

In certain situations, however, the inherently technical character of an exchange movement is clearly discernible, not only in retrospect but already while it is in progress. The main criterion of a technical movement is that it is apt to occur independently of any development that would call for a theoretical explanation. A typical borderline case is an exchange movement that is due to a change in the views of the market on an unchanged basic situation.

We often talk about "firm" or "weak" exchanges without defining what exactly we mean by it. An exchange is unquestionably firm when it appreciates in terms of all important currencies, and it is indisputably weak when it depreciates in terms of all important currencies. When it is firm in relation to some exchanges and weak in relation to others then it is often

110

a matter of opinion whether to regard it as firm or weak. From the point of view with which we are concerned at present it is only strength or weakness against the principal currencies that matters. If sterling appreciates in relation to a number of inflated Latin American currencies this does not in itself justify us in regarding it as firm. But it may be regarded as firm even if it depreciates in terms of one or two leading currencies and appreciates in terms of several other leading currencies, provided that its depreciation in relation to some currencies is due to the fact that the currencies concerned are even firmer than sterling. Conversely, sterling may be regarded as weak even if it appreciates in terms of one or two unimportant currencies if this movement is due to the fact those currencies are even weaker than sterling.

The question is whether the appreciation or depreciation of an exchange is due to inherent strength or weakness, or whether it merely reflects the trend of other exchanges. Much depends on the relative importance of the two groups of currencies in terms of which it moves in opposite directions. From the point of view of sterling, for instance, the dollar is so overwhelmingly important that the trend of the sterling-dollar rate overshadows all other exchange movements in the London market.

Viewed from the market's angle, the immediate cause of changes in exchange rates is simply that dealers are unable to buy or sell at the prevailing rates the amounts they want to buy or sell, or that they think they might be able to buy or sell at more favourable rates. Banks may be induced to quote or accept rates less favourable to themselves, or to hold out for more favourable rates according to the relative strength of their bargaining positions, or according to their expectations of future exchange movements. They may have first-hand knowledge of an actual change in supply-demand relationship in the market or they may expect such change as a result of some concrete information, or they may simply have a vague feeling that the relationship has changed or is about to change.

Except on very dull days, supply-demand relationship never remains quite the same for any length of time. It changes through each new buying or selling inquiry of any substantial size that reaches the market, unless that inquiry happens to be offset by a simultaneous inquiry of a comparable magnitude in the opposite sense. Every now and again the market experiences pressure through additional buying or selling in excess of the amount of the counterpart that is forthcoming spontaneously at the prevailing rates. When there is such excess, but also when buying and selling are evenly balanced but selling is more urgent than buying or vice versa, rates have to be bid up or to be offered down in order to induce the required counterpart to come forward.

Textbooks on economic theory contain diagrams showing how supply curves and demand curves meet at a certain point that, in the case of foreign exchanges, is supposed to be the equilibrium rate of exchange at which supply and demand become equated. Such diagrams may convey the impression to those unfamiliar with academic economics that the impact between the same quantitative changes in supply-demand relationship and prices is claimed to be always arithmetically identical — that is, a certain extent of change in supply or demand always affects exchange rates to the same extent, and that a certain change in prices always reacts to supply-demand relationship to the same extent. Such assumption would oversimplify the highly complex and ever-changing relationships between quantities and prices in any market, and especially in the foreign exchange market which is usually extremely sensitive in its reactions to external influences as well as to influences generated within the market itself.

There is no such thing as a definite rate at which, given the amount of spontaneously forthcoming supply and of spontaneously forthcoming demand, and the initial quantitative discrepancy between them, the relationship must always necessarily balance once more after its temporary imbalance. In actual practice the rate at which dealers are prepared to provide the required counterpart, and those at which dealers who have taken the initiative are prepared to concede to a change of rates for the sake of obtaining the counterpart, depends on the assessment by both sides of the most favourable rate at which they expect to be able to close the deal.

Equilibrium rate is something essentially variable, fluid and elusive, and the extent of the adjustment is liable to change as and when the market's assessment of the situation changes, even in a complete absence of any change in the material facts, or their knowledge of the material facts, on which their assessment is based.

If market influences were purely mechanical and could be adequately expressed in terms of simple arithmetic the existing market mechanism could conceivably be substituted some day by a computer into which all buying and selling orders would be fed. The emerging weighted average of these orders would then produce the correct exchange rate of the moment. In real life, however, buying and selling orders exert their influences on rates through the intermediary of a multitude of human beings endeavouring to strike the best possible bargains and constantly changing their judgment about the rate which, in their view, represents the best possible bargains in prevailing circumstances. The figures at which dealers strike a compromise between their conflicting interests and divergent judgments and are prepared to conclude a deal are what medieval theologians described as the "just price reached by common consent". These rates express the collective judgment of all participants in the market and are influenced indirectly to a large degree by the sum total of individual judgments of those outside the market who feed the market by their buying and selling orders to their banks.

Important as quantitative factors are, their influence on exchange rates is liable to be modified by the human element — by the collective wisdom (or unwisdom) of all participants in foreign exchange transactions. Because of the human element involved the same changes in supply-demand relationship need not have an identical effect on every occasion on the collective judgment of the market. And even in the absence of quantitative changes exchange movements are liable to occur. The quantitative factor may be vitiated through the following influences:

(1) The direction from which the initiative for the transactions originate.

(2) The relative urgency of the proposed transaction for the two parties.

(3) The skill with which dealers execute their orders.

(4) The mood of the market.

(5) The nature of reports or rumours concerning changes or impending changes in the situation.

(6) Favourable or unfavourable comments concerning the position or prospects of the exchanges.

(7) The volume of the turnover.

(8) The extent to which foreign exchange departments are already committed in respect of an exchange.

(9) The volume of funds at the disposal of foreign exchange departments.

(10) Changes in financial markets other than the market in spot exchanges.

Any one of the influences listed above, or any combination of them, is liable to modify the effect of quantitative influences on exchange rates. For this reason, while on some days additional buying or selling pressure of a certain magnitude may hardly cause any change, on other days an identical pressure is unable to attract a counterpart unless and until the rates change substantially. The same change in exchange rates may produce on some occasions a very marked effect on supply-demand relationship, while on other occasions it hardly makes any difference.

The importance of the initiative factor cannot be stressed sufficiently. Banks are of course familiar with it, but it is apt to be underrated by economists, not only when dealing with technical influences — which they usually ignore or underrate in any case — but also when dealing with fundamental influences. They are aware, for instance, that foreign exchange requirements arising from an import surplus find their counterpart as a result of an increase in the country's external short-term indebtedness. Bankers on their part are aware that an import surplus means that buyers of foreign exchanges have to take the initiative for attracting a counterpart by bidding up the rates, thereby inducing holders of foreign exchanges to acquire holdings of the currency of the importing country.

When a bank has to take the initiative for buying or selling, and cannot await the spontaneous advent of a counterpart through the initiative of other banks, usually it has to concede rates less favourable to itself.

This brings us to the relative urgency of buying or selling, another subject that deserves attention. Even if the total of buying and selling orders in the hands of foreign exchange departments happens to be identical at a given moment, rates might still tend to move according to which side is in a better position to wait in the hope of obtaining more favourable rates. If there is a surplus of spontaneous demand or spontaneous supply, the extent to which it affects rates is influenced by the relative urgency of the buying and of the selling. Situations are apt to arise in which, although the volume of buying enquiries that reach the market has exceeded that of selling enquiries, buyers are in a better position to wait, so that rates move only slightly, if at all, against them. Conversely, very urgent buying or selling of a relatively moderate amount is capable of moving rates to an extent quite out of proportion to the amount involved.

Of course dealers are not omniscient even about the total volume of buying and selling that has actually reached the entire market at any given moment, let alone about the potential volume that is liable to be attracted to the market by a change of a certain magnitude in the rates. But through their experience and their close touch with the market, they have a fair idea towards which direction the tendency is pointing and approximately how strong the tendency is. On the basis of their estimates of tendencies they have to take their decisions about the rates they quote, whether to modify their quotations, to maintain them or to withdraw them if they are not accepted immediately, and whether or not to accept the rates quoted by their rivals. If it were possible to calculate the average exchange rates that emerge from the multitude of bilateral bargains in the market at any one moment or during a given period it would in all probability differ on most occasions from the average that would be produced by the imaginary computer mentioned above. This is because the computer's result would be based solely on quantitative factors, while in a market those factors are subject to a variety of modifications through the influence of the human element.

Exchange rates are also influenced by the relative bargaining skill of dealers. The devices applied by them, described in detail in Chapter 3, may not as a rule produce more than a temporary marginal effect on rates, though on occasions when the market is hyper-sensitive even such minor movements might trigger off self-aggravating chain-reactions. For this reason the possibility of technical exchange movements resulting from dealers' tactics should not be ignored.

The mood of the market is something quite intangible. The atmosphere is liable to change through causes which very often cannot be defined or traced, or whose logic may appear to be quite perverse. The market's response to news reports and to rumours depends largely on the mood in which it receives them. On some occasions it is inclined to be highly responsive to reports, genuine or false, which it would ignore if it received them in a different mood. The same announcement or whispered rumour is liable to affect rates to a different degree, and at times even in a different direction, according to the mood of the market. When it is in a thoroughly pessimistic mood it is inclined to give unfavourable interpretation even to changes which would normally be regarded as favourable. Some drastic measure taken in defence of a currency might produce an unfavourable technical effect because dealers, in a pessimistic frame of mind, would regard it as a panic measure implying official admission that the situation is truly desperate.

According to a well-known philosophical theory, the collective reactions of a multitude of men are liable to differ materially from the sum total of the reactions of the individuals in that multitude. This rule applies to the foreign exchange market. Any mood that develops in it is apt to become contagious and self-aggravating. Dealers watch each other's behaviour closely and react to each other. In particular if they notice that some dealer who is considered to be usually well-informed or who is supposed to have dependable hunches takes a certain line they are all inclined to follow his line. Likewise, some financial commentator — a financial editor who had often been right in the past, or a leading banker making a public pronouncement, or an economist whose views happen to be fashionable — is apt to have a large following, not so much among dealers as among non-banking customers of banks. If a financial columnist was repeatedly right in his past forecasts or in the inside information he published, banks in foreign countries instruct their correspondents to communicate with them his news or comments as soon as they appear in print. In given situations such commentators may influence rates even if their reports were false or their comments mistaken, simply because many people believe in them and operate accordingly.

Exchange rates are affected by the volume of the turnover. In a lifeless market a relatively small transaction may move the rate quite disproportionately to the amount involved, while the same amount barely affects the rate when the turnover is large.

The response of dealers to developments varies according to the size of their existing commitments. If the banks are heavily committed it may take a relatively substantial change in the rate to induce them to increase their commitments, though a much smaller change might in given circumstances be sufficient to induce some of them to take their profits and reduce their commitments. If most of their resources available for that purpose are already committed in interest arbitrage profit-margins would have to increase substantially before they could be induced to increase their commitments further. Their response depends on their ability to increase the amount at their disposal if tempted by some attractive arbitrage opportunity.

Most British banks follow the practice of allocating a definite capital to their foreign exchange departments. But in other centres, for instance in Amsterdam, the practice has always been that the amount engaged in foreign exchange transactions varies according to the relative profitability of such employment of the bank's resources compared with yield on alternative use of them. The difference between the two practices is really one of degree, for London foreign exchange departments, too, re-lend any unused funds to their banks and are able to obtain the allocation of additional funds if they can convince their

117

managements that they can make profitable use of them. Under both systems the attitude of managements towards the size of the allocation is liable to change, though under the British system the amount does not change so frequently or so widely. It is apt to be affected by the extent to which the board and executive are foreign-exchange minded.

The same profit margin on arbitrage may or may not be sufficient to bring about foreign exchange operations, according to the attitude of various banks towards minimum profit margins. This depends not only on their own unused or available resources but also on yields on alternative uses of those resources. The ups and downs of the domestic demand for credit are an important factor. From time to time dealers and managements change their minds about the minimum profit margins for the sake of which they would be willing to allocate additional funds for the sake of a profitable transaction.

The choice of methods used by speculators, too, is an important factor. Changes in financial markets other than the foreign exchange market are liable to affect exchange rates not only through giving rise to additional supply or demand but also through their psychological effects. This is particularly true about changes in money markets which are watched closely by dealers, but it is also true about trends in Stock Exchanges. A boom or a slump in Wall Street could be an important influence even before it has affected the volume of capital transfers to or from New York. Anticipation, or even a change in the degree of anticipation of any such developments is liable to affect the foreign exchange market's mood.

Hitherto we have been dealing with technical movements arising from the different ways in which dealers are apt to react to extraneous influences and which modify the effects of such influences. In addition there are technical movements resulting from influences inherent in the market itself which are liable to affect supply-demand relationship. The following are the most important amongst them:

(1) Banks' attitude towards keeping open positions during the course of a day.

(2) Their attitude towards covering at the end of the day,

on the eve of week-ends and of holidays.

(3) Window-dressing operations at the end of calendar year, half year and quarter.

(4) End-of-month arrangements and middle-of-month arrangements.

(5) Covering operations for the returns that banks have to submit to the authorities.

(6) Reactions of markets after a substantial exchange movement in the form of taking profits or cutting losses.

(7) Changes of views in respect of prospects of long-short interest differentials and forward rate differentials.

(8) Intermediary role of a market or a currency.

The application of the textbook rule about covering all transactions at the earliest possible moments, or at any rate covering open positions at the end of each day, varies in practice from bank to bank and is liable to change. Any change of the extent to which the rule is to be applied is liable to produce technical influences on exchange rates. Although dealers and their managements are apt to change their attitude towards the rule under the influence of extraneous developments, they might also change it in the absence of any such direct cause.

Operations undertaken by banks for increasing their liquidity in general or for window-dressing dates in particular are liable to become a major technical factor from time to time. Although British commercial banks are not in the habit of engaging in foreign exchange transactions for window-dressing purposes, the London market and sterling are often affected by window-dressing habits of banks abroad. Their importance depends on the attitude of a great many banks, but also on the conditions prevailing in their local money markets and the extent of any squeeze which may occur, or may be expected to occur when the critical dates are approaching.

End-of-month and middle-of-month pressure in Continental centres is due to the custom of settling a multitude of financial transactions on *ultimo* or on *medio*. The extent to which banks are prepared to increase their liquidity through withdrawals of funds from abroad is affected by the cost of the transactions in the form of swap margins. In case of uncovered balances or

119

funds engaged in uncovered interest arbitrage it is affected by the extent to which the currencies are considered to be devaluation-prone or revaluation-prone.

On the approach of certain dates, especially of December 31, and to a less extent June 30, window-dressing considerations and considerations of liquidity are apt to prevail over considerations of yield or cost. But considerations of risk are apt to prevail over all other considerations. Whenever a currency is under suspicion even arrangements made on the eves of week-ends are liable to become a major technical influence on exchange rates. As we saw in the last Chapter, now that Saturday closing has become the general rule in foreign exchange markets the importance of such week-end influences has increased considerably. The value date for spot transactions concluded on Thursdays is now on the following Monday, for those concluded on Fridays is on the following Tuesday. Since during recent decades changes in parities were almost invariably announced during week-ends, whenever the market feels that there may be something in the air most banks are particularly careful in avoiding uncovered balances in devaluation-prone currencies or short positions in revaluation-prone currencies on the eve of week-ends. There is therefore a great deal of preparation for week-ends on Thursdays and on Fridays, and such operations are reversed on Mondays or Tuesdays. Wednesdays are practically the only days of the week that are comparatively free from week-end influences.

The way in which banks interpret the rules concerning official limits to their uncovered or covered holdings of foreign exchanges is by no means uniform. We saw in Chapter 9 that some of them at any rate are inclined to cover specially for the days for which they have to submit their returns. Such operations are apt to constitute an important technical influence on occasion.

There is an almost unlimited range of other possible technical influences that are liable to affect exchange rates. The wide variety of transactions and the shifting of their relative importance, the discovery of new types of arbitrage or the discontinuation of existing types, are all apt to influence exchanges in the absence of any changes in the basic situation. On the borderline between technical and fundamental causes are anticipations of regularly recurrent or otherwise predictable fundamental changes in supply-demand relationship. For instance, there is the effect of discounting autumn crop movements. As the resulting transactions arise from the trade balance their effects on exchange rates may be attributable to fundamental causes. Their anticipation comes under the heading of leads and lags, which are again fundamental causes. But insofar as dealers adjust their rates in anticipation of such anticipatory operations before they actually occur the effects on rates is of a technical character.

It may be arguable that, from a practical point of view, the distinction between technical and fundamental causes is purely academic, since in the market their effects merge into each other. But it is not without practical significance that, while technical influences are the foreign exchange market's own making, it merely acts as the channel through which fundamental influences produce their effect.

In normal circumstances technical influences produce a limited effect only. Unless the exchange movements they cause are intensified by some fundamental influence their extent is likely to remain moderate and they are apt to become reversed. As was pointed out earlier in this chapter, however, even technical movements are apt to become self-aggravating. When the market expects, rightly or wrongly, some fundamental influence to come into operation it might be inclined to seize upon a technical movement to allow its expectation to produce a marked effect on the rates. A market in a sensitive or nervous mood is apt to exaggerate a technical movement by interpreting it as being the beginning of a fundamental movement. Thus a movement arising from week-end influences is liable to develop into a major speculative movement setting in motion or aggravating the speculative or psychological factor.

For this reason it is always risky to assume that a movement that is correctly regarded as technical would necessarily remain technical. Whenever a market shows inclination to respond to technical causes too easily or to an unusually high degree it is always necessary to envisage the possibility that there might be a fundamental movement underlying it.

There is one important technical factor which is liable to influence exchange rates very considerably. It originates from the use of a currency or of a centre as an intermediary through which banks in other centres buy third currencies. London's position as an intermediary between the foreign exchange markets of Western Europe and New York is an outstanding instance. We saw in Chapter 7 that, because London is the best market in dollars, continental banks usually contact their London correspondents when they want to sell or buy large amounts which would move the rate against them in their own narrower markets. Sterling is bound to be affected by such operations. If the continental bankers buy dollars with the aid of sterling they already possess, it means selling pressure on sterling which tends to depreciate in relation to the dollar. Continental selling of dollars in London tends to strengthen sterling if the proceeds are left in London. If Continental bankers, in order to be able to buy dollars in London, have to buy sterling first, the result is an appreciation of sterling in relation to continental exchanges and a depreciation in relation to the dollar. Such movements have no bearing in the inherent strength of sterling or in the confidence it inspires. They are simply the results of technical influences arising from sterling's intermediary role.

Reference was made in Chapter 8 to the operation of the technical factor represented by arbitrage transfers to the New York market in Federal Funds. Even in the absence of any devaluation fears, sterling tends to be slightly weak in terms of dollars on Thursdays and Fridays as a result of such operations, and their reversal causes a slight appreciation of sterling on Mondays. Wednesdays are the only "neutral" days.

CHAPTER 11

BASIC TRENDS OF EXCHANGES

HAVING dealt with technical causes of exchange movements in the last chapter, our next task is to examine their fundamental causes. In doing so we enter the realm of foreign exchange theory. The theoretical aspect of foreign exchange is a vast subject and its detailed examination is a major operation which is outside the scope of this book. Within the limited space of the present chapter I can only give the bare outlines of the principal theories and can only cover their best-known version, without going into the controversies between supporters of the rival theories, or into the details of their various versions.

Foreign exchange dealers often follow theories, even though they may not be aware of doing so. In their everyday activities they are bound to base their views and their decisions on what are in substance theoretical rules about the way in which various influences are liable to affect exchange rates. They may not be conscious of pursuing a theory, any more than Monsieur Jourdain was aware of having talked in prose all his life. Nor would most dealers be able to express those rules in a sufficiently rigorous form to pass for theory in the academic sense of the term. But possibly it would help them if they were able to formulate more articulately the rules which they are in the habit of applying instinctively.

Theories actually followed by dealers may be divided into two categories — those concerned with parities around which exchange rates tend to fluctuate and those concerned with deviations of exchange rates from such parities. There is no sharp dividing line between the two categories of theories, for the same fundamental influences which are responsible for the anticipation of changes in parities also tend to cause exchange rates to deviate from their existing parities, and the difference between the two types of movements is merely one of degree.

The simplest and oldest of foreign exchange theories that concern changes in parities is the metallist theory, according to which exchange rates depend on the relative amount of precious metals represented by the monetary units exchanged against each other. This rule is seldom quoted nowadays and it seems to have faded into oblivion because, under the post-War system, none of the currencies are freely convertible into gold by private holders, or even by private arbitrage. Nevertheless it is still valid for a large number of currencies — amongst them those of member countries of the I.M.F. — because they have fixed parities in relation to gold and to the dollar, and the dollar is actually convertible by official holders into a fixed quantity of gold.

Metallic parities are not equilibrium rates in a sense that exchange rates would tend to remain at their parities so long as the market is at equilibrium, and their deviations from their metallic parities do not tend to become automatically readjusted. Exchange rates may be at equilibrium at a premium or at a discount, at any exchange rate at which supply and demand balance. We saw in Chapter 1 that the reason why metallic parities determine the approximate level of exchange rates under the post-War system is simply that any deviation beyond the support points related to parities is prevented by official intervention.

The metallic theory is certainly valid amidst post-War conditions. Changes in parities, or even their mere anticipation, constitutes probably the strongest influence affecting exchange rates.

Foreign exchange dealers take it for granted that any change in I.M.F. parities necessarily brings about a corresponding change in exchange rates. Whenever they envisage a devaluation or a revaluation their operations are based on the expectations of changes in exchange rates that would result from a reduction or an increase in the relative quantities of gold that the currencies concerned represent. Even if spot rates are held stable at their support points right to the moment of the change, forward rates tend to be affected by such anticipations to a large degree. The moment the change is announced dealers adjust exchange rates to their new parities as a matter of course, without waiting for the actual operation of the market-mechanism to produce such an effect through a change in supply-demand relationship. For it is taken for granted that, from the moment of the change the rate around which the exchanges are now supposed to fluctuate is the new ratio between the new theoretical metal content of the monetary unit and those of other currencies.

According to the State theory of foreign exchange, governments are in a position to determine the value of their currency. This theory, in the form in which it was put forward by Knapp at the beginning of the century, was only meant to apply to the domestic value of the national monetary unit. Indeed, Knapp himself went out of his way to emphasise that, since the Government's writ does not run outside the frontiers of its country, the State's power to determine the value of money is confined to the domestic sphere. In reality the State has almost unlimited power to determine the external value of the currency by changing its parity in relation to gold or in relation to some currency which represents a definite quantity of gold. For instance, when in 1959 the French Government equated 100 old francs to one new franc, foreign exchange dealers immediately adjusted the exchange rates accordingly as a matter of course. Likewise, when in 1961 the D.mark was revalued by 5 per cent the announcement was automatically followed by a corresponding adjustment of exchange rates in the market.

The adjustment of the exchange rate to changes in parities need not be arithmetically perfect, because prior to the change its anticipation had already affected the rates to some extent, and after devaluation or revaluation any anticipation of further changes is liable to influence them. Moreover, the new parity is not a pegged rate and actual exchange rates deviate from it in accordance with changes in supply-demand relationship and other influences. What matters from the point of view with which we are here concerned is that the moment the change is announced dealers throughout the world take it for granted, in accordance with the metallist theory and the State theory, that the new parity would be the new rate around which the actual exchange rates would fluctuate. Of course, insofar as a change in parity affects the balance of payments or the ratio between the price levels, the exchange rate towards which the currency will subsequently tend to gravitate in practice might come to differ from the new parities.

When mint parities were suspended after the first World War, and again during the 'thirties, it became fashionable to assume that in such a situation they were replaced by purchasing power parities — the ratio between price levels in the two countries concerned. This essentially academic concept became very popular even among practical experts, judging by the fact that most practical pre-War textbooks on foreign exchange contained lengthy dissertations on the purchasing power parity theory. It was unfortunate that the misleading terms "purchasing power parities" should ever have been applied at all instead of "purchasing power differentials". For the use of the former implies a high degree of similarity between purchasing power parities and metallic parities. Yet there are three basic differences between them:

(1) While mint parities are generally known, or at any rate they can easily be calculated on the basis of the official metal contents of the currencies, purchasing power parities are essentially vague and uncertain. The method of their calculation is a highly controversial question.

(2) While metallic parities are rigidly fixed and are hardly ever changed purchasing power parities virtually never stand still. Very often they change even before publication of the series of indexes of prices on which they are based, so that any published figures are apt to be out of date.

(3) Above all, while it was always mint parities that determined the approximate level of exchange rates, under inconvertible currencies with flexible exchange rate between them the relationship is reciprocal. Any substantial and prolonged undervaluation or overvaluation of exchange rates compared with their purchasing power parities is liable to affect the latter as well as the former. As often as not equilibrium between purchasing power parities and exchange rates is restored

through the effect of exchange movements on domestic prices.

Having regard to the above considerations it is essential that readers should not allow themselves to be mislead by the similarity of the terms "mint parities" and "purchasing power parities" and to assume that it is always exchange rates that are adapted to changes in the differentials between price levels without any reciprocity in the relationship. All the same the purchasing power theory deserves the attention of foreign exchange dealers, provided that they allow for its one-sidedness and exaggerations. They are right in allowing for the influence of changes in price levels on exchange rates, so long as they bear in mind that this theory has more pitfalls for the unwary than other foreign exchange theory. In the early 'twenties operations based on its dogmatic interpretation inflicted heavy losses on many people, besides misleading Governments into adopting the wrong policies. Dealers must always bear in mind that exchanges need not always be the effect of changes in prices but may often be the cause of such changes.

Deviations from parities are explained by a number of theories foremost among which are the following:

(1) The supply and demand theory.
(2) The theory of the market mechanism.
(3) The quantity theory.
(4) The trade balance theory.
(5) The leads and lags theory.
(6) The terms of trade theory.
(7) The capital movements theory.
(8) The interest rates theory.
(9) The psychological theory.
(10) The speculation theory.
(11) The elasticity theory.

Of these theories the first-named is by far the most familiar to foreign exchange dealers. Its operation has already been dealt with in the last chapter. Dealers know from their everyday experience that when buyers exceed sellers the exchange appreciates until it reaches a level at which buyers cease to consider it worth their while to buy it and at which it attracts adequate additional sellers to the market. When sellers exceed

127

buyers the exchange depreciates until it reaches a level at which holders cease to deem it worth while to sell and at which it attracts sufficient additional demand.

The operation of the market mechanism through the interplay between supply, demand and prices is substantially the same as in other markets, but owing to the very high degree of elasticity of both supply and demand in foreign exchanges it operates in the foreign exchange market as near to perfection as in any market. This does not mean that it operates perfectly. We shall see below that its operation is affected by the varying degrees of the elasticity of its supply and its demand. Even though foreign exchange dealers may not be acquainted with the theory of market mechanism — to be precise, they may be unaware of having any knowledge of that theory as such — they are perfectly familiar with its operation in practice. In fact the market mechanism operates through them. It is they and their clients through their intermediary who provide and absorb the supply of foreign exchanges and who have to make up their minds when an upward or downward movement of an exchange must be considered to have become overdone. Here we are confronted with another instance in which theory merges into technique with no borderline between them. Whether a dealer is successful or otherwise depends very largely on his ability to judge when a movement due to fundamental causes has proceeded too far so that a reaction bringing about a technical readjustment of the rate becomes due.

The quantity theory is in substance a more sophisticated version of the supply and demand theory. From the 14th century onward foreign exchange dealers have been aware of the existence of relationship between the quantity of money available in the market for the purpose of acquiring foreign bills. Already in the 16th century Gresham, a practical dealer in foreign exchanges, was able to express this relationship very clearly: "The waye to rayse th'exchange for England, . . . By making money scaunte [*i.e.* scarce] in Lumbard Strete".

We saw in the last chapter that foreign exchange dealers in our days are only too familiar with a "quantity theory" in a much narrower sense. The volume of their own operations is affected by the amount of funds placed at their disposal by their banks, plus the amount they are authorized to borrow through swap transactions, in the Euro-currency market, in the inter-bank sterling market or on their *nostro* accounts.

In a much broader sense the quantity of money that deter-mines the exchange rates is not the quantity available in the foreign exchange departments, or even the quantity of the total liquid resources available in the money market, but the entire volume of currency and credit in the two countries concerned. In the course of the bullionist controversy during the Napo-leonic Wars and again in the course of the foreign exchange controversy after the first World War this version of the quan-tity theory of money emerged as the purchasing power parity theory of foreign exchange. It is concerned not with changes in the volume of funds actually in foreign exchange markets but with changes in the total monetary circulation. Even if the dogmatic exaggerations of this theory are discounted it contains sufficient truth to make it necessary for bankers to keep a watch-ful eye on changes in the volume of money both in their own countries and in foreign countries. In advanced countries with a modern credit system it is not the note circulation that matters but the volume of bank money. Anything that points towards its expansion — for instance in the U.K. an increase in the amount of Treasury bill issue — must be looked upon as foreshadowing higher costs and prices and therefore an adverse change in the trade balance.

This brings us to the most popular foreign exchange theory — the trade balance theory. All dealers are thoroughly aware that an export surplus makes for an appreciation of the ex-change concerned, while an import surplus makes for its depre-ciation. They are well placed for ascertaining the operation of such influences, because these influences operate through their medium. They know when the big tobacco-importing firms cover seasonal dollar requirements and are familiar with the effects of large-scale operations by the international oil com-panies, and so on and so forth. Even though each foreign exchange department only covers a fraction of the total opera-tions arising from imports and exports, the news about large

F   129

transactions usually gets round the market long before balance of trade figures come to be published.

Foreign exchange dealers are indeed well aware that there is inevitably a time lag between changes in the balance of visible trade and the publication of the relevant figures, and a considerably longer time lag as far as invisible imports and exports are concerned. Nevertheless, they are often inclined to allow themselves to be influenced by the published trade figures, although they know that those figures refer to a past period. If the trade returns of the United Kingdom for the past month show an increase in the adverse balance through an increase of imports, for instance, it inspires pessimism towards sterling in the market, although dealers must surely know that most of the demand for foreign exchange arising from the additional imports has already passed through their hands — especially insofar as imports consist largely of raw materials which are paid for immediately — so that it could not possibly affect the future trend of sterling. In any case, since importers having to pay in foreign currencies at some later date and exporters having to receive foreign currencies at some later date often cover the exchange risk in advance, their transactions affect the exchange rate when they carry out the necessary forward exchange transactions and not when the goods are registered in the customs returns, or even when the actual payment for the goods is due. Seasonal adjustment of trade figures is unrealistic.

We must not confine our interest to grand totals but have to analyse the details of imports and exports and we must pay attention to leads and lags. For instance, if increase in an adverse balance is due to purchases of manufactures of the kinds that are usually bought against medium- or long-term credits then it is advisable to expect a delayed effect. British exports consist mainly of manufactures, and a large proportion of them are capital goods sold on a long-term credit basis, so that their increase could not possibly have affected sterling favourably during the month for which they were included in the customs returns.

Those who seek to apply the balance of trade theory in order to explain exchange movements must know a great deal about actual or customary terms of payments in the various lines of exports and imports in order to form an idea when they have affected, or are likely to affect, exchange rates. Since bankers know much more than economists about credit terms granted to exporters and importers in various lines, they are in a better position to form an idea about changes in leads and lags. This should assist bankers in the correct use of balance of trade figures for interpreting or forecasting exchange rates.

Practical experience should enable bankers to avoid the fallacious conclusion that the balance of payments could not possibly affect the exchange rate because "it must always balance". It is true that in a good foreign exchange market any one-sided buying or selling pressure is always offset through movements of short-term funds in the opposite sense, so that in the balance of payments, as in balance sheets, the total debit and credit items must always equate each other. But the process through which they equate each other entails a change in exchange rates.

Just as the fact that two sides of a balance sheet must always be equal does not mean that no firm could therefore ever become insolvent, so the fact the two sides of a balance of payments must always balance does not prevent a deficit from causing an exchange to depreciate or a surplus from causing it to appreciate. Foreign exchange dealers, ever since the time of Davanzati, the 16th century Florentine banker who may be regarded as the father of foreign exchange theory, have been aware that if there is an excess demand for an exchange it finds a counterpart, and the gap is filled, as a result of an adjustment of the exchange rate. We already touched upon this subject in the last chapter.

The theory of leads and lags was popularised by economists during the post-War period. It recognises that the timing of the pressure on exchange rates depended very largely on the decisions of their commercial customers whether to cover their foreign exchanges well in advance or to defer the payment as long as possible. As already observed, bankers are favourably placed for interpreting foreign trade figures in the light of their knowledge of payments terms customary in various trades.

They are in a fair position to judge the extent to which seasonal import requirements, for instance, are covered well ahead. They have a good idea when leads and lags tend to lengthen or shorten.

The effect of imports and exports on exchange rates depends not only on their volume but also on their relative prices. An increase in the prices of imports by 5 per cent without a corresponding increase in the prices of exports produces the same effect on exchange rates as an increase in the volume of imports by 5 per cent with prices unchanged. Changes in the terms of trade — the relative value of imported goods and exported goods — are in fact one of the basic influences that affect exchange rates from time to time.

An import surplus or an export surplus is offset in the balance of payments by a corresponding adjustment in borrowing and lending abroad. In an ideal world such borrowing and lending would assume the form of spontaneous long-term capital transactions. In our world, however, international long-term capital movements need not produce a balancing effect. It happens very often that not enough long-term capital is exported by a country with an export surplus, and the country with an import surplus is unable to borrow enough long-term capital to fill the gap, which has to be filled by short-term borrowing. On the other hand, countries are apt to export more capital than they can afford to on the basis of their export surplus, and have to re-borrow the difference in the form of short-term borrowing. In all such situations deficiency of capital imports or overlending are apt to influence exchange rates. It is necessary, therefore, to take an interest in all forms of capital export and imports from the point of view of their impact on exchange rates.

The relative level of long-term interest rates in different countries is one of the many factors affecting capital imports and exports. But they are also affected by the availability of long-term capital and by a multitude of other influences. On the other hand, short-term interest rates are almost always an important influence affecting international movements of short-term funds and, through them, exchange rates.

From the 18th century, possibly earlier, dealers must have been aware of the modern version of the theory under which differences in the levels of interest rates affect exchange rates through giving rise to transfers of funds from the centre with low interest rates to the centre with high interest rates. It was a practical banker, Goschen, who first expressed that theory in a comprehensive form in his *Theory of the Foreign Exchanges*, published in 1861. In our days foreign exchange dealers are always on the lookout for changes or prospects of changes in interest rates in foreign centres. When a Bank rate changes they are quick to adapt their forward quotations to the changed interest parities. Spot rates, too, respond to changes in interest rates. Changes in the Bank rate are apt to induce dealers to revise their views on the economic prospects of the country concerned, and their reassessment of the prospects is liable to modify the material effect of the change on spot as well as forward rates.

All dealers are familiar, consciously or otherwise, with the psychological theory according to which material influences affecting exchange rates produce their effects largely through their psychological influences which are liable to modify the effects of material influences to a very large degree. As I already pointed out in the last chapter, the extent to which changes in supply and demand affect exchange rates depends on the market's moods to a very large degree. The same amount of excess of buying or selling may be absorbed on some days with the greatest ease with hardly any effect on the rates while on other days it triggers off a self-aggravating exchange movement. Anticipations of changes of every kind are an essentially psychological factor. Even after an anticipation has materialised its effect on the rates is influenced by reactions of thousands of dealers to the changed situation and, further removed, by the reactions of hundreds of thousands or even millions of commercial and other customers concerned with foreign exchange.

This is not, however, the sum total of the psychological theory which merges imperceptibly into the speculation theory. The effects of speculation operating through market-psychology are not confined to anticipation, exaggeration or mitigation of the effects of material factors. The foreign exchange market is capable of generating purely speculative movements unwarranted by any previous improvement or deterioration of the basic strength of currencies. An exchange movement of an essentially speculative character which was originally unjustified can become self-aggravating, first through the reciprocal influence of dealers on each other's attitudes, then through the response of their customers to the trend of the market and finally through the economic effects of a persistent speculative appreciation or depreciation.

A strong and prolonged exchange movement is capable of creating its own subsequent justification by influencing domestic prices in the country whose exchange depreciates or appreciates. Even a persistent heavy premium or discount on its forward exchange due to sweeping speculative pressure can produce such effects in a smaller degree. When it comes to a movement of the spot exchanges they are liable to influence domestic prices to such extent as to cause a material change in purchasing power parities. They are also liable to influence domestic interest rates and the volume of credit, with far-reaching effects on the economy.

This means that the significance of an exchange movement must not be underrated on the ground that it is due purely to speculative or psychological forces. This is one of the reasons why practical men cannot believe in the all-curing effect of adopting a system of floating exchanges. Many academic economists imagine that if only Governments allowed exchanges to find their "natural" level through the operation of unhampered market influences the exchanges would settle at equilibrium rates at which the balance of payments would right itself. Those who think on such lines overlook the extent to which exaggerated and even entirely unjustified exchange movements are capable of changing the equilibrium level. Moreover the effect of an over-valuation or an under-valuation of exchange rates on the trade balance depends on the elasticity of supply of goods in the exporting countries and on the elasticity of demand for goods in imported countries.

Bankers must avoid dogmatism in respect of foreign exchange theories which have a bearing on their views on exchanges. Above all, foreign exchange dealers interested in theory must always bear in mind that no single theory can be relied upon for explaining all foreign exchange movements, let alone forecasting them, in all circumstances. No matter how firmly they may be convinced that one particular theory is right they must always bear in mind that it can only contain part of the truth and that other theories, too, may contain parts of the truth. Unless they are able to retain absolute neutrality between the wide variety of alternative theories, and unless they realise that each one in turn, or any combination of them, might account for exchange movements in given situations, it would be infinitely better for them to close their minds altogether to any theories and rely exclusively on their practical experience and instinct. One-sided support of a particular theory may bring fame to economists because it attracts more attention than a well-balanced attitude towards it. But as far as bankers are concerned, instead of bringing them fame, it might easily cost their banks a great deal of money.

CHAPTER 12

MOVEMENTS OF FORWARD RATES

ALTHOUGH we often talk about "forward exchange market" in practice there is no real separate market for forward dealing. It is true, in Continental countries where the practice of daily meetings of foreign exchange dealers has survived their activities are confined to spot transactions. But in the "unofficial markets" — where the turnover is usually much larger than in the "official markets" — spot and forward exchanges are dealt in as indiscriminately as in the Anglo-American markets, even if some dealers and brokers specialise in forward exchanges. For one thing, the bulk of forward business transacted between banks assumes the form of swap operations which are a combination of a spot and a forward operation. They are inextricably bound together, both from a market-technical point of view and from the point of view of the reciprocal influences of spot and forward rates.

Most of what was said in Chapter 10 about technical influences affecting spot rates applies equally to forward rates. Since spot exchanges bought and sold are not delivered immediately but two days after the conclusion of the deal the difference between them and forward exchanges, which are delivered after three days or more, is merely one of degree. Forward rates, like spot rates, are determined by the ever-changing relationship between supply and demand, this law being subject to the same reservations as it is when applied to spot rates. Forward rates, too, are liable to be influenced by technical factors and by fundamental factors of the same kind as those which are liable to affect spot rates.

In additional to being affected by all those factors, forward rates are also influenced by changes in spot rates, just as spot rates are influenced by changes in forward rates. Very broadly speaking, spot rates and forward rates tend to move in sympathy — subject to a great many important reservations and expectations, some of which are to be discussed below. In particular if spot rates change as a result of changes in parities, forward rates — though not forward margins — tend to follow them as a matter of course, even if the change is seldom identical and at times widely divergent. Just as spot rates fluctuate in the vicinity of their I.M.F. parities forward rates tend to fluctuate, very broadly speaking, in the vicinity of the spot rates and, therefore, they too, fluctuate around the I.M.F. parities.

While, however, under I.M.F. rules member Governments are under obligation to prevent any appreciation or depreciation of spot rates beyond their support points, they have no such obligation concerning forward rates which can, and at times do, deviate quite substantially from spot rates and therefore from support points and I.M.F. parities. Nevertheless, rigid maintenance of spot rates at support points necessitates measures which tend to keep forward rates within support points, or to restore them after a while to within support points. Under the gold standard there were automatic forces at work, in the form of gold shipments through private arbitrage, preventing any but purely fractional temporary deviations of spot rates from gold points. Under the Bretton Woods system no such automatic forces are at work, but intervention by the monetary authorities in accordance with the I.M.F. rules produces a similar result even more effectively. Neither under the gold standard nor under the Bretton Woods system are there any automatic forces at work to keep forward rates within support points. It is the psychological factor — the degree of confidence in the maintenance of gold points or support points — that prevents or moderates the deviation of forward rates from these limits fixed for spot rates.

In actual fact there have been a number of recent instances of substantial and persistent discount on forward rates bringing them well outside the support points for spot rates. But restoration of confidence in the maintenance of parities is liable to restore forward rates to within support points even in the absence of official intervention to that effect.

Swap rates — that is, the margin between spot and forward rates expressed in terms of premium or discount — tend to be equal to their interest parities — that is, the differential between comparable interest rates in two financial centres. This is because any discrepancy between forward margins and interest parities tends to correct itself automatically by means of giving rise to interest arbitrage operations. It is mainly from this point of view that forward rates are subject to influences that differ from those affecting spot rates. It is true, as we saw in the last chapter, interest rates exert a powerful influence also on spot rates. But they do so in a sense opposite to the sense in which they influence forward margins. An increase in the Bank Rate tends to cause spot rates to move in favour of the country concerned, but at the same time it tends to cause forward margins to move against it.

Moreover, while the effect of changes in interest rates on spot rates is vague and indistinct, their effect on forward margins tends to be clear-cut and arithmetically distinct. It operates largely through interest arbitrage which tend to reduce and remove any discrepancies between interest parities and forward margins, partly through the effect of the former on the latter, but in given circumstances also through the effect of forward margins on interest rates. So long as there are funds available for interest arbitrage, and so long as the profit margin is sufficiently wide to make it worth while, such operations tend to readjust interest parities and forward margins to each other.

In theory swap margins are at equilibrium when the percentage per annum they represent is equal to their interest parities. This theory, like so many other economic theories, oversimplifies the real situation which in practice is highly involved. There is not one interest parity for a swap rate of any particular maturity but a number of them. This is because in financial centres there are usually several alternative sets of interest rates which are capable of influencing forward rates. As we saw in Chapter 8, a swap rate for a particular maturity can only conform to one interest parity at a time and must therefore necessarily deviate from its other interest parities. More often than not it does not conform perfectly to any interest parity but is in the vicinity of the most important amongst them, while allowing to some extent for differences between that parity and the parity that is next in order of importance.

Nor are interest arbitrage transactions necessarily confined to transfers of funds into the same type of short-term investment in which they were held prior to their transfer. Prospects of higher yield are liable to induce banks to change the form in which they employ their funds at the same time as transferring them into another currency. They may choose a different type of investment or different maturities. For this reason there is a very wide variety of possible interest differentials between two centres which, like London and New York, have a wide choice of short-term investment facilities. Moreover, transfers of bank funds are sometimes undertaken, not mainly for the sake of higher yield, but largely for the sake of changing the composition of a bank's short-term assets.

Although Bank Rates determine, very broadly speaking, levels of interest rates, and changes in them have always an immediate and at times dramatic effect on forward rates, the ratio between them does not constitute one of the interest parities. Interest rates determining forward rates are those actually received by investors of short-term funds engaged in forward exchange operations. Before 1929 it was the London rate for fine bank bills and the New York rate for Wall Street loans that were most of the time the most important from the point of view of interest arbitrage between the two cities. After the resumption of exchange dealings in 1951 it was the ratio between U.S. and U.K. Treasury bill rates which was regarded for a long time as the standard interest parity for the forward sterling-dollar rate. In actual fact there were all the time also other sets of interest rates the differentials between which provided arbitrage opportunities because, since swap rates tended to be in the vicinity of the principal interest parities, they were bound to deviate from the various secondary interest parities. We saw in Chapter 8 that there are from time to time distinct changes in fashions in respect of favoured interest parities. At the time of writing differentials between Euro-dollar and other Euro-currency rates are of overwhelming importance but a fair volume of arbitrage transactions is based also on differentials between Euro-sterling rates and inter-bank sterling rates or rates on loans to British Local Authorities. In New York the rates paid on Federal Funds over week-ends attracted a certain amount of arbitrage in the 'sixties, but they were only important from the point of view of very short forward rates.

It is not only arbitrage in the narrower sense that is relevant from the point of view of interest parities. Decisions by banks, merchants, industrial firms, investors, etc., whether to borrow or lend in this currency or that are also largely determined by relationship between interest parities and forward rates. This is an additional reason why forward rates tend to gravitate automatically towards their interest parities to a much larger degree than spot rates tend to gravitate automatically towards I.M.F. parities.

There is a tendency towards adjustment, even in the absence of actual arbitrage transactions, owing to the anticipation of such transactions, on the assumption that so long as discrepancies exist they are liable to induce such transactions. Moreover, when a change in the Bank Rate is expected dealers are inclined to adjust their forward commitments in anticipation of the resulting changes in interest parities. Following an unexpected change in the Bank Rate which has not been discounted in advance in forward rates dealers adjust their forward quotations immediately to the level to which they expect these rates to settle down on the basis of the new Bank Rate. Interest rates themselves also tend to anticipate Bank Rate changes, but anticipatory changes in swap rates often surpass such anticipatory changes in interest rates.

It would be idle to try to establish strict arithmetical relationship between changes in supply and demand in forward exchanges and changes in forward rates, or even between changes in interest parities and forward rates. In respect of the latter, practice approximates more closely to theory. A change in the Bank Rate, for instance, creates a new equilibrium level towards which forward rates will tend to gravitate, but any adjustment following the change is seldom arithmetically perfect. For one thing, as we saw above, such changes are often widely expected and produce part of their effect in advance, so that when the anticipations materialise a smaller degree of subsequent adjustment is sufficient to restore equilibrium. Moreover, there is no reason why there should not remain in existence after the change some degree of discrepancy between the equilibrium level and the actual rates just as there had been before the change, even though it is not likely to be the same degree. There is indeed no reason why this discrepancy should be identical with the previous one. The change itself is liable to influence the judgment of the market concerning the prospects of spot rates and of forward rates, a judgment which itself tends to influence forward rates. One of the ways in which such changes of market opinion are liable to affect forward rates is by affecting the relative proportion of covered and uncovered commitments. While prior to a widely expected devaluation most claims in the devaluation-prone currency are covered, the need for doing so becomes much less imperative after the devaluation unless the market feels that the devaluation, having been "too late and too little", is likely to be followed by another devaluation. Anticipation of long-range effects of Bank Rate changes on the level of domestic costs and prices and on the balance of payments also tends to affect the supply and demand situation in forward exchanges.

Even in the absence of changes in parities changes in spot exchange rates within their support points are liable to influence swap margins. Devaluations are usually followed by a sharp reversal of swap margins as a result of profit-taking covering operations. Moreover, if dealers feel, following on a depreciation of the spot rate through devaluation or even within support points, that it is not likely to depreciate any further, their optimism will express itself in an adjustment of forward margins in that sense. This rule operates when under the Bretton Woods system spot rates approach their support points, provided that the maintenance of the support points is trusted. In such a situation forward rates do not go beyond support point. For once the spot rate has depreciated to its support point those expecting payment in that currency may feel safe in leaving the exchange risk uncovered rather than covering it at a forward rate which would be lower than the limit for the possible depreciation of the spot rate. We saw in Chapters 7 and 8 that if a spot rate reaches maximum support point those who have to make payments at some future date in that currency may deem it unnecessary to cover the forward exchange because they do not expect to be exposed to losses through a further appreciation above support point. Conversely, those who have to make future payments in a currency which has reached minimum support point are likely to cover the risk of its recovery while those who expect to receive payment in a currency which has reached maximum support point are likely cover against the risk of its depreciation.

The influences resulting from this attitude are apt to begin to operate even before spot rates actually reach their support points. Always on the assumption that the maintenance of support points is trusted, forward margins tend to narrow as and when spot rates approach their support points, so that actual forward rates do not go beyond support points. This means that while there is a discount or a premium on very short forward exchanges until support points are actually reached, the margin, expressed in percentage per annum, begins to narrow for long forward rates — at any rate up to three months — long before spot rates have reached their support points. When dealing with time arbitrage in Chapter 7 we saw that this phenomenon gives rise to discrepancies between long and short forward rates and provides opportunities for time arbitrage.

Once the maintenance of spot rates at support points comes to be distrusted the above rule ceases to operate. In that case supply-demand influences and psychological influences are allowed to produce their effects on forward rates, which are liable to depreciate or appreciate well beyond support points. Official intervention prevents the anticipation of a devaluation or of a revaluation from producing its effect on spot rates unless and until the anticipated change actually materialises, but its anticipation expresses itself to a very large degree in changes of forward rates. The authorities are under no obligation to prevent movements of forward rates beyond support points, but under a practice that has developed in the early 'sixties they very frequently deem it expedient to do so. Official forward operations and their effects on forward rates are discussed in detail in Chapter 17.

Forward rates are liable to be affected by changes in the market's preference for working on certain interest parities, or by the banks' attitude toward the minimum profit margin for the sake of which they deem it worth while to co-operate. Above all, as we pointed out earlier in this chapter, they are affected to a very large extent by the volume of funds at the disposal of foreign exchange departments for the purpose of interest arbitrage. This is a factor of first-rate importance in abnormal circumstances when, owing to the persistence of a relatively wide profit margin on covered interest arbitrage, foreign exchange departments are liable to exhaust their resources available for that purpose. In that case forward rates are liable to lose touch altogether with their interest parities, for the widening discrepancies are unable to give rise to sufficient interest arbitrage to arrest and reverse their appreciation or depreciation. The widening of profit margins may induce some banks, however, to increase the volume of funds they place at the disposal of their foreign exchange departments. It depends largely on the profit margins that they can earn on alternative uses of their liquid funds and also on the volume of liquid funds which they are in a position to divert to such use without having to victimise their regular domestic customers by diverting these funds for use in arbitrage. To a large extent the general liquidity of banks is an important factor in determining the extent to which forward rates can depart from their interest parities. Even though foreign exchange departments may be permitted to procure additional funds by borrowing in the Euro-currency markets, the priorities for the use of such funds also depend largely on their bank's general liquidity.

In centres where the granting of credits to foreign banks is not effectively prevented by exchange restrictions the liquidity factor is liable to influence forward rates to a much higher degree. If foreign banks find it cheaper to cover exchange risk by borrowing the currency that is under attack and selling the spot exchange they do so in preference to incurring the high cost of selling forward exchange. To the extent to which such operations are possible they tend to keep down the discrepancy between interest parities and forward rate, but in such situations the interest parities are based on the high interest rates charged on overdrafts on *nostro* accounts or on alternative forms of borrowing. Since, however, such operations increase the burden for the authorities to support the spot exchange they usually discourage it, if not by means of official or unofficial bans on credits to foreign banks, at any rate through making money tighter in the domestic market. Alternatively or additionally they may reduce the benefit derived from forward operations through supporting the forward rate.

We saw in Chapter 9 that the development of Euro-currency markets has introduced a new element into the situation. Hitherto the extent to which the alternative method of speculating by means of borrowed funds in preference to forward exchange transactions depended on the willingness and ability of local banks to grant credits. Now those who wish to cover exchange risks or to create short positions are able to do so independently of the facilities obtainable from local banks, by borrowing Euro-currencies. For instance, although exchange control in the U.K. prevents non-resident banks from obtaining sterling overdrafts in London they are in a position to borrow Euro-sterling — that is, sterling deposits owned by non-residents — and sell the proceeds in preference to selling forward sterling at a wide discount. They are likely to do so up to the limit of their capacity to borrow Euro-sterling, so long as Euro-sterling rates do not exceed the cost of selling forward sterling. It is partly for this reason that forward sterling tends to be in the close vicinity of the ratio between Euro-sterling and Euro-dollar deposit rates.

A consideration which is seldom stressed sufficiently is that relationship between forward rates and interest parities is essentially reciprocal. While changes in interest rates affect forward rates changes in forward rates in turn tend to affect interest rates. For a detailed analysis of this relationship the reader is referred to my books *A Dynamic Theory of Forward*

Exchange and *The Euro-Dollar System.* The reciprocal character of the relationship is particularly in evidence in respect of interest parities based on Euro-currency rates. While the volume of forward exchange transactions is usually smaller then the turnover in a highly developed local money market it is usually much larger than the turnover in Euro-currency markets, so that changes in forward rates brought about by causes other than previous changes in Euro-currency rates are bound to react on Euro-currency rates. We saw above that when there is strong pressure on forward sterling the resulting widening of the discount causes a rise in interest rates on Euro-sterling deposits.

Forward rates are liable to depart from their interest parities as a result of changes in supply or demand, especially for maturities other than standard dates. Their interest parities vary, of course, according to maturity because differentials between long and short interest rates are seldom, if ever, identical in different markets. We saw in Chapter 7 that there is a theoretical equilibrium line representing interest parities between interest rates for various maturities at a given moment, and forward rates for the same maturities tend to gravitate towards this equilibrium line. There are, however, many influences at work which cause forward rates to deviate from their equilibrium line.

CHAPTER 13

INVESTMENT CURRENCIES

THE system of multiple exchange rates, that developed mainly in Central Europe during the 'thirties and came to be applied very widely in many countries during and after the War, gave rise to many special practices and techniques in foreign exchanges. There was, for instance, for a number of years a wide market in transferable sterling which assumed considerable importance in Zürich and in other centres. The progressive elimination of multiple exchange systems during the 'fifties and early 'sixties has greatly reduced, however, the practical need for studying the infinite variety of practices arising from them. They are still in force in a number of Latin-American countries and, to a much less extent, even in some countries in Europe. In the U.K. there are no multiple currencies apart from investment dollars, property dollars and external account sterling. These exchanges are the last survivals of the many types of sterling that developed during and after the War as a result of exchange control. Investment currencies are important and transactions in them deserve attention, because they differ in some respects from ordinary foreign exchange operations.

Investment dollars are for the use of U.K. residents for the purpose of acquiring securities and other assets in non-sterling countries. Security sterling was until 1967 for the use of non-residents in the U.K. for the acquisition of sterling securities. Similar markets are in operation in other countries. For instance, in Belgium and in Holland there is a market for foreign currencies which can be used by Dutch and Belgian residents for the acquisition of foreign securities. Dollars are not the only currency which can be transacted in London by U.K. buyers or sellers of foreign securities. But since the investment dollar is by far the most important investment currency, and

146

the rates of other investment currencies are based on investment dollar rates, we propose to confine ourselves in this chapter to the latter.

From an American point of view investment dollars differ in no way from other dollars held by U.K. residents. From the point of view of U.K. residents, however, the difference is that, while their holdings of ordinary dollars can only be used for the acquisition of goods or the payment of liabilities, their holdings of investment dollars — variously called also "security dollars", "premium dollars" or "switch dollars" — can also be used for the acquisition of any eligible non-sterling securities quoted on a recognised stock exchange. Their holders are entitled to sell them as ordinary dollars, and for this reason investment dollars could never go to a discount. Because they can be used for investment in non-sterling securities they are almost always at a very substantial premium that is subject to very wide fluctuation.

U.K. residents are only entitled to buy foreign securities if either they or some other U.K. holder of foreign securities had sold their holdings so that investment dollars (or other investment currencies) are available or can be purchased for that purpose. Since 1965 sellers of foreign securities have to sell 25 per cent of the proceeds in the market for ordinary dollars.

The market in investment dollars and other investment currencies differs materially from the market in ordinary foreign exchanges. Dealings in such currencies are transacted to a large but diminishing extent outside the foreign exchange market proper, often between stock departments of banks and stock exchange firms specialising in foreign securities. This is because it is they who handle transactions in such securities, so that it is convenient for those concerned if they handle also the investment dollar transactions connected with them. But because a certain proportion of transactions in investment dollars is not connected directly with security transactions, in recent years foreign exchange departments have been taking an increasingly active hand in transactions in investment dollars. In addition to banks that are authorised dealers in foreign exchanges, all stockbrokers dealing in foreign securities,

London branches of American brokers, solicitors and other firms who are authorised depositaries of foreign securities are entitled to deal in investment currencies. Only a small proportion of them are, however, really active in the market.

Firms with a large turnover are often able to marry buying and selling orders of their clients, thereby circumventing the market altogether. They do not use foreign exchange brokers. Even foreign exchange departments usually deal in investment dollars direct with each other, or with stockbroker firms. In some foreign exchange departments one or more dealers specialise in investment dollars. Investment dollars, and to a much less extent other investment currencies, are often acquired and held by banks who have no intention to use them for the purchase of foreign securities. Since 1965, however, banks are not supposed to hold investment currencies in excess of their customers' expected requirements.

Investment dollars can be bought and sold for forward as well as for spot delivery. In the absence of arrangements to the contrary spot investment currencies are due to be delivered two days after the conclusion of the deal, the practice being the same as in the foreign exchange market and in the Euro-currency market. But whenever a transaction is directly connected with a security purchase the delivery date of the investment currency is usually synchronised with the settlement of the security transaction. In the late 'sixties considerable delays developed in the deliveries of Euro-bonds bought in the secondary market, and the dates of settlements became uncertain. It is impossible for the buyers to guess the date for which they would require the investment dollars. The usual practice is to instruct their bank to buy them and keep them on their account.

It is possible to arrange delivery on the same day or on the day following the conclusion of the deal. There is also a fair amount of forward dealing. When a dealer sells investment dollars for forward delivery he immediately covers the premium risk by buying spot investment dollars. He has the use of the dollars until the forward contract matures and may lend it in the Euro-dollar market or may carry out a swap transaction in ordinary dollars. When a dealer buys investment dollars for forward delivery he immediately sells spot investment dollars out of his holding, or borrows Euro-dollars and sells the proceeds, or carries out a swap transaction in ordinary dollars. The charge to the customer is usually based on the current swap rate on ordinary dollars and on the premium on investment dollars. The practice of making two-way quotations applies to a large extent to investment dollars. There is a fairly regular market in forward investment dollars up to three months but it is possible to arrange deals up to six months.

In theory the maximum supply of investment dollars is represented by the total of quoted dollar securities and other eligible foreign securities held by residents in the U.K. In reality only a small fraction of the total is ever offered for sale or is available for the requirements of the market at any given moment, or even over a period. Most dollar securities are held firmly by institutional or private investors. Conceivably a very sharp rise in the premium on investment dollars might induce many of them to sell their holdings in order to take their profit on their investment dollars. In actual practice in most cases, in order to tempt holders to part with their investments, the premium would have to rise to such a high figure as to deter potential investors from acquiring investment dollars.

There is always a certain amount of liquid investment dollars held by investors intending to reinvest it at the right moment, but since 1965 25 per cent of the investment currencies sold has to be sold as ordinary currencies. Between 6 and 12 months that proportion increases to 50 per cent, and thereafter to 100 per cent. When the premium is high, dealers are liable to keep down their holdings of investment dollars for fear of losses through a contraction in them. For this reason the premium is apt to be sensitive when it is high, and comparatively small transactions are liable to move it disporportionately to the amount involved. When the premium is low a counterpart is not readily forthcoming out of investment dollar balances and must be produced by means of stock transactions which have to be made worth while through a rise in the premium to a tempting level.

Sellers of dollar securities have to reinvest the proceeds within six months. Otherwise they have to surrender another 25 per cent of their investment dollars as ordinary dollars. The total surrendered between April 1965 and August 1968 was $750 million.

While occasionally the premium on investment dollars moves in sympathy with the trend of the dollar, more often than not it is largely independent of it. In addition to the influence of changes or anticipated changes in exchange rates, the investment dollar rate is also affected by influences affecting Wall Street or the London Stock Exchange, by measures or prospective measures of taxation in the U.K. or the U.S.A., by the amounts of new dollar issues in Europe, etc. For detailed discussion of this highly involved subject the reader is referred to my book *The Euro-Bond Market*.

Whenever some institutional change brings additional types of investors into the market for dollar securities or increases the proportion of their recourses available for investment in such securities, the result is an increase in demand for investment dollars. Buyers of dollar securities may want to hedge against the investment dollar risk by selling investment dollars forward, while those buying options on dollar securities may buy investment dollars forward in order to secure the exchange rate in case they should take up the option. In both cases they only do so if they anticipate a change in the premium to their disadvantage.

The ups and downs of the investment dollar premium are indeed apt to be perplexing. To add to the complications the authorities are in a position to influence the rate without intervening directly, by granting or witholding permits for the use of investment dollars for direct investment abroad. Conversely, in approved instances the use of ordinary dollar holdings is permitted for approved portfolio investment to avoid an unwanted rise in the premium.

In many quarters the investment dollar premium is looked upon as barometer indicating market opinion on the prospect of the sterling-dollar rate. Indeed on various occasions in the post-War period when sterling came under a cloud the premium widened because dollar securities were bought as a hedge against devaluation. The experience of the devaluations of 1949 and of 1967 proved that the use of investment dollars, or even of dollar securities bought with the aid of them, for hedging against devaluation was utterly futile. On the eve of both devaluations the premium on investment dollars was 36 per cent and immediately after the devaluation it went down in excess of the extent of the devaluation. As a result those who had bought investment dollars shortly before the devaluation lost more than they gained through the rise in the basic sterling-dollar rate. If they waited a little longer the premium rose once more to a level at which they would be able to make a moderate profit. Even so, the experiences of 1949 and 1967 proves that the holding of investment dollars is not a suitable hedge. For one thing it is seldom possible to be certain about the imminence of a devaluation or about its extent. It is of course much cheaper to hedge against devaluation by means of forward exchange operations, especially for brief periods. But U.K. residents are only permitted to operate in forward exchange in connection with foreign trade or other approved international transactions.

Political prospects are an important factor in determining the premium. The prospects of a Socialist victory during 1963–4 were largely responsible for a rise in the premium on investment dollars. Following on the Labour Party's victory, however, the premium narrowed considerably, largely because of fears of a ban on dealings and of a commandeering of dollar securities. The announcement of the measure by which 25 per cent of the proceeds of foreign securities have to be sold as ordinary exchange cause a sharp rise in the premium, because holders felt that "it might have been worse".

The market in security sterling sought to ensure that while there should be no reduction in the total of foreign long-term capital in British portfolio investment overseas holders of sterling securities should be in a position to realise their holdings by selling them to other overseas investors. The market was somewhat similar to that of investment dollars inasmuch as there are dealings both within and outside the foreign exchange market proper. As in the case of investment dollars, much of the business was transacted between stock exchange firms and stock departments of banks. This system was brought to an end in April 1967 when security sterling was converted into external account sterling. This meant that non-resident holdings of sterling securities became unblocked. This act of liberalisation was ill-timed, as it must have contributed to no slight extent to the pressure on sterling some months later, which culminated in the devaluation in November.

CHAPTER 14

THE EURO-DOLLAR MARKET

THE most important change in the foreign exchange market since the War has been the development of an active market in foreign currency deposits during the late 'fifties and the 'sixties. It has broadened the scope of foreign exchange departments by the addition of an important new section to the market, by the increase of the resources available to them, and by the increase of the variety of types of transactions. It has thus provided additional work and additional opportunities, but also additional complications and the need for foreign exchange dealers to acquire additional techniques.

The bulk of the turnover in Euro-currencies consists of transactions in Euro-dollars. For the sake of simplifying matters I shall propose to confine myself therefore largely to the Euro-dollar market with only casual reference to other Euro-currencies. For a detailed treatment of the subject I must refer the reader to the revised edition of my book *The Euro-Dollar System — Practice and Theory of International Interest Rates.*

Euro-dollars are not a special type of dollars and there is absolutely nothing to distinguish them from ordinary dollars held on deposit accounts with banks in the United States beyond the fact that their original holders have lent the deposits to some European bank. Their holders can employ them in exactly the same ways as they can any other dollar deposits. There is no separate exchange rate for Euro-dollars. When we talk about "Euro-dollar rates" we mean interest rates at which Euro-dollar deposits are lent and borrowed. American banks have usually no means of knowing when, and if, a dollar deposit they hold becomes a Euro-dollar deposit through being lent by the depositor.

The term "Euro-dollar" has come into popular use for want

153

of better, but it is not strictly accurate because there is no basic difference between dollar deposits re-deposited in Europe or in other continents outside the United States. Euro-dollars can be lent or borrowed by American, Canadian, Latin-American or Middle East residents. Even the term "deposit" is to some extent a misnomer, for properly speaking the "placing" and "taking" of Euro-currency deposits is a loan transaction. In view of the fact, however, that regular takers of such deposits include some of the world's largest banks, they would not care to admit that they are borrowing. They are not supposed to take the initiative for borrowing but simply "accept" deposits offered to them on the initiative of other banks. One of the reasons why this formula came to be accepted in London, where the system originated in the late 'fifties, was that, while under the exchange regulations banks in the U.K. are entitled to accept deposits in terms of foreign currencies, borrowing in terms of foreign currencies would require authorisation by the Bank of England. So the Euro-dollar deposits are "accepted" even when the receiving bank has instructed a foreign exchange broker to find a bank willing to offer it such a deposit.

For all practical purposes Euro-dollar transactions are loan transactions in terms of dollars. If in spite of this they are not handled by the money market departments of banks but by their foreign exchange departments it is because in a large proportion of instances Euro-dollar transactions are linked with foreign exchange transactions and because foreign exchange departments are more familiar with the names of banks operating in this market. Nevertheless the fact remains that the Euro-dollar market is a money market which is parallel with the local money market, providing facilities that compete with those of the conventional money market. The standard dates for which most transactions for Euro-dollars are concluded are substantially identical with those of the discount market and the money market.

Under British exchange control regulations only banks authorised to deal in foreign exchanges may transact business in Euro-currencies. No official limits are imposed on the amount of Euro-dollars lent or borrowed by banks in the U.K.

Most authorised dealers who are active in foreign exchange are more or less actively engaged in Euro-currency transactions, even though, following on some unfavourable experience towards the close of 1963, some of them withdrew temporarily from the market or curtailed their operations. In foreign exchange departments, and also in foreign exchange brokers' dealing rooms, some dealers specialise in foreign currency deposits. All dealings take place in the same way as foreign exchange dealings, by means of private telephone lines between banks and brokers, and in dealings with foreign centres by means of long-distance telephone or teleprinter.

London is by far the most important market in Euro-dollars. It is practically the only market where it is possible to deal in large amounts in both ways at any time. London has also the advantage of having the largest foreign exchange market in dollars and excellent local short-term investment facilities for the use of the proceeds of Euro-dollar deposits.

Paris is the second important Euro-currency market, with the largest turnover in Euro-sterling. Other Euro-dollar markets include Frankfurt, Amsterdam, the Swiss banking centres, Milan, Montreal and Toronto. There is some activity also in Nassau, Vienna, Stockholm, Beirut, Tel Aviv and Cairo.

In London most of the foreign exchange brokers act as intermediaries in Euro-dollar transactions. The use of brokers is not so general as in the case of foreign exchange transactions, but most banks prefer to use them most of the time. In Paris all Euro-currency business is transacted through foreign exchange brokers.

The London Euro-dollar market is very efficient, capable of absorbing large and sudden changes in the supply or in the demand without unduly affecting the rates, except for those of very short deposits which are very sensitive to changes in market trends. The spreads between borrowing and lending rates were rather wide during the early stages of the market, but later they narrowed considerably, only to widen again somewhat following on the unfavourable experience referred to above. They tend to widen whenever a feeling of uncertainty develops in the market.

155

A Textbook on Foreign Exchange

Non-banking customers often place Euro-dollar deposits with banks or borrow Euro-dollar deposits from them. From about 1963 a large proportion of the supply of the Euro-dollars consisted of deposits lent by corporations in the United States. Unspent proceeds of Euro-bond issues are often held in Euro-dollars ; the rates quoted in the market do not apply to business transacted with non-banking customers, except possibly to a few very large firms of international standing such as the big oil companies. The spread between borrowing and lending rates, which is apt to be very narrow in the market is much wider in relation to firms outside the market, though even they can usually borrow at a lower rate, or lend at a higher rate, than in the domestic market in the United States, or in terms of the local currencies in the centres concerned.

Banks find it possible to "marry" transactions in Euro-dollars, placing with a customer a deposit placed with them by another customer. Much more often, however, a counterpart outside the market is not readily available so that if they want to re-deposit the deposit immediately they have to find the counterpart inside the market, even though it means a much narrower profit margin. Since rates are normally lower for short deposits than for long deposits there is a strong inducement for borrowing short and re-lending long. In times of currency scares short rates become abnormally wide.

In Euro-currency dealings brokers have to disclose the borrower's identity to the lender before the deal is concluded, as soon as they are satisfied that the latter really intends to proceed with the transaction and not just to sound the market. The reason why potential lenders are not content with the assurance — which they usually accept for a foreign exchange transaction — that the potential counterpart is a first-class name, is the possibility that their limit for that name may have already been reached. We shall see in Chapter 16 dealing with risks that all Euro-dollar transactions are unsecured credits, hence the importance attached to names and limits. When the lending bank for some reason does not wish to renew maturing deposits it usually resorts to the excuse that some of its own large Euro-dollar depositors were not renewing their maturing deposits, so that it has to call in some of its deposits. Debtors faced with such a situation, if they are first-class names, find no difficulty in replacing the deposits, even though in order to avoid bidding up the rate for long deposits they may find it expedient to borrow for a short period in the hope of being able to arrange later for a longer deposit on more satisfactory terms.

Certain amount of Euro-currency business between foreign centres is transacted through international brokers specialising in such business. There are several such firms in Germany, Switzerland and France. They have both banking and non-banking clientèle. It occurs sometimes that international brokers arrange for a deposit to be given to a London bank and re-lent immediately to a foreign borrower, possibly to one resident in the original depositor's own country. The transaction amounts to a guarantee of the loan by the London bank in return for the difference between its borrowing and lending rates.

The commission paid to foreign exchange brokers in London on Euro-dollar transactions is $\frac{1}{32}$ per cent by each party. In Paris it is $\frac{1}{16}$ per cent, which partly accounts for the relative wideness of margins in Paris. Brokers specialise in certain Euro-currencies, but most of them transact business in Euro-dollars. Some of them specialise in certain types of transactions such as deposits for long periods or for broken dates. Standard maturities are similar to those of the forward exchange market — deposits at call, for seven days, one month, three months and six months. It is usually possible to obtain quotations for almost any day up to twelve months. It is also possible to negotiate deposits for long periods up to a maximum of five years, even though this became more difficult towards the end of 1964.

The practice relating to the confirmation of the transaction concluded by telephone and to instructions to the placers of the deposits are the same as in the case of foreign exchange transactions. Unless otherwise stipulated, all dealings in foreign currency deposits are treated as spot transactions which means that lenders have to deliver the amount of the deposit on the third clear business day. It is possible, however, to transact business for delivery on the same day or on the second day. It is also possible to stipulate delivery in more than three days, usually up to seven days as a matter of routine. For longer periods the arrangement is a matter of negotiation. Such forward deals in Euro-dollars are not very frequent. They really amount to deferred loans of Euro-dollars. The lender covers himself by a long-short transaction.

For instance if somebody wants to borrow in a month's time Euro-dollars for three months the lender borrows a deposit for four months and re-lends it for one month. The net result is that he gains possession of dollars in a month's time for a period of three months and re-lends them for the same period. It is possible to negotiate options in respect of the date on which the borrower takes up the Euro-dollars he borrowed. Options in respect of the decision whether or not to avail himself of the loan are not transacted by many banks and are usually arranged only for the benefit of goods customers about whom the bank is satisfied that they really intend to avail themselves of the loans so arranged.

Euro-dollars transacted in items of large round amounts. The standard unit is $1 million, although items of $500,000, $250,000 and even $100,000 often change hands. Single transactions up to $5 million are not infrequent and there are occasionally transactions of $10 million and even more. Rates for such large transactions are always a matter of negotiation, owing to the time it takes for the lender to undo his commitments in the market without moving the rates against himself. Transactions between bankers and their customers are usually in smaller amounts, but they are also in round figures and seldom in broken amounts. Smaller dollar deposits are accepted by banks from non-banking customers, but interest paid on them is distinctly lower than that obtainable in the market or that allowed to non-banking customers on large amounts.

As in the case of forward exchange commitments, banks usually give their foreign exchange departments a free hand to maintain discrepancies between maturity dates. Their instructions are usually aimed at limiting the total net amount lent or borrowed that is outstanding at a given moment, and they are at liberty to exceed the limit so long as the excess is offset by

a transaction in the opposite sense, even if it is for a different
maturity. They may job in and out of the market for the sake
of earning the margin between lending and borrowing rates.
Some banks are prepared to take a risk by taking a view on the
future of Euro-dollar rates, lending long and borrowing short,
or vice versa. Some foreign exchange departments are instructed never to swap into other currency while others systematically swap the Euro-dollars into the local currency or into a
third currency.

Practices in dealing with other foreign currency deposits are
substantially identical with those of dealings in Euro-dollars,
subject to modifications due to exchange control regulations
or local practices in the country concerned. In Britain, for
instance, only sterling deposits held by non-residents can be
subject to Euro-sterling transactions. In theory there is
supposed to be no market in Euro-sterling in London, but in
practice it is possible to deal in it on non-resident account
and of combining a Euro-dollar transaction with a sterling-
dollar swap — which amounts for all intents and purposes to a
Euro-sterling transaction.

Dealings in foreign currency deposits further increase the
intricacies of the international monetary system by adding
borrowing, lending and investment facilities and by creating
additional sets of interest parities affecting forward exchanges.
The choice between various short-term investment facilities for
use in interest arbitrage has widened through the creation of
these new interest parities between the various Euro-currency
rates, and also between them and the various national interest
rates. The increase in the variety of interest parities has
increased the likelihood of lasting and relatively substantial
discrepancies for the benefit of interest arbitrage. Situations in
which it is profitable to move funds in both directions at the
same time because at a given moment a forward margin is over-
valued in relation to one of its interest parities with a currency
while it is under-valued in relation to another of its interest
parities with the same currency are now liable to arise much
more frequently as a result of the development of the Euro-
currency market.

A reason why the appearance of foreign currency deposit rates has created additional arbitrage possibilities is that, while local interest rates in a market tend to move, broadly speaking, in the same direction under the influences of domestic developments, Euro-currency rates are liable to be affected by conflicting international influences. The Euro-dollar is subject to a set of influences operating outside the United States.

Parities between Euro-currency rates have come to play a very important part in interest arbitrage. As we saw in Chapters 8 and 12, this does not mean that forward rates are necessarily determined by changes in those parities. More often than not it is Euro-currency rates that are influenced by changes in forward rates. This is particularly true about Euro-currencies other than Euro-dollars because, while the latter has a wide market, other Euro-currencies have a much narrower market, so that if changes in their rates were to determine forward rates it would mean that the tail is wagging the dog.

It is indeed remarkable that arbitrageurs have been concentrating on Euro-currency parities at the cost of neglecting attractive opportunities arising from discrepancies between forward margins and their other interest parities. Operating on Euro-currency parities has of course the great advantage of being able to carry out the entire transaction within the foreign exchange department. If a London arbitrageur wanted to switch into dollars in order to employ the proceeds in U.S. Treasury bills it would have to invest its dollars through a New York bank. But if he wanted to employ the dollars in the Euro-dollar market his colleague across the dealing table who specialises in Euro-dollars could settle the matter in a matter of seconds. Even so, it would be doing less than justice to the enterprising spirit that certainly prevails in post-War foreign exchange department to explain the fashion favouring Euro-currency parities as a minor matter of convenience. Yet there is no other obvious explanation.

As the authorities in London do not impose a limit on Euro-dollar commitments the market in Euro-currencies has provided banks with opportunities to increase their supplies of funds available for arbitrage. The development of the Euro-currency system has provided additional arbitrage opportunities of the following types:

(1) Space arbitrage to take advantage of the discrepancies between Euro-dollar rates quoted at a given moment in various markets.

(2) Interest arbitrage between Euro-dollars and other Euro-currencies.

(3) Interest arbitrage between Euro-dollars and conventional short-term investments.

(4) Time arbitrage between long and short Euro-dollars.

(5) Time arbitrage between long and short Euro-dollars on the one hand and other long and short Euro-currencies on the other.

(6) Time arbitrage between long and short Euro-dollars on the one hand and long and short dollar swaps on the other.

(7) Arbitrage between Euro-dollars and forward gold.

(8) Lender or borrower arbitrage, covered or uncovered, between Euro-dollars and other Euro-currencies.

(9) Hedger-arbitrage between Euro-dollars and other facilities.

(10) Trader-arbitrage between Euro-dollars and other facilities.

(11) Speculator-arbitrage between Euro-dollars and other facilities.

We saw in Chapter 9 that the advent of Euro-currency markets has provided speculators with alternative and additional facilities. This cannot be prevented unless the Government concerned resorted to the extreme measure of blocking foreign deposits. So speculators are in a position to choose freely between selling forward the currency in question or borrowing it in the Euro-currency market and selling the spot. Their choice depends on the relative cost, hence it constitutes "speculator-arbitrage". In the same sense, decisions by lenders, borrowers, hedgers and merchants, whether to engage in Euro-currency operations or in conventional operations constitutes arbitrage-decisions.

While the role of Euro-currencies in speculation is apt to overshadow its other roles from time to time, in the long run it plays an important and constructive role in providing additional means for arbitrage. Above all, the foreign exchange market, in creating this new section, has greatly contributed towards increasing and redistributing the world's international liquid resources.

The importance of the Euro-dollar market has increased considerably during the late 'sixties. By the end of 1967 the amount of outstanding Euro-dollar deposits rose to $16,000 million and it continued to rise in 1968. The London Euro-dollar market came to be used by American banks extensively for borrowing systematically, as an alternative to borrowing in the New York money market. While in the early 'sixties doubts were entertained in many quarters about the permanent character of this market, by the late 'sixties it came to be realised that the system has come to stay. Recognising its importance, the Board for International Settlements and several Central Banks adopted the policy of intervening in the Euro-dollar market in order to steady movements of rates and to counteract unwanted tendencies.

CHAPTER 15

THE INTER-BANK STERLING MARKET

In addition to developing the Euro-currency market, the post-War foreign exchange market may also claim the lion's share of the credit for the creation of another money market which is in many ways of a similar character — the market in inter-bank sterling. Its activities consist of the placing and taking of sterling deposits between London banks, including London branches and subsidiaries of overseas banks. In reality these deals, like Euro-dollar deals, are credit transactions. Unlike Euro-dollar transactions, they are in terms of sterling and unlike Euro-sterling transactions, they can be in terms of sterling on resident account. The reason why a description of this market is not out of place in a book on foreign exchange is not only that it has originated largely through foreign exchange departments and is operated very largely by them, but also that it has a bearing on interest arbitrage transactions even if actually no foreign currencies are involved as far as the London market is concerned.

Although inter-bank deposits in terms of a local currency are no innovation, it was not until the early 'sixties that an active market came to develop in such deposits in London. Its creation must have been inspired by the successful experience with the market in Euro-currencies. Its expansion into a factor of major importance, which occurred in the concluding months of 1964, must be attributed to the sterling crisis that followed the advent of the Labour Government. Owing to fears abroad that exchange restrictions interfering with withdrawals of foreign funds might be adopted inward arbitrage declined because many foreign banks were reluctant to hold sterling even with the forward exchange covered, or even to lend Euro-currency deposits in London. This attitude led to reduction of

163

the resources of the London foreign exchange market at a time when foreign banks were reducing their sterling deposits and their sterling balances on *vostro* accounts to a minimum. The high yield of Local Government loans provided attractive short-term investment opportunities just when the banks' resources available for the purpose were declining. Operations in inter-bank sterling provided the means by which the local resources could be utilised more completely.

The inter-bank sterling market need not necessarily be confined to resident sterling. Indeed after the fears of rein-forced exchange control subsided foreign holders of sterling came to look upon the new market as providing alternative short-term investment facilities to those of the Euro-sterling market. While under the existing exchange control regulations banks in the U.K. are not entitled to lend sterling on a resident account to a non-resident bank, they are entitled to accept non-resident sterling deposits from the latter. If and when rates prevailing in the inter-bank sterling market are attractive and no reinforcement of the exchange control is expected, the short-term investment facilities of the new market, though not its short-term borrowing facilities, are at the disposal of non-resident banks. That they have not made much more extensive use of it up to the time of writing is due to the fact that, owing to frequently recurrent pressures on sterling, the market in Euro-sterling in Paris and Zürich often offers more attractive yields to holders of non-resident sterling accounts.

In any case it is only natural that sterling deposits which can be lent to banks either within or outside the U.K. should command higher interest rates than those which can only be lent within the U.K. If in spite of this the inter-bank sterling market does attract at times foreign-owned sterling it is largely because the names of U.K. banks command high confidence everywhere and foreign holders may want to spread their risk by re-depositing with them some of their sterling holdings even at slightly less attractive rates.

There are many points of similarities between the inter-bank sterling market and the Euro-currency market.

(1) Both markets transact deposits between banks.

(2) Lenders require no security.

(3) Lenders ask no questions about the purpose for which the money is required.

(4) Business is transacted in a speedy and informal way.

(5) Lenders may decline names if they do not consider them good enough for unsecured credits.

(6) Alternatively, lenders may expect of such borrowers interest rate above the standard rates.

(7) Transactions are always in large round amounts.

On the other hand there are in some respects differences between the two markets:

(1) While Euro-currencies are transacted entirely in the foreign exchange market, inter-bank sterling deposits are often transacted outside that market.

(2) The nature of inter-bank sterling rules out its direct use in space arbitrage, though indirectly it is apt to play an active role in that sphere.

(3) Nor is there nearly as much time arbitrage between long and short inter-bank sterling as between long and short Euro-currency deposits. In the inter-bank sterling market money borrowed for short periods is usually re-lent for short periods while money borrowed for long periods is re-lent for long periods. The markets for long and short inter-bank sterling constitutes separate departments.

There is a close connection between inter-bank sterling market and the market in loans to Local Authorities. In fact the interest rates prevailing in the former are usually somewhere halfway between rates quoted in Lombard Street for corresponding maturities and those quoted in the market for Local Authorities. Normally inter-bank sterling rates are about a quarter per cent above rates prevailing in the conventional money market, which differential is fully justified on the ground that in Lombard Street loans are secured while in the inter-bank sterling market they are unsecured. In normal conditions differentials between long and short maturities tend to be similar to those prevailing in Lombard Street and tend to fluctuate in sympathy with them. Abnormal conditions are likely however to affect the inter-bank sterling market to a larger extent. For instance the anticipation of a Bank Rate reduction in the early months of 1965 had a more pronounced effect on inter-bank sterling rates, because they had been much higher for short periods than for long periods.

While the Bank of England considers it as one of its principal tasks to regulate the supply of funds in Lombard Street it leaves the inter-bank sterling market entirely to its own devices. As a result wider fluctuations are more likely to occur there, especially in short rates.

The inter-bank sterling market is more likely to be affected than Lombard Street by ups and downs of the demand for funds by foreign exchange departments for interest arbitrage. This is because, while foreign exchange dealers have no direct access to Lombard Street and would have to borrow there through the intermediary of the treasurer or the money market department of their bank, in many banks they are in a position to borrow inter-bank sterling directly from other banks, which saves time and trouble. They are entitled to use such sterling for interest arbitrage within the limits imposed on them by the authorities and by their own managements. In some banks, however, inter-bank sterling transactions are handled by the management, or by the money market department, or even by a special small department set up for the purpose.

Dealers often quote two-way rates in the inter-bank sterling market, in the same way as in the Euro-currency market. This is done regularly by active participants in the market, who aim at making a profit through jobbing in and out of the market. They benefit by the spread between their two-way quotations and by a rise of inter-bank sterling rates between the time they borrow and re-lend. They risk losses if the rates decline in the intervals.

The standard amount of inter-bank sterling transactions is £100,000 and larger deals are usually in its multiples, though it is possible to deal in items of £50,000. On the other hand, many single transactions run into millions of pounds. The total turn-over on a really active day may exceed £100 million.

As in the Euro-dollar market, each bank has a limit for every name. Money-brokers and other intermediaries play the same part as in the Euro-currency market in helping lenders to avoid the awkwardness of having to refuse lending to a bank whose name is not acceptable or whose limit has been reached. The practice is the same as the one described in Chapter 14 — the broker discloses to the would-be lender the name of the would-be borrower but withholds the former's name from the latter until after the conclusion of the transaction. Not all foreign exchange brokers act as intermediaries in inter-bank sterling transactions, but in addition to them some bill brokers and some stockbrokers also specialise in this market — usually the same firms which act as intermediaries for loans to Local Authorities.

Standard rates quoted to first-rate names are usually more or less identical for all borrowers at any given moment, though they are liable to fluctuations. On the other hand, the rates quoted to smaller banks — they too must be of good standing, otherwise their names would not be taken at all for unsecured loans — or even to leading banks which are known to have been borrowing heavily, vary within a wide range at any given moment and is subject to wider fluctuations than standard rates. Lenders also differentiate according to whether the borrowers are in the market exclusively as borrowers or whether they usually lend as well as borrow.

Interest rates in the inter-bank sterling market are closely linked with the trend of foreign funds. We saw above that during the sterling scares of 1964–65 foreign funds were withdrawn and their owners were reluctant to return them. Some London banks had to replace the foreign balances withdrawn from them at short notice by borrowing inter-bank sterling. From time to time a squeeze developed in the inter-bank sterling market, because some lenders had to call in their deposits owing to withdrawals of their foreign deposits. At the same time there was an increase of demand for such deposits by new would-be borrowers.

On normal days the market is usually tighter in the mornings because many members are inclined to be on the safe side in case deposits at call borrowed by them should be called before noon. Once the conventional hour for such notices or withdrawals is past conditions are inclined to turn easier. In the afternoon many banks may want to place their idle surplus funds in the inter-bank sterling market. Funds are borrowed sometimes in that market for a few hours, as an alternative to "daylight overdrafts", that is, overdrafts arranged for a few hours and repayable on the same day.

Merchant banks are the most active participants in the market, but London overseas banks and London branches of foreign banks are also active. Discount houses do not, of course, participate but, as we saw above, some billbrokers act as intermediaries. The attitude of clearing banks towards the market has changed considerably during the concluding months of 1964 and in 1965. Originally most of them kept altogether aloof from this market, but later their subsidiaries which handle their Euro-currency transactions began to participate in these operations. At first they were lenders only, but more recently they came to operate in both ways, their transactions achieving at times a considerable turnover.

Although inter-bank sterling, like Euro-dollars, are for all practical purposes loans, for accounting purposes they are treated as deposits both by the borrowing bank and by the lending bank. Lenders include them among their liquid assets for the purpose of calculating their liquidity ratio. They cannot, of course, include them among assets eligible for the purpose of calculating their cash ratio. On the other hand borrowers are in the position to add the proceeds of the deposit to their cash supply, unless they re-lend the proceeds in which case the amount figures both in their liquid assets and in their short-term liabilities. This means that since both sides increase by the same amount their liquidity ratio improves.

The Bank of England does not intervene in the inter-bank sterling market any more than in the Euro-dollar market. Its attitude may be described as one of benevolent neutrality. While the Euro-dollar market is apt to introduce additional liquid resources at a time when the official policy is in favour of restriction, the inter-bank sterling market merely reallocates existing resources, apart from any influx of inter-bank sterling deposits from foreign banks which is usually only a fraction of the turnover. When inter-bank sterling deposits are lent and borrowed all that is happening is that a larger proportion of the funds available is lent without security and a smaller proportion with security.

It must be borne in mind, however, that individual banks which have used up all their available securities for borrowing in Lombard Street are now in a position to raise additional funds through borrowing in the inter-bank sterling market. Supplies of funds which would remain otherwise inactive are thus lent to banks which make active use of them. The grand total of market resources may remain unchanged but their velocity of circulation — that is, the number of times they change hands in a given period — increases. The authorities are, of course, well in a position to mop up any unwanted surplus of funds resulting from the activities of the inter-bank sterling market even if their action is confined to the conventional money market.

In a sense the authorities may find this market helpful. Before its existence the money market was liable to develop too easy conditions in the afternoon if clearing banks decided to unload large surpluses in Lombard Street. The Bank of England had then to deal with such unwanted ease. Now the surpluses are likely to be absorbed by the inter-bank sterling market which obviates the necessity for official action. It is outside the Bank of England's responsibilities to meet any unsatisfied demand in this market or to intervene directly for absorbing its surplus, even though it cannot be altogether indifferent to the ups and downs of inter-bank sterling interest rates.

As the inter-bank sterling market has been in operation for a much shorter time than the Euro-dollar market its structure and its practices have yet to assume their permanent form. It is already clear, however, that its operation constitutes a valuable addition to the facilities and efficiencies of the London financial markets. The high degree of confidence between London banks of standing is the basis of this institutional development. To the extent to which the market is operated by foreign exchange departments it has added to the importance of the London foreign exchange market.

CHAPTER 16

RISKS, PROFITS AND LOSSES

FOREIGN exchange departments fulfil an essential social function — they relieve merchants, and others engaged in socially useful international financial transactions, of the risks they would have to bear in the absence of covering facilities provided by banks. Some of the risks involved are obvious. Importers and exporters who have to make or receive payments in foreign currencies at future dates would be exposed to losses through adverse exchange movements if banks were not prepared to provide them with facilities to cover such risks. Banks are better qualified than they are for assessing such risks and for making provisions against them. This does not mean, however, that banks fulfil the same social function as insurance companies which take upon their own shoulders the entire risk that would have to be borne by their clients. Even insurance companies usually reinsure a large part of the risk they assume. Banks, having relieved their clients of exchange risk, usually aim at covering the risk thus assumed by undoing the transaction in the market or by adjusting their balances on their *nostro* accounts or their other holdings of foreign currencies accordingly. Nevertheless there is always a certain amount of risk attached to their function of providing their customers with exchange cover.

Risks arising from this function are by no means the only kind of risk attached to banks' foreign exchange operations. There are others, either inherent in the activities of foreign exchange departments or assumed by them deliberately. They may be summarised as follows:

(1) There are apt to be time lags between concluding small deals with customers and covering them in the market when their total has reached a large enough figure to give rise to a market operation.

(2) Unduly narrow profit margins on transactions with large customers might easily be wiped out by a slight adverse movement of exchange rates even if the covering is immediate.

(3) Uncovered balances on *nostro* accounts are exposed to depreciation.

(4) Covering of some balances on *nostro* accounts may be costly if the forward exchange is at a discount.

(5) Loss of interest on balances in *nostro* accounts may not be offset by direct or indirect profits derived from their maintenance.

(6) Open positions arising from discrepancies between the amounts of the transactions to be covered and standard amounts that are dealt with in various currencies in market transactions might lead to losses.

(7) If covering is deliberately delayed in anticipation of a favourable change in the exchange rates, an adverse change might cause losses.

(8) Discrepancies between maturities of forward commitments might lead to losses through an unfavourable change in forward rates.

(9) There may be at times arithmetical miscalculations or other mistakes on days when the market is hectic.

(10) Adoption of new exchange control measures or more efficient enforcement of existing measures might result in frozen claims.

(11) Defaults by clients and even by banks on forward exchange contracts might result in a loss of exchange differences.

(12) There is the possibility that the seller of foreign exchanges, having collected the purchase price, fails to deliver the foreign currencies in the foreign centre concerned.

Most transactions with clients are too small for banks to cover in the market immediately. They have the choice between two solutions. They can try to anticipate their clients' seasonal or other predictable requirements by going long or short in the currencies in question, or they can accumulate a number of small orders and cover subsequently after the balance between buying and selling orders in the same currency assumed a sufficiently large total to be covered in the market.

171

The banks' choice may depend on the view they take on the prospects of exchange rates, but in either case they take some degree of risk. If they assume an open position in anticipation of their clients' orders those orders may not be forthcoming. To undo the resulting open position is liable to cost money even if the exchange rate has remained unchanged because of the spread between buying and selling rates, unless the rates charged to customers fully allow for the spread. Such losses increase if the rate moves against the bank, in which case they might suffer a loss even if the customers' orders are forthcoming in accordance with anticipation. For the rates they have to quote to clients must be based on the market rate of the moment. On the other hand, if banks prefer to accumulate customers' orders and cover them subsequently the rates might move against them by the time they are ready to operate in the market.

Banks have to quote to many of their customers firm rates for transactions of a fairly large size, and these quotations have to be competitive, especially when dealing with large customers. It is not always easy to cover in the market at rates which secure a profit. This is particularly true during periods of fluctuating exchanges in a narrow market, or in a one-way market, when the covering of a substantial operation is itself liable to move the rate against the bank concerned. Growing competition for large accounts has enabled big firms to get very fine quotations from rival banks, and in many instances profit margins narrowed to vanishing point during the 'fifties. This increased the risk of incurring losses.

There is also a risk involved in keeping balances on *nostro* accounts, especially in devaluation-prone currencies, but also in any currency which is above minimum support point and is, therefore, subject to depreciation to its lower point. If such balances are not covered the banks are liable to suffer a loss through a devaluation or a depreciation. If, in order to avoid such losses, they cover their balances the cost of covering is usually very high whenever devaluation or depreciation is expected. On such occasions the forward exchange goes to a discount in excess of the extent to which it is warranted by

172

interest parities between two centres. In any case no interest is allowed on current account balances in most countries, or the rate allowed is quite inadequate. This, together with the cost of covering, or the alternative risk on uncovered balances, is the reason why banks usually keep their working balances on *nostro* accounts down to a minimum, especially in devaluation-prone currencies. Even so certain amounts must be kept on each *nostro* account to meet current requirements. Moreover, banks in some centres, especially in New York, usually insist on relatively large minimum balances.

There is always the risk that the cost of maintaining such balances — of interest and forward covering at a discount — may exceed the direct profit derived from their use, even though indirect profits in the form of additional business received from the banks concerned or from banks and non-banking clients with which foreign exchange business is transacted must also be taken into consideration.

Business in the market is transacted in large items of round figures. Uncovered differences are liable to arise from the discrepancies between the standard amounts for single items in various currencies. For instance, the usual minimum amount of individual transactions in sterling between large banks is £100,000, while the minimum for transactions in dollars is either $250,000 or $300,000. Now if a bank, having an open position of $250,000, comes across an acceptable quotation for £100,000, it concludes the deal in order to cover its open position in dollars, even though the equivalent of £100,000 is about $240,000, so that the transaction still leaves it with an open position of $30,000 which cannot be covered in the market until other items raise it to $250,000. Actually big banks seldom deal in minimum items, they prefer to deal in items of millions, in which case the discrepancies between round figures representing multiples of the standard amounts in various currencies are even wider. Thus the covering of an open position of £1,000,000 through a transaction of $3,000,000 leaves an amount of $600,000 uncovered.

Dealers make, or hope to make, a large part of their profits through choosing the right moment for covering their open positions. Very often they can only do so on the basis of a more or less lax interpretation of the rule against open positions at the end of each business day. Delays in covering may secure profits, but they certainly entail the risk of losses.

A bank with an oversold or overbought position is exposed to losses not only through changes in spot rates but also, in given circumstances, through changes in forward margins. A dealer with a short position may decide to cut his losses because of an improvement in the prospects of the currency concerned. In such situation the discount on the forward exchange is liable to contract, however, so that if the dealer covers by means of a forward purchase for the unexpired period of the forward contract he has to do so on the basis of a narrower discount than the one that prevailed at the time when he originally sold the currency for forward delivery. Likewise, if a dealer, having a long forward position, changes his mind about the prospects before it matures, the covering of his position by a forward sale for the unexpired period of the original contract is liable to entail a loss as a result of a decrease in the premium or an increase of the discount on the forward exchange since the conclusion of the original deal.

Banks with open positions are also exposed to losses through changes in the swap margins if they want to renew their open positions on maturity and if in the meantime the forward margins have moved against them. When the open position was originally created it was possible to go short or long at a low cost, because forward rates were still within support points or because they were officially supported at an artificial rate. If in the meantime they depreciated or appreciated beyond support point the change confronts dealers with the choice between cutting their losses or renewing their position at a higher cost than the one they had originally envisaged.

Although the risk of changes in forward margins is of a smaller extent than the risk of changes in spot rates through devaluations or revaluations, it materialises much more frequently than that of changes in parities. After all, devaluations and revaluations are very infrequent occurrences, but devaluation scares or revaluation scares, which are sufficient to cause forward rates to move beyond support points, are much more frequent.

So long as the maintenance of spot rates within their support points can be relied upon bankers know the maximum extent of their possible losses and profits through changes in spot rates and can arrive at a decision whether the prospects of profits justify the risk of losses. From this point of view they are now incomparably better placed than during the period of floating rates, and even better than under the gold standard when gold points were liable to change.

They can avoid, moreover, even such limited and roughly calculable risk by covering operations. They can also reduce their risk through their familiarity with predictable changes, recurrent or otherwise. Such changes may occur through regular requirements for foreign exchange arising from seasonal trade influences, window-dressing operations at certain dates, eves of week-ends and holidays, etc. Some non-recurrent influences such as the transfer of the proceeds of a new issue, or the repayment of a maturing foreign loan, can also be discounted by well-informed dealers. For the reduction of the risk arising through unpredictable developments some knowledge of theories of exchange rates is helpful, though there is always the risk that the effect of identified influences may become vitiated by the effects of unpredictable or unidentifiable factors.

The incalculable risk arising from the latter can be reduced but can never be eliminated by following as closely as possible any developments that are liable to give rise to such influences. To possess inside information on developments not yet known to the market as a whole is, of course, a great advantage. There is, however, the ever-present risk of unexpected market reactions to unpredictable developments which are liable to upset the calculations even of the best-informed and most experienced dealers. Moreover, since official intervention has now become more frequent, the unknown factor represented by unpredictable changes in official policy and tactics constitute a considerable additional risk.

Commitments consisting of discrepancies between maturity dates of claims and liabilities entail risk of losses through changes in forward rates. These risks were discussed in detail in Chapter 7.

Risk arising from the adoption or more effective enforcement exchange control may be remote in respect of the leading currencies but it can seldom be said to be completely absent. Unexpected developments in the international or domestic political sphere might lead to new measures impeding the freedom of international transfers, of a kind that might prevent banks from meeting their liabilities in terms of foreign currencies and might block deposits or investments in foreign centres. Such situations arose all over the world during the 'thirties and again during the War in countries that came under enemy occupation. Since the War too there have been many such instances.

In spite of the skill of foreign exchange dealers and the modern equipment at their disposal, occasional mistakes may occur in calculations and quotations especially on hectic days when they are rushed. What is indeed remarkable is how seldom such mistakes occur, having regard to the speed with which dealers must take decisions. They would have to be superhuman to be wholly infallible. On the rare occasions when mistakes occur they are apt to cost their banks money. It was pointed out in Chapter 3 that when the discrepancy between their quotations and the rates prevailing in the market at the moment is sufficiently wide to make the error obvious it is one of the unwritten laws of the foreign exchange market that the banks concerned must not take advantage of it.

Although banks in their dealings with non-banking customers may require security in order to be safeguarded against losses through defaults on forward exchange contracts, they are liable to be caught out if they overrate the standing of their customers or if they underrate the possible extent of exchange movements.

There exists also a risk of default in dealings in the market between banks, which is sought to be reduced through refusing to take the name of banks that are considered to be of dubious standing, and by placing a limit on the amount for which even the best names are taken. This is all the more necessary as the practice of asking for a deposit to cover risk from exchange transaction is never applied in inter-bank dealing. The name of a bank is either taken or it is not taken in the market, but if it is taken no security is ever asked for or given. The risk of losses arising through major changes in exchange rates is similar to that arising from transactions with customers, with the difference that in the case of inter-bank transactions no part of it is covered by a deposit.

There is, moreover, another kind of risk in inter-bank dealing — the delivery risk, or *valeur compensé* risk. It arises from the circumstance that in foreign exchange transactions payment by buyer and seller is supposed to take place simultaneously — "here and there" — in two different financial centres. If a London bank buys dollars against sterling it has to pay the purchase price in sterling in London on the "value date". It does so on the assumption that the dollars are paid simultaneously in New York into its account with the New York bank indicated in its instructions to the seller. Discrepancies between the actual moment of the payment are bound to arise, however, and there is always some degree of risk — its extent varies according to the standing of the bank that had sold the dollars — that the London bank, having made the sterling payment, might not receive the dollars. In dealings between first-rate banks such a risk is of course negligible. But the fact that some banks have a relatively low, if elastic, limit for foreign exchange transactions for most names for delivery due on any particular date shows that the existence of this risk is recognised. While the limit for good names for total forward transactions may be very high, the limit for transactions to be executed on any one date is much lower.

Delivery risk is apt to be enhanced by discrepancies between market hours in various centres. While the discrepancies were small between London and Continental centres — they disappeared altogether between London and Western Europe since the change of London time — they are large between London and New York. Sterling payment due to be made in London at a given date is now simultaneous with the payment of the equivalent in Continental currencies in some Western

177

European centre. Payment in London is certain to be much earlier than the payment of the dollar equivalent in New York, especially as it is the practice of New York banks to make payments at the very last minute, shortly before 3 P.M. New York time, equal to 9 P.M. London time, long after banks in London are closed. Even if the New York correspondents of a London bank that had been notified to expect a large dollar payment informed the London bank immediately about a default the advice only arrives the following morning. Meanwhile the seller, having collected the sterling on the previous day, may have disappeared. It is no wonder the *valeur compensé* arrangement is known to have been referred to as *voleur compensé*! The risk is increased by the practice of many banks not to advise their correspondents about payments they are to expect but await simply the advent of the credit advice from them. It is not until such advice becomes overdue that a default would come to be discovered.

The attitude of banks differs widely in respect of limits to transactions with each bank. There are three different kinds of such limits.

(1) Limits to outstanding forward exchange transactions with the same bank.

(2) Limits to outstanding Euro-currency deposits lent to the same bank.

(3) Limits to transactions involving delivery on any one date.

Limits to forward exchange transactions are the highest because the risk involved is confined to possible exchange differences. Limits to Euro-currency lendings are lower because default might involve total loss. An alternative course is to charge higher rates to not altogether first-rate names. Limits to maturities on any one day are even lower owing to the delivery risk discussed above. In this case there can be no question of charging higher rates.

There are two schools of thought in respect of limits according to whether they should apply to net balances between transactions offsetting each other or to the gross amount that would be affected in case of default. Some banks, while strict about limits on Euro-currency transactions, are easy-going about forward exchange limits and do not concern themselves at all with limits to deliveries on particular dates. Others, on the other hand, are very strict about all limits and are known to have refused loans to banks bigger than themselves because their limits for those banks have been reached.

In addition to the various risks of actual losses foreign exchange departments also risk losing potential profits if tempted by marginal profit possibilities on interest arbitrage. They tie down their resources and subsequently have to forgo opportunities for much more profitable operations.

It goes without saying that the prospects of operating profitably are related to the extent of risks that dealers are allowed to take and are prepared to take. Any banks which impose very rigid rules against taking risks and any dealers who are temperamentally unprepared to assume such risks have to be content with smaller profits, unless they are able to discover unexplored arbitrage possibilities and are able to conceal them for some time from their rivals.

In his otherwise excellent book Lipfert puts forward a theory that foreign exchange departments can only make profits at each other's expense and that the profit of one department must necessarily be the loss of some other department or departments. This theory conjures up a picture of gamblers sitting round the card table, who are unable to win unless somebody else amongst them loses the same amount. Indeed Lipfert goes even further by stating that, since foreign exchange departments have very substantial overheads, the total of the net losses of all foreign exchange departments is bound to exceed the total of their net profits. If that were so many banks would be unwilling to participate in the market, even though indirect advantages gained through participating might tempt them to put up with the probability of direct net losses.

If Lipfert's theory were correct, or even if dealers in general came to believe it to be correct, it would create an almost intolerable atmosphere in the foreign exchange market. The present atmosphere in which the attitude of "live and let live" is alternating with the attitude of "the survival of the fittest" would be replaced by an unmitigated cut-throat attitude. Instead of regarding each other as colleagues in the same profession who work together for the benefit of all, and who can afford to be generous to each other because there is enough to go round, they would behave like gladiators facing each other in the arena, knowing only too well that, in order to survive, they must defeat and kill their opponent. To avoid this effect as well as to discover the true facts for truth's sake, it is most important to submit this theory to a searching scrutiny.

There is every reason to believe that the grand total of the net profits made by all successful foreign exchange departments considerably exceeds in normal circumstances the grand total of net losses made by all unsuccessful foreign exchange departments. This in spite of the fact that substantial and ever-increasing overhead expenses have to be deducted from profits and have to be added to losses. For there are many ways in which all foreign exchange departments can make profits that are not losses to some other foreign department. The following is a list of some of these ways:

(1) Profit on customers' transactions that are "married".

(2) Profit-margins between rates charged to customers and those at which such operations are covered in the market.

(3) Execution of customers' instructions to buy or sell "at best".

(4) Profit made at the expense of the monetary authorities.

(5) Arbitrage of every kind.

(6) Foreign currency deposits re-lent at higher rates, especially to borrowers outside the market.

(7) Inter-bank sterling operations, insofar as they are transacted by foreign exchange departments.

For commercial banks, but also for many other types of banks, dealings with customers constitute an appreciable proportion of the turnover. Much of these deals can be "married" within the bank. In any case the spread between buying and selling rates is usually wider than in the market, so that foreign exchange departments, unless they are particularly unlucky, ought to be able to cover customers' transactions at a profit. On transactions to be executed "at best" they can make a profit without taking any risk. Such transactions constitute a fair proportion of their turnover and include practically all small transactions with customers on which a commission is charged, though admittedly the multitude of small items involve much clerical labour which costs much nowadays. Banks may receive instructions to buy or sell "at best" from overseas markets which keep different hours from London. But, in keeping with the spirit of chivalry that prevails among high-class banks, they go out of their way on such occasions to satisfy their correspondent, and themselves, that they are worthy of the trust placed in them, by charging an infinitesimal margin of profit.

An unsuccessful attack on a currency defended at support point by the authorities concerned is liable to inflict losses on the attackers. But on a number of occasions, when the authorities feel compelled to modify or abandon a rate between support points after a prolonged effort to hold it, the attackers profit. In the infrequent instances of widely-anticipated devaluations or revaluations such profits were very substantial for departments which created open positions at the right moment.

Profits made by banks on space arbitrage are not made at each other's expense, except to the extent to which the rate moved in favour of one bank and against another bank before the transaction is finalised. In time arbitrage changes in the forward margin may mean a profit to one partner and a loss to the other partner. But in interest arbitrage, when borrowers of the receiving centre pay a higher interest rate, they would not do so unless they in turn had some profitable use for the money borrowed. Likewise in transactions in foreign currency deposits the willingness of the ultimate borrower to pay higher interest rates may ensure profit to all banks through whose hands the deposit had passed before reaching its final destination. Nevertheless, by jobbing in and out of the market banks are liable to make profits at each other's expense, if borrowers have to re-lend at a loss owing to a decline in the Euro-currency rates.

It is true, if dealers with open positions miscalculate the

trend they suffer losses while their more fortunate colleagues whose judgment or instinct has proved to be correct make profits at their expense. On the face of it this might lead to the conclusion that, whenever exchange rates fluctuate, those with open positions can only make profits at each other's expense in a similar way to profits and losses of speculators on stock exchanges. But the foreign exchanges they buy and sell at the right moment need not always necessarily be bought from or sold to other banks. Or the latter may have covered the risk. Since banks are better informed than others about prospects of exchange rates they stand a better chance of operating at the right moment than others concerned with foreign exchange transactions. It is probable that the banking community as a whole, by knowing better when to buy and when to sell, and being on the spot, makes a profit at the expense of the rest. While luck may help anyone indiscriminately, the odds are in favour of professionals. As far as familiarity with calculable influences go, bankers are distinctly at an advantage.

It is necessary to differentiate between profits which are actually losses to other banks and those which may only mean missed opportunities to other banks. Allowing for all these considerations, I have no hesitation in concluding that foreign exchange dealing is a most profitable branch of banking and, given a reasonable degree of caution, skill and — last and by no means least — hunch, the result should justify the risk involved. In any case the indirect advantages derived from being able to provide their customers and their correspondents with much-needed and highly-valued services should go a long way to outweigh moderate direct losses.

CHAPTER 17

OFFICIAL INTERVENTION

ALTHOUGH instances of official operations in the foreign exchange market can be traced back to a very early period, the importance of such intervention has greatly increased since the War. We are not concerned here either with its theoretical implications or with its broader monetary policy aspects. But a textbook on foreign exchange would not be complete without containing an outline of the practice of official intervention. Familiarity with its aims, tactics and technique has become essential for bankers and for anyone concerned with the foreign exchange market for the following reasons:

(1) Official operations constitute from time to time a very high proportion of the turnover in the market.

(2) In a one-way market they are apt to be virtually the only source from which counterpart for an excess of buying or selling is forthcoming.

(3) They are frequently the main influence affecting exchange rates.

(4) The estimated extent of intervention gives an idea of the strength of the buying or selling pressure on the exchange concerned.

(5) The nature and extent of official operations, indeed their presence or absence, give an idea about the aims of official policy and tactics.

(6) Pegging of exchanges at an artificial rate provides opportunity for buying or selling on relatively advantageous terms.

Before 1914 intervention was seldom practised systematically and was regarded as a weapon for use by weak countries, or in emergency only. The monetary authorities of strong countries deemed it sufficient to buy and sell gold at official prices and relied on the mechanism of gold movements to maintain the stability of exchanges. During the inter-War period the authorities in a number of countries came to intervene occasionally, and even systematically, from time to time. But it was not until the 'sixties that such intervention became an integral part of the foreign exchange system.

Since the resumption of free dealings in foreign exchanges the authorities of countries associated with the International Monetary Fund have been under obligation to operate in foreign exchanges as a matter of routine in order to comply with their undertaking to maintain spot rates between support points. They are under obligation to buy their currency to an unlimited extent whenever it threatens to depreciate below its lower support point and to sell their currency to an unlimited extent whenever it threatens to appreciate above its upper support point. In actual practice many Central Banks play in a great many known instances a more active role in the market. They very frequently intervene even when their exchanges are at some distance from support points, buying or selling foreign exchanges in order to prevent their depreciation or appreciation to support points, and at times in order to bring about an appreciation or depreciation to a convenient level.

The reasons for the increased extent of official intervention may be summarised as follows:

(1) The automatic forces that tended to maintain the stability of exchanges under the gold standard no longer operate. Stability of all member currencies other than the U.S. dollar under the Bretton Woods system can only be maintained through intervention.

(2) Even the United States deem it expedient in given situations to supplement the stabilising effect of official gold purchases and sales by official operations in foreign exchanges.

(3) Post-War expansion in the volume of commercial and financial transactions now tends to create wider gaps between normal supply and demand, and it is essential to cover them by providing official counterparts.

(4) Owing to the increase in the size of foreign holdings of liquid funds, and of realisable long-term investments abroad, their potential disturbing effect has increased.

(5) The practice of hedging against devaluation risk on direct investment has become much more prevalent.

(6) Pre-War prejudice against foreign exchange operations by Central Banks has disappeared almost completely, so that decision for or against intervention is now looked upon purely as a matter of expediency.

(7) Central Banks have become much more familiar with tactics and techniques of foreign exchange operations.

Intervention is passive when the exchange is supported at a certain level and initiative for transactions is left to private operators in the market. It is active when the authorities take the initiative to buy or sell, or when they deliberately change the rates at which they operate without being forced to do so by market pressure. The authorities may intervene at support points or between support points. Even the final stand made by Central Banks in compliance with I.M.F. rules is often made a shade inside support points, in order to leave room for brokers' commission. Otherwise the rates at which business is actually transacted would be slightly outside support points.

Very frequently the authorities buy or sell dollars long before support point is reached, in order to prevent support point being reached or approached. The argument in favour of such tactics may be summarised as follows:

(1) When pressure on an exchange is strong support point is bound to be reached in any case sooner or later, so that intervention merely anticipates inevitable operations.

(2) It is deemed to be a matter of prestige for Central Banks to intervene voluntarily rather than intervene when they are compelled to do so.

(3) Depreciation of an exchange to its support point produces an unfavourable psychological effect which is liable to accentuate the pressure on it.

(4) The official character of operations between support points may be less obvious than those effected at support points.

(5) The scope for manœuvring becomes greatly reduced if rates are held at support point. The authorities have then very little freedom of action.

(6) The extent to which speculators could be squeezed is lessened by a reduction of the distance between the *de facto* intervention point and the opposite support point.

On the other hand, intervention undertaken before support point is reached has also some disadvantages which may be summarised as follows:

(1) Inducement for dealers to operate in the same sense as the authorities is reduced if profit prospects are less than that allowed by the spread between support points.

(2) The inducement to operate against the authorities is strengthened because, apart altogether from any anticipation of changes in parities, there appear to be prospects of some profit from an appreciation or a depreciation of the exchange within support points.

(3) Even if the rate is pegged between support points the market is usually aware when it is held artificially by official intervention.

As we pointed out in Chapters 1 and 9, Central Banks are under no obligation to maintain forward rates at support points. In practice on many known occasions ever since the 1890s they intervened by means of operating in forward exchanges or influencing forward rates by other devices. An account of such interventions is given in my *Dynamic Theory of Forward Exchange*. Such interventions became much more systematic during the 'sixties. Until then several leading Central Banks were firmly opposed to official operations in forward exchanges, and even those which had not been dogmatic about this had looked upon that device as one to be applied on special occasions only. Between 1961 and 1967 forward exchange operations became part of the normal routine of a number of Central Banks. The reasons for this change of attitude are as follows:

(1) Closer co-operation between Central Banks has greatly improved technical facilities for such intervention.

(2) The risk run by Central Banks in selling forward a foreign currency in excess of their resources available to meet their liabilities has become reduced by the availability of more ample facilities to meet the forward contracts on maturity if necessary.

(3) Better realisation of the extent of the potential disturbing influence of forward exchange operations has led to acceptance of the need to intervene.

(4) The development of the Euro-currency market has increased the importance of influencing forward rates.

(5) Growing opposition in many countries to conventional credit squeeze and to other "stop-go" devices has made it politically expedient to experiment with alternative devices.

(6) The success of the defence of sterling and the dollar in 1961, largely with the aid of intervention in forward exchanges, has strengthened the arguments in favour of such intervention.

(7) Improved knowledge of the theory and technique of forward exchange in official quarters has removed one of the causes why in the past they preferred to confine intervention to operation in spot exchanges.

(8) It is deemed expedient to prevent an undue increase in the cost of hedging that would induce hedgers to realise considerable assets and repatriate the proceeds.

(9) In countries with revaluation-prone currencies official forward operations have been found an effective device for preventing an unwanted influx of hot money.

On the other hand, the tactics of preventing the forward discount from widening has a number of disadvantages:

(1) It encourages speculation and hedging by keeping its cost artificially low.

(2) It encourages a one-sided tendency to cover.

(3) Central Banks may incur considerable forward liabilities in a foreign currency.

(4) As the extent to which the liabilities have to be met is incalculable the authorities have no means of knowing the full extent of their eventual losses of reserves.

(5) As the operations defer the losses of reserves they also defer the application of measures necessary in order to stop the drain.

(6) The failure of the defence of sterling in 1967, and the resulting gigantic losses on forward commitments, strengthened the arguments against such intervention.

In my *Dynamic Theory of Forward Exchange* (revised edition), I examine the arguments for and against intervention in forward exchanges and arrive at the conclusion that, while in many situations the case for intervention is very strong, unlimited support at a fixed rate against strong and persistent adverse pressure is inexpedient. I see no reason for altering that conclusion on the basis of the experience of the intervening years.

Monetary authorities in several countries have greatly relaxed their former attitude of secrecy in respect of their forward exchange operations and in respect of their intervention in general. A much larger volume of information is now released, and some of the monetary authorities have acquired the habit of explaining their foreign exchange operations in general and their forward exchange operations in particular.

Although in the majority of instances the object of official intervention is to prevent a depreciation of the forward exchange in order to obviate the adverse material and psychological effect of such a depreciation, the device can be operated and is at times operated in reverse — to prevent an unwanted appreciation of the forward exchange. In July 1964 the Federal Reserve Bank of New York, with the Bank of England's consent, intervened actually to cause a widening of the discount on forward sterling beyond support point in order to prevent an unwanted movement of funds from New York to London through covered interest arbitrage which would have been profitable in the absence of such intervention. Earlier, in July 1961 when the Swiss National Bank, acting as agent for the American monetary authorities, sold forward Swiss francs in the market in order to divert short-term funds from Switzerland to the United States by making covered outward arbitrage profitable. This latter instance proves that official intervention in forward exchanges need not always be passive. It can be applied not only for preventing movements of funds which are deemed to be disadvantageous but also for bringing about movements of funds which are deemed to be advantageous.

The rule that no Central Bank should intervene in another country's currency without consent has not been adopted solely for safeguarding the spirit of co-operation between monetary authorities. An even more important practical consideration is that any attempt on the part of two Central Banks to operate in an exchange at two different rates would reduce itself to absurdity. Arbitrageurs all over the world would buy unlimited amounts from the Central Bank which sells at a cheaper rate and would re-sell them to the Central Bank which is trying to hold the exchange at a dearer rate. They could make fortunes without running any risk. For instance, if in July 1964 the Bank of England had insisted that the discount on forward sterling must be kept narrow while the Federal Reserve Bank of New York intervened in order to cause it to widen, arbitrageurs would have bought large amounts of forward sterling from the Federal Reserve Bank and re-sold it in the London market where the Bank of England would have bought it at a narrower discount. Clearly no Central Bank would be prepared to distribute such free gifts to arbitrageurs. Unless an agreement is reached with the Central Bank whose currency is directly involved there can be no intervention.

The monetary authorities need not always be on the defensive but may take the offensive by bringing about "squeezes" and inflicting punishment on speculators in order to discourage their future activities. They can do so if they are in a strong enough position to enforce a change of the rates in a sense opposite to the market trend and if they can convince the market that they are not bluffing. Or, after a turn of the market trend, they can intervene to reinforce the reaction, thereby increasing the losses suffered by speculators. Such tactics may be used if Central Banks possess important information which is not yet known in the market. They must be played from strength, however.

Those in charge of official operations are in some ways at a considerable advantage against dealers of banks.

(1) Thanks to the highly developed co-operation between Central Banks and with the International Monetary Fund they are likely to possess resources which, while by no means unlimited, are sufficient to enable them to resist purely or largely speculative trends, and for a while to resist even basic trends.

(2) The authorities are bound to be better informed in many

189

respects than ordinary dealers. Thanks to the returns which banks have to submit to them about their foreign exchange positions and commitments, Central Banks are in possession of the overall picture of the banks in their own community even though they are not so well-informed about the overall picture of banks abroad. In this respect there is scope for exchange of information between monetary authorities.

(3) To some extent Central Banks are at an advantage also in respect of their advance knowledge of information concerning various balance of payments items, especially Government payments abroad.

(4) They are supposed to be familiar with impending changes of official foreign exchange policies — even though the Bank of England's experience in 1967 shows that this need not be so.

Having regard to all these circumstances it seems that the dice are loaded distinctly against the ordinary dealer in relation to official operators. But the latter are liable to be defeated in the long run.

It is important for dealers to be able to gather some idea what the authorities are doing, when and how they are doing it and why they are doing it, so as to make their arrangements accordingly. This is not always possible. Unless there is a one-way market in which the counterpart is usually forth-coming from the authorities the latter may be able to disguise their intervention if they wish to do so. It is not always to their interest to disguise their intervention, however. In certain circumstances it may suit them to draw attention to it and even exaggerate it in order to produce the maximum of psychological effect with the minimum of operations. On other occasions, however, it suits them to disguise their presence as far as possible. The market's reaction is liable to be different to an official operation than to a non-official operation of the same magnitude precisely because the authorities are in a position to operate on a larger scale. Yet very often Central Banks undertake an isolated operation with the limited purpose of sounding the market. They want to know whether a market trend is due to genuine pressure or whether rates have moved with very little actual business done. They can have their answer through ascertaining the market's response to their limited intervention. If the movement is due to genuine pressure a single transaction is not likely to halt it. If, on the other hand, the rates are simply marked up or down the appearance of a genuine order is liable to halt the movement or even reverse it.

The authorities may seek to conceal their presence in the market through making use of a number of channels for their intervention and changing them from time to time. They can operate in several markets. They may operate in both directions at the same time in order to confuse the market. When there is intervention on a large scale in a one-way market, however, all these tactics are useless. The market is bound to have a fair idea about the presence of the authorities and even about the approximate scale on which they operate, although their estimates in the latter respect are apt to vary.

Dealers must always reckon with the possibility that market influences are liable to be distorted at any moment by official intervention. That possibility adds another to the risks dealers have to face, not only if they have open positions but even if they merely have covered commitments. For a change in the forward rate is liable to upset their calculation in respect of such commitments. Moreover, if official intervention maintains the rate practically stable, whether in the close vicinity of support point or somewhere between support points, the absence of fluctuations reduces their chances of making a profit. On the other hand, since the hands of the authorities are tied by their obligation to maintain the rates at support points, or by a self-imposed pegging of the rate between support points, their intervention gives dealers a high degree of assurance that the rates would not move beyond that figure.

Provided that dealers trust the willingness and ability of the Government concerned to carry out its obligation under the I.M.F. rule they are safe in operating on that assumption. If they do not trust the Government and base their operation on the assumption that it would yield eventually to their pressure they expose themselves to losses, but without changes in parities such losses are limited to the spread between support points in both directions. One of the arguments of those in favour of floating rates, or at any rate in favour of a much wider spread between support points is that it would give the authorities much wider scope for manœuvring and it would greatly increase the risk attached to speculating against the maintenance of the exchange rate at support points. The weight of arguments is, however, overwhelmingly against both proposals.

It is very important for dealers to keep themselves informed all the time about what the authorities are doing. There is much exchange of information between dealers and brokers, but the bank which is at the moment in charge of carrying out official operations is bound to secrecy in the same way as if it were acting for some other client.

There are many instances for intervention in forward exchanges in the form of both outright and swap operations. In respect of the extent of forward operations the attitude of British authorities underwent a remarkable change in 1964. Until then the official view, as expressed in the evidence before the Radcliffe Committee, was against an unlimited support of the forward rate in case of a strong and persistent adverse movement. In the Treasury's memorandum to that Committee and in oral evidence by official witnesses suggestions in favour of pegging the forward rate were emphatically rejected, mainly on the ground that the size of gold losses arising from forward sales could not be estimated until the forward contracts matured. It might easily reach a figure which would approach the total of the gold and dollar reserves. If forward rates were pegged it would become known that the authorities were carrying an undisclosed liability to be charged against the reserves. At times of pressure therefore the published reserves would mean little. The knowledge that a substantial part of the reserve was already committed could have a calamitous effect on confidence.

Nevertheless, in November 1964 the British authorities resorted to those very tactics which a few years earlier they condemned in no uncertain terms. In addition to supporting spot sterling out of the proceeds of foreign credits, they also supported forward sterling on a very large scale, in order to prevent a

widening of the discount which, if allowed to occur, might have
led to massive outward arbitrage and might have inspired distrust in sterling. Admittedly, in 1964 they were on safer ground
than they would have been in 1957, because in the meantime
co-operation between Central Banks had made considerable
progress, and foreign credits were now at the disposal of the
British authorities to an amount well in excess of the gold
reserve. Their availability reduced the risk of overdrawing
their resources available for meeting forward commitments,
though there remained the risk of being unable to repay the
foreign credits if they had been drawn upon very extensively.

Having decided to adopt the tactics they had formerly
rejected, the British authorities deemed it necessary to profess
their belief that the bulk of these forward dollar transactions
were self-liquidating and would not entail any loss of dollars
when the contract matured. As every dealer knows, however,
it is extremely difficult to guess the identity and intentions of
the ultimate counterpart, as the forward exchanges sold by the
authorities are liable to change ownership between the conclusion of the contract and its maturity.

The United States authorities, too, have resorted on a
number of occasions to defending the dollar with the aid of
forward transactions because, apart from other reasons, they
could no longer depend on foreign Central Banks abstaining
from converting into gold the dollars they would acquire in the
course of their official transactions in support of the spot dollar.

Official intervention in forward exchanges may assume the
form of swap transactions outside the market. The Deutsche
Bundesbank has adopted the practice of providing German
banks with dollar swap facilities at rates which compare
favourably with prevailing market rates, so as to make it
profitable for them to transfer some of the unwanted foreign
money abroad. The disadvantage of having a dual set of
forward rates was that from time to time the funds thus transferred abroad found their way back once more into Germany,
because inward arbitrage was profitable on the basis of the
market rates while outward arbitrage was profitable on the
basis of the official rates. To prevent this the Bundesbank

eventually restricted the use of the official swap facilities for investment in U.S. Treasury bills which had to be held for the entire duration of the official swap contracts. Even this was not a watertight safeguard against such circular arbitrage, because the German funds invested in U.S. Treasury bills released a corresponding amount of money that became available for transfer to Germany.

The authorities are in a position to support their intervention in foreign exchanges by means of reinforcing exchange control measures, or at any rate by bringing unofficial pressure to bear on banks to abstain from certain types of operations. They are further in a position to exert their influence on exchange rates through modifying their attitude towards the Euro-currency market — by ceasing to lend their dollars, by preventing banks from borrowing Euro-dollars, etc. To a large extent the market had developed because Central Banks holding their reserves in the form of dollars wanted to obtain higher yields on their holdings. They lent their dollars to the market and thereby increased the volume of dollars available for speculative operations or for unwanted interest arbitrage. As a result of the increase in American deposit rates allowed on official deposits, and also of the realisation that the expansion of the Euro-dollar market is liable to weaken the control of Central Banks over their own money markets, a number of Central Banks have withdrawn their dollars from the Euro-dollar market.

Central Banks of countries whose banks borrow Euro-currency deposits are in a position to influence exchange rates by encouraging or discouraging such borrowing and external borrowing in general. This end can be achieved by changing reserve requirements in respect of such credits, or by fixing a maximum limit to interest rates borrowers are permitted to pay, or by modifying regulations regarding the switching of foreign credits into local currency.

The power to adopt such measures, in addition to the volume of actual and potential resources available for operating in the market, increases the ever-present risk of an unpredictable change in exchange rates brought about by official intervention.

Even if the authorities pursue the tactics of pegging the rates rigidly there is nothing to prevent them from suspending the peg — unless it is at support point — or changing it. But, as long as it is maintained at an artificial level, dealers are in a position to operate against them on favourable terms. The volume of an over-valued currency that can be dumped on the authorities is virtually unlimited if the forward rate is supported. There is, therefore, a strong case for supplementing intervention by other measures calculated to reduce the extent to which intervention is required.

Another powerful argument against unlimited official intervention, especially in forward exchanges, is that abnormally large commitments arising from official operations are liable to reduce the capacity of the market to transact legitimate business arising from transactions with customers. Because there is a limit to the amounts for which the names of banks are taken, as a result of official operations on a vast scale those limits are liable to become exhausted and, as a result, the market may find it increasingly difficult to transact its normal business. The only way to avoid this would be if the Central Banks were to indemnify the banks through which they intervene against losses arising from credit risk.

The failure of official support to forward sterling on an unprecedented scale in 1967 to save sterling from devaluation went a long way towards discrediting those in favour of unlimited intervention. It inflicted losses on the British Government estimated at hundreds of millions of pounds. It conclusively proved that intervention in support of the forward rate is unable to prevent a devaluation in face of persistent pressure.

CHAPTER 18

EXCHANGE CONTROL

IT is essential that foreign departments of banks and firms concerned with foreign trade or foreign exchange should be familiar with all the complicated sets of regulations restricting foreign exchange transactions. This is necessary not only to avoid transactions which are contrary to the law but also because the existence of exchange restrictions and any conceivable changes made in them is liable to influence exchange rates. Bankers are expected to have a thorough knowledge of the exchange restrictions operating in their own country, but they must also know a great deal about those in force in other countries in whose currencies or with whose banks or business firms they have dealings. Larger banks have a separate department specialising in exchange control, so that those engaged in foreign exchange dealings are only concerned with rules affecting operations in the market.

To cover the details of exchange restrictions affecting even the most important countries and currencies would require much more space than is available in a general textbook on foreign exchange. Moreover, the regulations are subject to frequent changes. The International Monetary Fund publishes every year a *Report on Exchange Restrictions* covering the situation right to the time when the volume goes to press. In addition to giving the outlines of the system in force in each country it contains a list of the changes that were made in each country during the past twelve months. At least a dozen of such changes are usually registered in the sections of most countries, which gives an idea of the immensity of the task to keep abreast with ever-changing exchange controls.

Foreign departments of banks are equipped with files containing the latest available information. They have a system to keep their files up to date by following closely relevant news items in the financial press, not only those relating to their own country but also those concerning all countries in which they are interested. They also rely on their correspondents abroad to advise them immediately, on a basis of reciprocity, about changes and impending changes in their respective exchange regulations.

Apart altogether from the importance for bankers to avoid mistakes, they must be in a position to advise their clients on exchange restrictions insofar as they affect their clients' business. Most merchants and industrialists are much less favourably placed than bankers for following such changes sufficiently closely to be always up to date, and they naturally rely on their bankers for information and advice. It is the kind of service which they appreciate. They are also inclined to blame their bankers for any costly mistake made through having been given out-of-date or inaccurate information, and even for failure to notify them about recent changes. Although some banks, when opening *loro* accounts for their clients, require them to sign a declaration stating that the clients do not hold them responsible for any losses arising from such accounts, it is nevertheless to their interest to advise holders of *loro* accounts whenever some new development that is liable to affect them occurs or is expected.

The present chapter is confined to giving the outlines of the restrictions in the U.K., with only occasional comparisons with systems in other countries. Although the general trend since the war has been towards a relaxation of exchange controls there is hardly a country in which some form of restriction is not still in force. Even in countries such as Switzerland or West Germany there are some restrictions, but they are directed against an unwanted influx of foreign funds. In the overwhelming majority of countries the main object of the restrictions is to safeguard the national currency against selling pressure due to an outflow of domestic funds or to speculative operations. Nevertheless in many instances, apart from those of hard-currency countries, the inflow of funds is also subject to some degree of control precisely in order to safeguard against the risk of their subsequent withdrawal at an inopportune moment.

Exchange control measures in the U.K. and in most other countries differentiate between transactions on the following basis:

(1) According to the residence of those engaged in the transactions.

(2) According to the destination of the funds to be transferred.

(3) According to the nature of the transfers, *e.g.*, whether serving current or capital transaction.

(4) According to the currency involved.

Non-residents enjoy in the U.K. and in many other countries a high degree of freedom to transfer abroad their liquid funds, and also the proceeds of their realised long-term investments. Residents are subject to a much more restrictive treatment, especially for capital transactions. This distinction is natural, for while potential withdrawals by non-residents are limited by the total of foreign balances, potential withdrawals by residents would be virtually unlimited. There are in most countries restrictions on borrowing by non-residents from residents, precisely in order to prevent the former from withdrawing funds in excess of what they actually own. There are also restrictions on borrowing abroad and on borrowing in terms of foreign currencies by residents.

There are in many countries distinctions according to the destination to which the funds are to be transferred. A number of currency areas are in existence and transfers between countries belonging to them enjoy if not complete freedom at any rate a much higher degree of freedom than transactions with countries outside these areas. Under the British exchange control measures there is almost unrestricted freedom of transfer to the following countries, referred to as Scheduled Territories:

The British Commonwealth (except Canada, Rhodesia and the Anglo-French Condominion of the New Hebrides).

British Trust Territories, Protectorates and Protected States.

Burma.

Iceland.

The Irish Republic.

Jordan.

Kuwait.

Libya.

The Union of South Africa and South-West Africa.

Western Samoa.

The Persian Gulf and Trucial Sheikhdoms.

Transactions with residents of the above territories are subject to no restrictions, as far as transfers from the U.K. to the Scheduled Territories are concerned. A resident for the purpose of U.K. exchange restrictions includes any persons or firm residing permanently in any of the scheduled territories. They are entitled to open resident accounts and transactions involving transfers between such accounts and those of U.K. residents require no special authorisation.

Non-resident for the purpose of U.K. exchange control is any person or firm residing outside the U.K. and the scheduled territories. A resident is not entitled to make any payments in the U.K. to the credit or on behalf of a non-resident or to place any sum to the credit of a non-resident, or to make any payment in the U.K. to a resident on account of a non-resident. He may not buy, borrow, sell or lend any foreign currency from or to a person other than an authorised dealer. He may not make any payment without permit outside the U.K. either for the credit of a non-resident or for the credit of a resident. He is not entitled to surrender his claim or payment due from a non-resident, delay the sale of goods and the proceeds of goods exported outside the Scheduled Territories or, having been authorised to make payments for imports from outside the Scheduled Territories, delay the import of goods. Transfers from the Scheduled Territories are subject to the local exchange control regulations operating in the territories concerned.

Exchange control measures in most countries discriminate according to whether the object of the payment is a capital transaction or a current transaction, and sometimes even according to whether the current transactions represent payment for goods or for services. U.K. residents' capital transfers outside the Scheduled Territories are limited to £250 per head p.a., and to a tourist allowance of £50 p.a., subject to various provisions. Emigrants are entitled to a settling-in allowance of £5000 per family.

Capital export in the form of acquisition of securities is regulated by the system of investment dollars and capital withdrawals by foreign holders of sterling securities is regulated under the system of security sterling dealt with in Chapter 13. Transactions in investment currencies are subject to various regulations but do not require a specific permit. Direct investment abroad is subject to license, and the acquisition of real property abroad has to be financed out of the proceeds of the sale of such property by U.K. residents. Repatriation of foreign direct investment in the U.K. is also subject to licence, but in the case of approved direct investments made after 1950 its granting is a matter of form.

Payments for imports from outside the scheduled territories can be authorised by the importer's bank up to £2000. A list of such payments is submitted to the Bank of England by the banks in their returns of foreign exchange transactions. For imports amounting to more than £2000 the procedure is somewhat more involved but the permit is usually granted as a matter of form.

The proceeds of exports outside the Scheduled Territories have to be sold to an authorised bank within six months after the goods are exported. If payment is delayed beyond six months authorisation has to be applied for. Importers are entitled to cover their foreign exchange requirements up to six months in advance of the date on which payment is due.

U.K. exchange restrictions differentiate according to the currencies of transaction. There is no need to surrender currencies of the Scheduled Territories. Until 1967 payment had to be made for imports or exports either in sterling or in any of the "Specified Currencies", which were as follows :

Austrian schillings	Netherlands guilder
Belgian francs	Norwegian kronur
Canadian dollars	Portuguese escudos
Danish kroner	Spanish pesetas
Deutsche marks	Swedish kronor
French francs	Swiss francs
Italian lire	U.S. dollars.
Japanese yen	

Since 1967 all non-Sterling Area currencies have become specified currencies. This means that U.K. residents are now required to offer all non-Sterling Area currencies for sale to an authorised dealer, who is not required, however, to purchase them if they have no market in the U.K.

Payment for exports to countries outside the Sterling Area can now be received in any foreign currency other than Rhodesian pounds.

Until the liberalisation of the foreign exchange market in the U.K. in 1951 even banks were only allowed to transact foreign exchange in their capacity of agents on behalf of the Bank of England which institution was the ultimate buyer and seller of all foreign exchanges. Since the liberalisation of the foreign exchange market authorised dealers are at liberty to transact foreign exchange business in the foreign exchange market with each other, subject only to the limits imposed on the net totals of their open positions and on their covered foreign exchange holdings.

All banks of standing whose business is to deal in foreign exchanges may become authorised dealers. The authorisation is not granted, however, automatically to new applicants. When a new bank is established in London, or a new branch of an overseas bank is opened, its application to the Treasury through the Bank of England is subject to close scrutiny and it may be withheld if, in the opinion of the authorities, the bank does not appear to satisfy them that it could be relied upon to observe the exchange regulations. In this respect the attitude of the authorities is influenced by the new bank's choice of managerial and foreign exchange staff. If they include persons about whom the authorities are satisfied that they are familiar with the operation of the exchange control and are likely to abide by the regulations the authorisation may be forthcoming, otherwise the answer to the application is liable to be delayed until the authorities come to be satisfied that they may grant it safely.

Authorisations may be withdrawn if the bank's sphere of activities changes so that it no longer deals systematically in foreign exchanges, or if it violates the exchange regulations. Up to the time of writing no authorisation has been withdrawn on the latter ground, but the possibility of such penalty does exist.

The amounts of the limits to open positions and to covered holdings of foreign exchanges bear some relation to the turnover of the banks concerned, as judged by the authorities. The limit of covered holdings is much larger than the limit for open positions. The latter represents a net balance between the grand total of long and short positions in all foreign currencies. We already saw in Chapters 5 and 9 that banks may have long or short positions in one or several currencies in excess of the authorised limit, if it is offset by open positions in the opposite sense in terms of other currencies. The limits were drastically reduced during the crisis of 1966.

Banks in the U.K. — which includes, for the purposes of exchange control, branches and subsidiaries of banks overseas — have to submit to the Bank of England monthly returns about their foreign exchange transactions and their outstanding commitments, as at the last working day of every month, and it must be submitted by the third working day of the following month. In addition, they also have to submit every Friday weekly returns about their open positions and covered holdings in foreign currencies, as at the previous Wednesday. The weekly returns specify according to dollar and non-dollar commitments, monthly returns indicate the positions and commitments in each currency specified according to the countries of their debtors and creditors. They do not specify the amounts according to maturities.

A bank whose turnover has increased considerably may

apply for an increase of its limit which may be granted if
justified by circumstances. Banks may also ask for permission
to exceed their limits in special circumstances. If occasionally
they felt impelled to do so without having had the opportunity
to ask for advance permission from the Bank of England the
latter may overlook it if an acceptable explanation is offered.
Some banks interpret the limits as being applicable solely to
the dates for which returns have to be submitted, and they feel
entitled to exceed the limits between the dates, so long as the
excess can be eliminated in time for the date of the return.
Although this interpretation is open to question, the fact that
the positions and commitments have to be within the authorised
limits every Wednesday goes a long way towards discouraging
excessive positions or commitments, owing to the risk of having
to cover at an awkward moment.

In the U.K. there is no time-limit for forward exchange
transactions but in some countries there is a time-limit. In
France, for instance, they are only permitted up to six months.

While residents other than authorised dealers are not entitled to borrow or lend in terms of foreign currencies without
licence authorised dealers are entitled to do so so long as the
transactions do not increase their open positions beyond the
authorised limit. According to this interpretation, if they
borrow Euro-dollars and re-lend them either in dollars or in
any other foreign currency, or even in sterling, it does not create
an open position, nor does it create covered commitment in
relation to sterling. This is why it is possible for authorised
dealers to operate in the Euro-currency market on a very extensive scale. If they sold the proceeds of their Euro-dollar
deposits and lent the sterling thus obtained without covering
the forward exchange it would create an open position which
would have to be included under a limit. If, however, they
swapped the dollars into sterling it does not create an open
position nor does it create a covered commitment which, by
definition under exchange regulations, means the purchase of a
foreign currency and the covering of the open position thus
created. In the instance which we have under consideration no
dollars are bought and by means of swapping into sterling the

repayment of the dollars is ensured. It is because of this interpretation of the rules that it has become possible for U.K. banks to lend to Local Authorities very large amounts with the aid of dollars borrowed in the Euro-currency market and swapped into sterling.

Transactions in Euro-sterling are confined to sterling held on non-resident account. These include balances of non-resident subsidiaries of the U.K. banks with their parent offices. Although the main market in Euro-sterling is in Paris and other foreign centres, it is possible to transact business also in London with the aid of sterling on non-resident account. In given circumstances it is advantageous for non-residents to buy sterling for the sole purpose of lending it in the Euro-sterling market.

There is nothing to prevent London banks, if asked by a Continental bank, to quote simultaneously their Euro-dollar lending rate and their swap-and-deposit rate for the conversion of dollars into a Euro-sterling deposit. In practice such a combined quotation amounts to a quotation of a Euro-sterling rate, but it has to be included among the U.K. banks' covered commitments. There can be, and often there is, active dealings in Euro-sterling in London, in spite of the ban on transactions on resident account, but it is a one-sided and restricted market. For once Euro-sterling is borrowed by a resident it becomes resident sterling pure and simple for the duration of the loan. The borrower is not entitled to re-lend it or to sell it to a non-resident, so that the deposit has to be held in sterling until it matures London banks are only permitted to lend sterling to non-residents without licence for specific purposes.

This brings us to another restriction operating in the U.K. Resident banks are not allowed to grant sterling credits abroad for the purpose of speculation against sterling. Owing to this limitation Euro-sterling rates in Paris and other continental centres are apt to rise very high during periods of sterling scares when speculators and others have to renew maturing short positions in sterling. In order to do so without having to pay the high discount on forward sterling they borrow Euro-sterling and then sell the proceeds. Because they cannot borrow resident sterling such a demand on a limited market is apt to drive rates abnormally high, especially for very short periods.

We saw in Chapter 15 that U.K. banks are entitled to accept sterling deposits from non-resident banks and this enables the latter to operate in the inter-bank sterling market if they deem it convenient. On the other hand U.K. banks are not entitled to keep sterling deposits with non-resident banks.

Since 1968 there are exchange restrictions in the United States in addition to those concerning transactions with Rhodesia, Communist China, Cuba, North Korea and North Vietnam affecting direct investments in Europe — with the exception of Finland and Greece — and to a less extent in other continents. There are virtually no restrictions in Canada, Saudi Arabia, Kuwait, Mexico, Haiti, Honduras, and Panama. We saw above that restrictions in operation in Germany and Switzerland are not directed against outflow of funds. In most other countries the restrictions are in many ways stricter than those of the U.K. In a number of countries the proceeds of exports have to be surrendered after a much shorter interval than in the U.K. In France banks are not allowed to have any open positions whatever.

Restrictions on the influx of foreign funds usually assume the form of a ban of their investment in certain forms or a ban on the payment of interest on them. Restrictions in the U.K. on dealings in gold assumes mainly the form of prescribing payment in dollars or External Account sterling and banning purchases for domestic hoarding as distinct from purchases for domestic industrial use.

CHAPTER 19

FOREIGN EXCHANGE POLICIES

The last two chapters, dealing with official intervention and with exchange control, stressed the need for being thoroughly well-informed about such measures. It is equally important to know a great deal about the policies that are behind the actual measures, and also about policies that aim at making such measures unnecessary. Although it is actual intervention and exchange control which affect foreign exchanges directly, it is familiarity with the basic policies which enables us to form an opinion about the official attitude and its probable effects on exchange rates. It may assist in taking a view about the probable extent and duration of official intervention and about the prospects of adopting, altering or abandoning various official measures affecting exchanges.

In order to understand official tactics we must follow as closely as possible any changes in the ultimate objectives pursued by the official measures, not only those bearing directly on foreign exchanges but also broader economic policy measures and even measures outside the economic sphere. We must have an idea about the aims of our Government and Central Bank, and also those of foreign countries.

Governments have to choose between conflicting policy aims. They all have their lists of priorities and anyone wishing to be informed about influences affecting exchanges must follow the ever-changing official preferences for one objective or another. Priorities are liable to be changed at any moment, and any such change might produce far-reaching effects on actual policy measures. The following are the principal ends which are liable to occupy a high place in Governments' lists of priorities and are therefore liable to influence their foreign exchange policies:

206

(1) Stability of the exchange rates.

(2) Stability of the domestic value of the currency.

(3) Expansion of production.

(4) Raising the standard of living.

(5) Achieving and maintaining full employment.

(6) Improving the balance of payments.

(7) Changing the terms of trade.

(8) Accumulating gold or foreign exchange reserves.

(9) Attracting foreign funds.

(10) Diverting unwanted foreign funds.

(11) Influencing domestic interest rates.

(12) Pursuing economic warfare.

If the maintenance of a stable external value of a national currency is given a high priority this end may be served, according to the degree of stability aimed at, by the adoption of the following policies:

(*a*) Exchanges can be pegged rigidly with no scope whatsoever for fluctuations. This policy is pursued in respect of rate between Britain and other Sterling Area countries.

(*b*) Fluctuations can be confined within narrow, well-defined limits. This is the system adopted by most countries that are associated with the I.M.F. Fluctuations between support points may be kept down by official intervention, or the rates may be left uncontrolled until they actually reach support points.

(*c*) A limited degree of stability can be pursued by abandoning parities and support points but maintaining in practice fluctuations within comparatively narrow limits. This policy was pursued for a long time by Canada during the post-War period.

Stability of the domestic purchasing power of a currency is not normally incompatible with the stability of its international value. Situations are apt to arise, however, from time to time when Governments have to choose between the two aims. During the 'thirties the British Government and other Governments adopted from time to time a policy of causing or accepting a depreciation of their exchanges in order to safeguard the domestic value of their currencies from the effects of

207

"imported deflation". In other words, they did not wish to accept a decline in domestic prices that would have resulted from the declining trend of world prices if the exchanges had remained stable. Instead they aimed at restoring the balance between higher price level at home and lower price level abroad by a deliberate policy aiming at bringing about a downward adjustment of the exchange value of sterling. Much more recently in the early 'sixties Germany and Holland revalued their exchanges by 5 per cent for the sake of preventing inflation abroad from causing a decline in the domestic purchasing power of their currencies.

There are frequent conflicts between the basic aim of safeguarding the stability of exchanges and that of expanding production, or that of raising the standard of living, or that of achieving and maintaining full employment. A victory of expansionism need not necessarily affect parities, or at any rate not for a long time. The Government concerned may not go so far as to decide in favour of devaluation in preference to sacrificing its expansionary aims. But it may abstain from applying deflationary measures in the hope that even in their absence it might be possible to maintain existing parities with the aid of borrowing, or realising foreign investments, or as a result of a windfall in the form of inflation abroad. If the market does not share the official optimism and assumes that in the absence of adequate defensive measures the currency would have to be devalued sooner or later, this is liable to depress spot rates within their support points and cause forward rates to move well beyond the support points of spot rates. An inflationary rise in the cost of production and in domestic consumption in the absence of deflationary measures means an adverse trade balance which itself tends to depress the exchanges, apart altogether from any speculative anticipation of an eventual devaluation.

For this reason, those interested in exchanges must follow closely the eternal conflict between the expansionist school — or, as it is often called, the inflationist school — and the stabilisationist school — or, as it is often called, the deflationist school — and watch the ups and downs of their influence over the

Government. Any evidence that one school or the other is gaining the upper hand is important, because it foreshadows the future trend of the exchange. In the long run it might even determine decisions whether to maintain existing parities, change them, or suspend them altogether.

Even if there is no reason to suspect the Government of intentions to devalue, any evidence that it gives expansion priority over stability is liable to affect the exchange unfavourably, in spite of frequent official disclaimers, because of the effect of such attitude on market opinion. Premature or unfounded the view may be that the Government would avoid deflation, even at the cost of devaluation, if it is held widely enough, is sufficient to depress the exchange towards support point, and to cause the forward discount to widen. Exchange movements within support points are liable to be influenced by the market's interpretation of the Government's attitude towards expansion, deflation and devaluation, so that it is very important to be well-informed about the official preference as between expansion and stability.

It is equally important to follow policies of foreign Governments. Sterling, for instance, is liable to depreciate not only because of the British Government's unwillingness to adopt deflationary measures in its defence, but also as a result of the willingness of other Governments to resort to such measures in defence of their own currencies, or even because of their unwillingness to resist or neutralise an unwanted export surplus by measures that would mitigate the firmness of their exchanges.

If improvement of the trade balance is given a high priority it means that the authorities concerned will adopt deflationary measures to make production costs competitive, to keep down domestic consumption, or they will curtail external Government spending. There is, however, also the alternative method of trying to safeguard the trade balance by means of higher import duties, quotas or other physical controls, or by means of bilateralist trade or exchange practices. Such steps, even if improving the trade balance, tend to accentuate the fundamental disequilibrium between domestic and foreign prices and foreshadow devaluation in the long run.

Changes in the terms of trade — the relative value of imported and exported goods determining the volume of imports obtainable for a given volume of exports and vice versa — are apt to affect the trade balance in the same way as changes in the volume of imports or exports. In given situations the Government may be tempted to devalue in order to increase exports and reduce imports. But if the view is held in official quarters that the effect of a devaluation on the terms of trade would wipe out the effect on the volume of exports and imports the idea of a devaluation is likely to be rejected. In given situation a Government may feel tempted to revalue its currency in order to benefit from its effect on the terms of trade. Such a decision may appear to commend itself if the exports of the country concerned are a sellers' market, so that the rise in their prices through a revaluation would not affect the volume of the exports. But if they are a buyers' market the increase in the volume of exports may not even be sufficient to compensate the trade balance for the adverse change in the terms of trade.

Official policy in respect of the maintenance or accumulation of gold and foreign reserves is of considerable importance from the point of view of exchange rates. A Central Bank, by accumulating a reserve, may deliberately prevent an appreciation of its exchange that would take place, for the sake of increasing its reserves. Conversely, the authorities may be willing to accept a decline of their reserves for the sake of avoiding disinflationary measures. This was the declared British policy in the spring and summer of 1964.

Official policy may aim at attracting foreign funds or at resisting their influx. This end may be attained by raising or lowering interest rates. Any such changes are liable to react on exchange rates, both spot and forward, and on Euro-currency rates. Similar results may be attained by changing reserve requirements against foreign funds. The authorities may prefer to influence the movements of funds by direct intervention in forward exchanges in order to affect the direction and extent of covered interest arbitrage. They can influence uncovered interest arbitrage by widening or reducing the margin between spot rates and support points.

Foreign exchange policy may aim at influencing movements of foreign funds for the purpose of expanding or reducing the total volume of credit available for domestic purposes, or for the purpose of raising or lowering domestic interest rates. Thus, changes in interest rates, as indeed changes in the volume of credit or domestic prices, may be either the means of foreign exchange policy or they may be the ends for the sake of which foreign exchange policy measures are applied.

In exceptional circumstances, foreign exchange policy may also aim at influencing interest rates in a foreign centre. This brings us to the role of foreign exchange policy in economic warfare. Such warfare has very ancient traditions. Thus during the Hundred Years War the repeated debasement of French coinage is said to have pursued the end of causing financial embarrassment to the English invader of France. There are many more recent instances quoted in my *History of Foreign Exchange*. Economic warfare by measures relating to foreign exchange can also be pursued in time of peace. For instance, President de Gaulle's decision in 1965 to withdraw gold from the United States and to try to persuade other Governments to act likewise aimed at weakening the dollar's position as a world currency. French official encouragement of speculation against sterling in 1965–67 pursued the same ultimate end through seeking to enforce a devaluation of sterling as a means of undermining confidence in the dollar.

Exchange movements are liable to be affected not only by official policies deliberately adopted for the purpose of influencing them but also by those adopted for other purposes. They may be incidental effects and even unwanted effects of various policies which were adopted either because the authorities had been unaware of the probable repercussions of their measures on foreign exchanges, or because they had not been sufficiently concerned with such consequences of their decisions. Inflationary or deflationary policies are liable to be undertaken purely or mainly for the sake of their effects on the domestic economy. They tend to affect exchange rates nonetheless. Import restrictions or export drives may be undertaken for the benefit of domestic industries even by countries whose exchanges are strong and whose reserves are adequate. "Buy American" policies pursue the policy of protection, and had been applied long before it became necessary to support the dollar. Decisions affecting public spending, taxation or debt management are taken very often independently of considerations of foreign exchange policies. All such decisions and many others in the financial, economic, social, political and military spheres are liable to produce far-reaching unintentional effects on exchange rates. Decisions in respect of the maintenance of armed forces abroad, for instance, are an important factor. Everybody concerned with foreign exchanges must follow them, therefore, closely and must try to assess their probable effects on exchange rates.

The aim of bringing about deliberately a depreciation or an appreciation of an exchange may be achieved in various ways. A depreciation may be effected by devaluation, by engineering a controlled downward movement, or by simply allowing an adverse trend to produce its effect on the exchange. Depreciation accompanies every devaluation but every depreciation is not a devaluation. Nor is every appreciation a revaluation, even though every revaluation means an appreciation. If the currency is allowed to find its level, as was the case with sterling in 1931, its resulting fall is a depreciation and not a devaluation. The downward movement may be controlled by frequent official intervention and market forces may not be allowed to produce their effects unhampered.

A policy favouring appreciation may be pursued by means of a revaluation — an upward adjustment of the parity or the raising of the peg at which the exchange had been held over a period. Or it may assume the form of bringing about a controlled or uncontrolled appreciation of the exchange.

Should the Government decide to abandon the system of stable exchanges it has the choice between the system of flexible exchanges and that of floating exchanges. These two terms are often used indiscriminately, though there is an essential difference between them. Flexible exchanges mean relatively frequent changes of fixed parities or of the peg at which an exchange is held. Floating exchanges mean a complete suspension of parities or of any attempt at pegging the rates, though not necessarily a complete suspension of official intervention. There is also the policy of the "crawling peg".

When an exchange movement is in progress, the authorities may be "neutral" towards it, or they may seek to accentuate it, or they may aim at moderating it — to "iron out" its fluctuations, as the British authorities did in the 'thirties. This may be a matter of policy decisions or it may be in the realm of tactics.

Hitherto we have been dealing with foreign exchange policies that concern exchange rates. A different set of policies concern the relative degree of control and freedom in foreign exchange transactions. The two spheres may overlap, because exchange control often aims at preventing foreign exchange transactions at rates other than those officially approved, instead of suspending free dealings in the foreign exchange market altogether. In most instances, however, exchange control is a policy aimed at maintaining stable exchanges by means of suppressing or limiting free dealings. If a policy of giving absolute priority to expansion, full employment and the raising the standard of living is carried too far the resulting disequilibrium between costs and prices at home and abroad, unless corrected by an adjustment of exchange rates, leads to the necessity of suppressing the freedom of foreign exchange deals. Under a system of controlled exchanges it is possible to isolate the domestic economy from the international economy and maintain the exchange value of the currency at an artificially high level, at any rate for a limited period.

Such a policy was pursued by Germany from 1931 and by a number of belligerent countries during the second World War. It took a number of years during the post-War period before most countries gradually relaxed this policy and resorted to more or less free exchange dealings. We saw in Chapter 18 that, apart from a small number of countries, mostly on the Western Hemisphere, the post-War foreign exchange system of the free world is the outcome of a compromise between control and freedom. Policies of changing the relative degree of control and freedom are of considerable interest to foreign exchange dealers. During the run on the pound that followed the advent of the Socialist Government in Britain in October 1964 the adverse pressure was due at least to the same extent to fears of a reinforcement of exchange control as to fears of devaluation.

Hitherto we have been dealing with national foreign exchange policies. It is possible, however, to pursue foreign exchange policies on an international plane:

(1) Through a uniform application, by agreement, of foreign exchange measures.

(2) Through the creation of currency areas.

(3) Through close co-operation between national monetary authorities.

(4) Through the creation and maintenance of international monetary authorities.

(5) Through the adoption of international monetary policies, such as the creation of Special Drawing Rights.

Between the two World Wars a number of central banks attempted to codify the rules of the gold standard as it operated between 1925 and 1931. One of the main objects of the Bank for International Settlements was precisely to assist in the achievement of that end. A similar end has been pursued much more systematically since the second World War in respect of the Bretton Woods system. As such rules have a bearing on foreign exchanges any reinterpretation, modification, curtailment or extension of their application is apt to react on exchange rates, and may affect the relative degree of freedom and control of dealings in foreign exchanges.

Arrangements relating to currency areas are of considerable importance from the point of view of foreign exchange dealers. For instance, the establishment of a currency area by the European Economic Community would have far-reaching implications calling for a revision of opinions about the prospects of the exchanges concerned. In the existing currency areas changes, such as the admission of a new member or the secession of an existing member, are important not only because of their effect on the position and prospects of the exchange directly concerned but also because they are liable to open or close

214

loopholes for the evasion of exchange control in the currency area and are liable to affect the strength of the remaining exchanges in that area.

The existence of currency areas makes it necessary to follow closely developments affecting not only the country in whose exchange dealers are interested but developments affecting the entire area. For instance, sterling is liable to be affected not only by changes relating to the U.K. but also by influences such as gold smuggling in India or a good wool export season in Australia. The monthly foreign trade returns of the U.K. present an incomplete picture without corresponding figures for the rest of the sterling area. Such figures are only available after considerable delay and no figures about trade of the whole sterling area with non-sterling countries are easily and promptly accessible. The policy adopted by most Sterling Area countries to 'diversify' their reserves instead of holding them in sterling only has reduced the direct effect of their balances of payments on sterling.

Another sphere in which international foreign exchange policy has been playing an increasingly important part relates to co-operation between Central Banks. This has increased in importance very considerably since the War, both in respect of the techniques used and in the extent of reciprocal assistance.

It is impossible for dealers to take a view about the prospects of official intervention unless they keep themselves informed about the nature and extent of co-operation between monetary authorities which largely determines the resources available for supporting an exchange. As a result of progress in such co-operation, which is always a major matter of policy on an international plane, the extent of official intervention has greatly increased since 1961 and the tactics adopted have improved materially.

Even before that development, co-operation through the International Monetary Fund became an important factor in the foreign exchange market, and increasingly so, as and when the resources of that institution were increased. Substantial drawing facilities are now automatically available to member Governments, or can be made available by special agreement.

The willingness or reluctance of the I.M.F. to make such facilities available for the defence of a currency that is subject to attack affects considerably the prospects of official intervention. In the case of the attack on the lira in 1963 and of the attacks on sterling in 1964–68 it was of great importance. The capacity of the I.M.F. to assist Central Banks will greatly increase through the creation of Special Drawing Rights.

Since 1961 the resources of the I.M.F., besides being further increased, have been supplemented by Central Bank facilities made available either directly or through the Bank for International Settlements, and also by reciprocal bilateral swap arrangements between individual Central Banks.

Under such arrangements two Central Banks place at each other's disposal each other's currencies in the form of direct swap transactions, up to an agreed maximum limit. These limits, which have been increased gradually, must be taken into consideration when forming an opinion about the strength of the defences of the currencies concerned. The use of such facilities assists in resisting pressure on the exchange that is subject to attack, while the gradual liquidation of the resulting liability is calculated to mitigate the effects of a subsequent buying pressure. All arrangements and the resulting transactions — about which much detailed information is published nowadays by Central Banks, by the I.M.F. and by the B.I.S. — must be followed closely, as they affect the prospects of the exchange concerned.

International monetary policy is largely in the hands of a group of leading Central Banks which decides such major matters as the establishment of the "two-tier" system of gold prices, the consolidation of official Sterling Area sterling balances, etc. The countries represented are the U.S., the leading Western European countries and Japan.

CHAPTER 20

PAST AND FUTURE OF FOREIGN EXCHANGE

A DETAILED account of the evolution of foreign exchange in all its aspect is outside the scope of the present book. Changes in the system through the centuries, trends of exchange rates, the emergence of a foreign exchange theory and the history of foreign exchange policies is described in detail in my *History of Foreign Exchange*. The present chapter is confined to giving the bare outlines of the past development of foreign exchange and forecasting the lines on which it is likely to develop in the future. This brief account of the changes in its basic character through the ages should make it clear to the present generation that there is no reason to regard the system of foreign exchange that is at present in operation as being necessarily the definitive form of that institution. Indeed, while in the past it took centuries for a new system of foreign exchange to emerge and gradually to supersede the previous form, the last four decades alone witnessed the operation of four fundamentally different systems — the gold standard, floating rates, exchange control and a combination of stable rates with a limited control. Evidently the system has become more easily adaptable than it had been at its earlier stages of evolution. It would be unrealistic not to envisage the possibility of further institutional changes, possibly even during the lifetime of the present generation.

The history of the evolution of foreign exchange may be divided into five main phases:

(1) Dealings in coins.

(2) Dealings in foreign bills of exchange.

(3) Dealings in foreign notes.

(4) Dealings in mail transfers and later in telegraphic transfers.

217

(5) Dealings through telephone and teleprinter.

There are no distinct borderlines between these phases which had merged into each other gradually and which had overlapped each other to a large extent. Even in our days, although most of the dealings are in telegraphic transfers transacted by means of telephone or telex, the earlier forms still survive to some extent. Ever since the emergence of paper moneys in the Western world dealings in notes came to play a part in foreign exchange, coexisting with other forms of foreign exchange, their relative importance varying considerably. Today notes, and to a smaller extent even coins, are still dealt in, but their markets are insignificant compared with those of more modern forms of foreign exchange. Dealings in bills, too, survived, although their significance has declined considerably.

Foreign exchange dealing during the Ancient Period and the early Medieval Period was confined almost entirely to dealings in coins. Originally changing hands by weight, some of the more trustworthy coins came to command sufficient confidence at a more advanced stage to be exchanged against each other by tale. This marked the beginning of the foreign exchange market which must have emerged during the 6th century B.C. It is true, there were isolated instances of foreign exchange by means of bills between Babylonia and her neighbours, and also instances of letters of credit in terms of foreign currencies, or mail transfers, in Greece and Rome. But systematic dealing in foreign exchange was confined for a very long time to dealings in coins. It was not until about the 12th century A.D. that dealing in foreign bills came to develop between Italy and other Mediterranean countries, and later in other parts of Europe.

The profession of money-changing was highly developed throughout the Ancient Middle East and the Mediterranean area. There was a certain amount of space arbitrage to take advantage of discrepancies due to the artificial parity between gold and silver coins in Persia and other countries, and even some interest arbitrage between Israel and Babylonia. The multiplicity of coinages in the Ancient Greek city-states kept money-changers busy in Athens and elsewhere. In the Roman Empire the profession of money-changing carried certain privileges amounting to monopoly, but it entailed some onerous duties, especially during the long period of debasements from the 2nd to the 4th century A.D. There was an important foreign exchange market in Alexandria where Roman coins were exchanged in trading with the East. Later, after the disappearance of the Western Roman Empire, Byzantium became the main foreign exchange market, though Alexandria remained active for some centuries.

During the advanced Middle Ages the centre of gravity of foreign exchange operations shifted to the Italian cities, especially to Genoa and Venice, and later to Florence. In Spain, too, active foreign exchange dealing developed after the liberation from Moorish occupation. In Northern Europe money-changing became important in Flanders, especially in Bruges, and in England where it was for a long time under close State control.

The main problems of foreign exchange dealers during this primitive phase in the evolution of the system were as follows:

(1) Lack of uniformity in the value of coins of the same coinages.

(2) Technical difficulty of ascertaining their metal content.

(3) Multiplicity of coin types in circulation.

(4) Frequent debasements of coins.

(5) Difficulty, delay, risk and expense of transporting coins.

(6) Frequent changes in restrictions on dealing and transfer of coins.

(7) Uncertainty of specie points at which transfers became profitable.

From the 12th century onward foreign exchange assumed increasingly the form of transactions in bills. Merchants and others found that this form of international payments was preferable to the costly, slow and risky method of conveying bullion or specie from one country to another. Owing to the cost and delay involved, very wide discrepancies had developed between exchange rates quoted in various markets — even in markets of the same country — and it usually took a long time before arbitrage could reduce them. Transactions in bills tended to reduce and keep down such discrepancies, though the slowness of communications — even for bills, although their conveyance to their destination required no armed escort — continued for a long time to maintain them relatively wide.

Foreign exchange dealers of the late Medieval Period and early Modern Period had to contend with the following problems:

(1) Uncertainty of the quality of the coins in which the bills were payable.

(2) Risk of debasement or devaluation of the coins before the bills became due.

(3) Unexpected changes in exchange rates through official manipulations of the market.

(4) Losses through defaults by debtors.

(5) Changes in exchange restrictions.

(6) Penalties for infringement of anti-usury laws.

The Church played an important part in the development of active markets in foreign bills. Transfers of the proceeds of Papal collections and financial transactions arising from the Crusades provided a very high proportion of the activities in early foreign exchange markets. Moreover, the Church law against charging interest had led to large-scale circumventions by disguising loan transactions under the form of foreign exchange transactions, with interest charges concealed in exchange rates. A very high proportion of bills in the markets were in fact fictitious bills serving that purpose. Yet the Church authorities were reluctant to apply the law too strictly, for fear that it would handicap legitimate trade which was under considerable disadvantage through the inadequacy of coin supplies during the Middle Ages.

The quarterly fairs in the trading centres of Champagne and elsewhere provided occasion for a high proportion of foreign exchange transactions during the late Medieval Period and the 16th century. There were by then a number of permanent foreign exchange markets in Italian cities, in addition to Venice, Genoa and Florence, also in Lucca, Piacenza, Milan, Bologna, Siena and Rome. Markets in other parts of Europe were also controlled almost entirely by Italian merchant bankers who had branches or agents in all important cities, such

as Lyons, Besançon, Paris, Avignon and Rouen in France,
Seville, Valladolid and Medina del Campo in Spain, Bruges and
Antwerp in the Low Countries, Geneva, London, Constan-
tinople until its occupation by the Turks, and to a less extent in
Germany — Lübeck, Cologne and Nuremberg. Such foreign
exchange markets, in addition to transacting business in bills,
also acted as loan markets where Governments and municipali-
ties were able to borrow.

Activity in foreign exchanges greatly increased after the
discovery of the gold and silver resources of America. Transfers on Government account through foreign exchange markets
came to play an increasingly important part in the 16th century.
Agents of the Emperor and other monarchs assumed from time
to time a virtual control of foreign exchange trends in Antwerp,
Lyons, Genoa and other principal markets. Princes financed
their allies or collected subsidies from them by means of foreign
exchange transactions, and remitted funds abroad for the
requirements of their military operations. In many instances
they raised loans "by exchange" — their fiscal agents in
Antwerp, Genoa or other markets sold bills of exchange drawn
on their own countries and met them on maturity by means of
selling new batches of fictitious bills. Such operations were
carried out systematically, among others, by the Fuggers for
Philip II of Spain for a period extending over decades.

During the late 16th century and in the 17th century the
monopoly of Italian bankers declined gradually, though they
continued to play an important role for a long time. The
Spanish markets increased in importance owing to the arrival
of gold and silver shipments from the New World but later they
declined gradually as a result of the decline of Spain. For a
long time the foreign exchange market of Antwerp reigned
supreme in Northern Europe, but in the late 17th century
Amsterdam came to overshadow it, mainly owing to the freedom of gold exports in Holland. London and some German
cities also advanced gradually. In the 18th century Vienna,
Hamburg, Berlin, Leghorn and Lisbon became also important,
the latter owing to gold shipments from Brazil which became
all-important after the exhaustion of the resources of the

Spanish colonies. The Church ban on interest was gradually relaxed, so that foreign exchange markets ceased to serve the purpose of disguising loan transactions. Bills became transferable from the middle of the 17th century.

A rudimentary forward market in bills on Amsterdam developed in London in the early 18th century. By that time private transfers of capital came to assume a considerable importance as factors in the foreign exchange market. From an early period foreign exchange brokers made their appearance. A system of fixing official exchange rate at the quarterly fairs had developed, though it was permissible to deal at other rates. From time to time Governments attempted to apply various forms of exchange restrictions, but they were usually extensively evaded and were abandoned sooner or later, or they fell into disuse, only to be revived again whenever the exchanges came again under adverse pressure.

Paper currencies, from their earliest origins in Europe towards the close of the 17th century and during the 18th century, came to be transacted regularly in foreign exchange markets. In some countries such as France and Portugal it was made compulsory to accept the payment of bills at least partly in inconvertible notes. Bill rates came to depend, therefore, largely on the fluctuating value of such paper money. During the French Revolution forward dealings developing in inconvertible paper money, the *assignats*, and throughout the 19th century we encounter forward markets in inconvertible paper moneys whenever they were subject to wide fluctuations.

The main preoccupations of foreign exchange dealers during this phase were as follows:

(1) Changing convertibility prospect of notes.
(2) Circulation of forged notes.
(3) Problems of transporting notes in quantities.
(4) Devaluation of notes.
(5) Deterioration of coins.
(6) Recoinages on unfavourable terms.

To safeguard themselves against losses through such contingencies, the practice of issuing bills in fictitious units representing a definite quantity of metals was adopted from an early stage. In the late 17th century the Bank of Amsterdam and later other banks adopted the system of holding deposits in full valued coins, and payments were made through transfers between such deposits.

During the 19th century exchange parities became more precisely defined and the process of narrowing the spread between specie point made considerable progress as a result of declining transport costs and speedier communications. Although dealings in paper currencies assumed from time to time considerable importance they were overshadowed most of the time by the market in foreign bills which, until about the last quarter of the 19th century, constituted the bulk of foreign exchange dealings. The relative importance of dealings in mail transfers and later in telegraphic transfers increased considerably during the concluding decades of the 19th century and the years preceding the first World War, although an active market in bills had survived.

Until the closing years of the 19th century all foreign exchange markets were real markets in the physical sense, being meeting places of bankers engaged in the transactions. To an increasing extent, however, business came to be transacted outside such meetings. With the adoption of the telephone there was a fundamental change in the character of dealings. Foreign exchange markets throughout the world came to assume gradually their present form consisting of a network of private telephone lines. Later, with the development of long-distance telephones, closer contact came to be established between banks in various countries and the market became increasingly international. Long before that stage was reached dealings in telegraphic transfers gradually increased in importance.

During the Wars of the French Revolution and the Napoleonic Wars Hamburg replaced Amsterdam as the world's leading foreign exchange market. Danzig too assumed some importance. Immediately after Waterloo the London and Paris market came to share the lead, with Amsterdam as a good third. Other foreign exchange markets of importance during the 19th century were Brussels, Frankfurt, Hamburg, Berlin,

Vienna, Trieste, St. Petersburg, Stockholm, various Italian and Spanish cities, Zürich and other Swiss centres, Lisbon, Istanbul, New York, Alexandria, various Latin American capitals, Bombay, Shanghai, Hong Kong, Singapore, Batavia, Tokio and Yokohama. A foreign exchange market developed in New York even before the United States became independent, but for a long time a large proportion of transactions in sterling bills was done in New Orleans, Boston, Baltimore and, later, during the gold rush and again during the Civil War, in San Francisco.

The establishment of closer relations between banks greatly helped the progress of the foreign exchange market. There was an all-round increase of mutual confidence. Banks in leading foreign exchange centres adopted the habit of keeping permanent balances on accounts with each other for the requirements of their foreign exchange business. They also came to trust each other sufficiently to accept informal mail instructions for transfers, and to grant each other overdraft facilities, instead of necessarily discounting bills of exchange. The invention of telegraphy and the laying down of overseas cables was a very important element in the development of foreign exchange transactions between Europe and other continents. By the 'nineties telegraphic transfers were used regularly and on an increasing scale, thus greatly reducing the minimum time lag for transfers between distant countries.

By far the most important change during the 19th century was the development of regular and active forward exchange dealings. Fluctuations during the French Revolution and the Napoleonic Wars stimulated the emergence of an active forward market which survived during the subsequent more stable period. Before forward exchange facilities became available exchange risk had been covered mainly by means of long bills. Forward exchange transactions came to be preferred, however, among other reasons because they did not involve immediate capital outlay for the buyer. It seems probable that Vienna was the first truly modern forward exchange market, having originated through the fluctuation of the Austrian currency during the second half of the 19th century. There was a forward market both in foreign notes and in bills and mail transfers, with elaborate exchange arbitrage and interest arbitrage operations. Forward exchange markets developed also in Berlin, St. Petersburg, Valparaiso, Shanghai and many other centres. Many formerly unstable currencies remained inconvertible even after their stabilisation, and arbitrageurs as well as merchants continued to play for safety and cover their operations.

During the second half of the 19th century London's importance as a foreign exchange market remained relatively small, because most of Britain's foreign trade as well as that of other countries was financed in sterling. This state of affairs continued right until the first World War. Nevertheless, during the concluding years of the 19th century and the early years of this century a number of foreign bank branches in London, and also London merchant banks, gradually increased their activities in foreign exchanges.

The importance of capital transactions and of various types of arbitrage increased in the foreign exchange market during the concluding decades of the 19th century. As and when the gold standard came to be adopted by country after country, a growing volume of gold arbitrage gave rise to a growing volume of foreign exchange transactions. There was an increase in stock arbitrage in the 'nineties. Likewise, space arbitrage and interest arbitrage became increasingly popular among banks. The expansion of the latter greatly increased the importance of interest rates among the factors affecting exchange rates and gold movements.

The period of instability that followed the first World War led to a considerable increase in the volume of foreign exchange business, a large proportion of which was of a speculative character. Fluctuations of exchange rates made it imperative to cover commercial and genuine financial transactions. During the early inter-War years there was a great deal of business in foreign notes, some of which had developed extensive markets. Gambling in depreciating mark notes was followed by large-scale speculation in French franc notes, lire notes and other Continental currencies. But by the middle 'twenties transactions in telegraphic transfers assumed predominant importance. During the early inter-War years regular dealings between markets through long-distance telephone calls developed considerably, though for many years they remained handicapped by the inadequacy of the telephone service.

Above all, dealings in forward exchanges, which existed already long before the first World War but were suspended during the hostilities, assumed considerable importance during the 'twenties both as a means of speculation and as a means of safeguarding legitimate interests against the effects of speculation. Forward exchanges have gradually replaced the long bills as the means for covering exchange risk on commercial transactions.

The London foreign exchange market increased in importance during the inter-War period, largely because of its role as an intermediary between Europe and the other continents. The clearing banks, which had kept more or less aloof from foreign exchange business before 1914, came to establish foreign exchange departments and became very large dealers. Continental foreign exchange markets that were important during the inter-War period included Paris, the three principal Swiss centres — Zürich, Geneva and Basle — Amsterdam, Berlin, Frankfurt, Milan, Brussels, Madrid, Stockholm, Copenhagen, Oslo, Vienna and Budapest. Outside Europe New York became the leading foreign exchange market but, in spite of the prominent role of the dollar in international finance, it could not become the world's principal foreign exchange market owing to the differences in business hours in New York and in the leading European centres. Other important markets on the Western Hemisphere were Montreal and Toronto, Valparaiso, Buenos Aires and Rio de Janeiro.

Extensive international borrowing through the foreign exchange market in the form of swap-and-deposit transactions developed during the 'twenties and played a decisive part in filling the temporary vacuum created through the destruction of capital resources by inflation in Germany, Austria and other countries.

The effect of speculative operations was greatly reinforced

by heavy and frequent international movements of "hot money" shifted from one currency into another mainly in anticipation of devaluation or depreciations. Such movements were largely responsible for the suspension of the gold standard during the 'thirties in Britain in 1931, and in the United States two years later. Amidst the resulting mutual distrust foreign exchange business suffered a temporary reverse, but by the middle 'thirties normal conditions gradually returned. The continued existence of floating exchange rates encouraged, however, speculation and nervous movements of "hot money" on a large scale. By then official intervention in the foreign exchange markets to support the national currency or to iron out its excessive fluctuations came to assume a prominent role.

During the second World War stability of exchange rates was maintained in most countries through a complete suspension of dealings and the adoption of advanced exchange control. That system continued until the early 'fifties when foreign exchange markets came to be reopened gradually. London recovered its supremacy as the leading foreign exchange centre in spite of the survival of some degree of exchange control and in spite of the vulnerability of sterling which reduced its use as an international currency, especially after its devaluation in 1967, which revived the atmosphere of uncertainty.

Since the end of the first World War the foreign exchange markets experienced two major periods of floating exchanges — between 1919 and 1925 and again between 1931 and 1939 — a brief period of stability through the operation of the gold standard, a more prolonged period of stability through exchange controls and, more recently, a period of stability through the operation of the Bretton Woods system. Apart from the fundamental changes from one system to another there have been several major institutional changes such as the emergence of the Euro-currency system before the very eyes of our generation. Similar major developments in the future are well within the realm of practical possibility.

Having dealt with past developments, our next task is to cast a glance into the future. As the foreign exchange system is conditioned by changes in the monetary, economic and political background against which it operates, it is difficult to predict its likely course with any degree of certainty. In one respect we are now on safer ground than we would have been thirty years ago. Amidst the conditions prevailing in the 'thirties it appeared even conceivable that the whole foreign exchange system might be replaced by exchange clearing. That system was making headway during the years preceding the second World War. It came to be adopted between quite a number of countries and its wider adoption was seriously considered for some time as a possibility. Even in our days Switzerland still operates some exchange clearing agreements with some countries, but most other financially advanced countries have long abandoned the idea. The system of free exchanges has come to be considered as the definite system, even if its actual form is subject to major modifications. It is true the inter-War experience is likely to be remembered if world finance should ever relapse into chaotic conditions comparable to those of the 'thirties. But should the world revert to exchange clearing or to advanced exchange control it would be looked upon as a temporary evil and a return to free exchanges would be regarded as the ultimate goal in the countries of the free world.

Major financial or political crises are likely to lead to a reinforcement of the surviving exchange restrictions. Although the post-War trend has been towards a higher degree of freedom in international trade and finance some countries have already felt impelled to revert to some forms of official or voluntary restrictions. Under strong adverse pressure other countries might conceivably follow the same course in preference to devaluing their currencies or allowing them to depreciate. The fact that even the United States, confronted with a perennial balance of payments deficit, chose in 1965 a limited degree of unofficial exchange restrictions rather than raise the dollar price of gold is very significant from this point of view.

Although world conditions in the 'sixties do not contain anything like the elements of instability that existed between the Wars a return to currency chaos cannot be ruled out as impossible. Apart from the ever-present danger of a major international financial crisis that would produce that result, it is even conceivable that mankind might deliberately put the clock back by adopting a system of flexible exchanges. There is strong temptation for politicans and economists to favour that system which would enable Governments to inflate without having to worry about its immediate effects on the balance of payments and on gold reserves. There has been strong and growing pressure in that direction. The disadvantages of that system experienced during the 'thirties have faded into oblivion and a new generation has arisen which has only experienced the disadvantages of rigid parities and which feels an increasing nostalgia for the pre-War system it never experienced from close quarters. Any return to floating exchange rates, or even to a more flexible system with frequent changes of parities, or a considerable widening of the spread between support points, would create new uncertainties and might culminate in currency chaos.

But disregarding such extreme possibilities, there is scope for a further expansion in the activities of the foreign exchange market even under the stability maintained by the Bretton Woods system. In the absence of a major crisis international trade is bound to expand further and finance is likely to become further internationalised. Any major crisis would mean, however, a curtailment of international trade and a reaction from the trend towards internationalisation of finance. Already as a result of the balance of payments difficulties of the United States and Britain, both countries resorted to measures to discourage the export of capital.

Changes affecting the foreign exchange market which might conceivably occur may be summarised as follows:

(1) Closer international co-operation between Central Banks might lead to a further increase in official intervention, reducing the range of fluctuations of both spot and forward rates.

(2) On the other hand, member Governments of the I.M.F. might decide to increase the spread between support points, thereby widening the range of fluctuations without resorting to the floating or flexible system.

(3) In the absence of a crisis the remaining exchange restrictions might be removed or, at any rate, mitigated.

(4) On the other hand, a crisis or prolonged chronic difficulties might lead to a tightening of existing exchange restrictions, especially on capital movements.

(5) In the absence of disturbing developments discrepancies between swap margins and their interest parities and also between various maturities of forward exchange rates will tend to narrow down. This would reduce the market's prospects of operating profitably in arbitrage.

(6) On the other hand, recurrence of disturbing developments might widen discrepancies, though it is difficult to visualise a widening of discrepancies in space, owing to the improvement of communications which is likely to continue.

(7) Forward facilities and Euro-currency facilities might become obtainable for longer maturities.

(8) On the other hand, limits to forward transactions and Euro-currency transactions might become shorter as a result of uncertainty of conditions and of the outlook.

(9) Dealings in Euro-currency deposits might expand further in the absence of any major crises.

(10) On the other hand, any substantial losses suffered in this market are liable to lead to a sharp contraction in this branch of activity.

(11) Facilities for forward exchange for optional dates are likely to improve further under pressing demand for such facilities. Even facilities for optional purchases and sales might develop.

(12) The number of banks participating in the foreign exchange market and the number of centres in which they operate is likely to increase as a result of progress and consolidation in a number of countries which are at present either unstable or too undeveloped to play an active share.

(13) Progress towards integration within the European Common Market and other economic unions might conceivably lead to the emergence of unified currencies, reducing the number of hard currencies in the foreign exchange market.

(14) A disintegration of the Sterling Area would increase the number of foreign exchanges in the London market and other markets.

(15) The isolation of the New York market from the Euro-

pean market through the discrepancy of six hours between business hours is likely to be mitigated through expanding the recently developed practice of maintaining contact with New York after the London market is closed.

(16) The integration of international money markets on lines indicated by the growing importance of American activity in the London Euro-dollar market will continue.

(17) International arbitrage will be stimulated by a further widening of the choice of short-term employment facilities for funds.

(18) Continued expansion of the Euro-bond market will provide additional business for foreign exchange markets and for the markets in Euro-currencies.

(19) As a reaction to the misuse of international co-operation for bolstering up unsound policies, there might be a revival of economic nationalism in the sphere of foreign exchange policies.

(20) There might even develop economic warfare in the sphere of foreign exchange and gold policies : currency depreciation race, a division of the Western world into currencies based on gold and currencies detached from gold.

(21) The Soviet Union and the Communist Bloc in general might play a more active part in the foreign exchange market, providing an additional element of uncertainty.

(22) A new devaluation of sterling, or its depreciation following on the adoption of the system of floating exchanges, would be followed by a series of devaluations or by a widespread adoption of floating rates.

(23) A devaluation of the franc might produce a similar effect.

(24) A devaluation of the dollar, provided that it is sufficiently drastic to eliminate fears that it might be repeated, would go a long way towards restoring confidence in stability, if accompanied by an orderly all-round devaluation of all principal currencies.

(25) Movements of the gold price might cause trouble.

In many of the above forecasts we are necessarily in the realm of conjecture. Taking everything into consideration it seems on the whole probable that, barring major disasters, the post-War expansion of foreign exchange markets will continue. The system will play an increasingly important part in assisting towards a higher degree of international division of labour that would enable countries to produce the goods which they are able to produce under the most advantageous circumstances. It will also play an important part in being instrumental towards a more equal distribution of financial resources between countries.

All this depends, however, largely on conditions outside the foreign exchange system. A major war would lead to its breakdown, and so would unrestrained inflationary policies that would create an increasingly vulnerable position and would culminate in chaos. Ill-advised adoption of floating rates or detachment of the dollar from gold would produce a similar effect. Mankind would have to learn the lessons, taught by experience during the inter-war period, all over again, at incalculable costs in terms of financial, economic and social setbacks. Given a reasonable degree of wisdom in the management of human affairs, however, the foreign exchange system can be depended on making its maximum contribution towards the progress of mankind.

APPENDIX

THE A.B.C. OF FOREIGN EXCHANGE

THERE are few spheres of economic literature in which terms are apt to be applied so loosely as in the sphere of foreign exchange. Distinguished academic economists are in the habit of using the terms "devaluation" and "depreciation" indiscriminately as if they were synonymous. The same is true about "floating" and "flexible" exchange rates. Writings on theoretical aspects of forward exchange are full of examples of indiscriminate use of the terms "hedging" and "covering". Many other examples could be quoted, but the above should suffice for proving that the terminology of foreign exchange requires more attention than it has received.

Although various terms are defined throughout this book in the chapters in which they are used, it might help students and others if an extensive list of them is provided here in alphabetical order. I should like to draw particular attention to distinctions such as exist between foreign *exchanges* (note the plural!) and foreign *exchange* (note the singular!). The former indicates the actual means of payment in which business is transacted, and also the actual activity of transacting business in them. The latter indicates the system by which currencies are exchanges against each other and by which payments are made in foreign countries, and also the economic process resulting from the operation of the system.

APPRECIATION. A rise in the value of a currency in terms of foreign currencies.

ARBITRAGE. Simultaneous buying and selling of foreign exchanges for the sake of realising profits from discrepancies between exchange rates prevailing at the same time in different centres, or between forward margins for different maturities, or between interest rates prevailing at the same time in different centres or in different currencies.

ARBITRAGE POINTS, or ARBITRAGE SUPPORT POINTS. The limits of the fluctuations of member currencies of the I.M.F. other than the dollar in terms of each other, based on their official support points in relation to the dollar.

ARBITRAGEURS. Foreign exchange dealers (or foreign exchange traders in the U.S.) engaged systematically in arbitrage operations.

"AT BEST". Instructions to banks to buy or sell foreign exchanges on account of other banks or of non-banking clients at the most favourable rates obtainable in the market.

AUTHORISED DEALERS. Banks in the U.K., and in other countries with exchange restrictions, which alone are entitled to engage in foreign exchange transactions with each other, with non-residents, and with resident non-banking clients.

BALANCE OF PAYMENTS. Surplus or deficit on total current and external payments and long-term capital movements settled by a change in reserves, foreign credits or short-term capital movements.

BEAR. Speculator going short in anticipation of a depreciation.

BEAR SQUEEZE. Official intervention in the foreign exchange market aiming at forcing speculators to cover their short positions at a loss.

BLOCKED ACCOUNTS. Non-resident funds which cannot be transferred freely.

BRETTON WOODS SYSTEM of foreign exchange, under which member Governments of the I.M.F. are under obligation to maintain, by means of systematic intervention in the foreign exchange market, their exchange rates in relation to the dollar within 1 per cent on either side of their agreed parities.

BROKERAGE. Charges made by foreign exchange brokers to both banks engaged in a foreign exchange or Euro-currency transaction concluded through their intermediary.

BULL. Speculator going long in anticipation of an appreciation.

BUSINESS DAYS. See CLEAR DAYS.

BUYING RATES. Exchange rates at which dealers are prepared to buy foreign exchanges in the market from other dealers, and at which potential sellers are therefore able to sell foreign exchanges to those dealers.

CABLE TRANSFERS. See TELEGRAPHIC TRANSFERS.

"CERTAIN" QUOTATION. See "DIRECT" QUOTATION.

CLEAR DAYS or BUSINESS DAYS or MARKET DAYS. Days on which both markets concerned are functioning and which alone count when reckoning the value dates on which foreign exchange contracts or Euro-currency contracts have to be executed.

CLIENTS or CUSTOMERS. Buyers or sellers of foreign exchanges who have no direct access to the market and who buy or sell through a bank with access to the market.

CLOSING A COMMITMENT. Allowing a covered foreign exchange position to expire on maturity, or reversing it before maturity by means of a swap operation, or allowing it to close through the incidence of transactions in the opposite sense.

CLOSING A POSITION. Covering open long or short positions by means of a spot operation or outright forward operation, or by allowing it to be balanced through the incidence of transactions in the opposite sense.

COMMISSION. Charge made by banks on foreign exchange transactions with their customers.

COMMITMENTS. Positions covered by means of forward transactions.

CONVERTIBILITY. In the post-War system it means the right of holders of a currency to transfer their funds into another currency, or the right of official holders of dollars to withdraw gold at a fixed price. Before the War it meant convertibility into gold for all holders, or for specific holders such as exporters of bullion.

COUNTERPART. Buying or selling orders of foreign exchanges that meet selling or buying orders.

CROSS RATE. The ratio between the exchange rates of two foreign currencies in terms of a third currency.

CURRENCY AREAS. An association of countries which maintain fixed exchange rates in terms of each other's currencies and between which international transfers are reasonably free.

DAYLIGHT OVERDRAFTS. Facilities granted for a few hours, repayable on the same day.

DEALERS, or FOREIGN EXCHANGE DEALERS (in the U.S. FOREIGN EXCHANGE TRADERS). Bank employees in Foreign Exchange Departments engaged in operations in the market with other banks or with foreign exchange brokers.

DEPOSITARIES OF FOREIGN SECURITIES. Firms authorised by the British authorities to hold foreign securities quoted on a recognised foreign Stock Exchange.

DEPRECIATION. A decline in the gold value or exchange value of a currency either within its support points, or beyond them, in the absence of support points.

DEVALUATION. A downward change in the official parity of an exchange, or of an exchange rate at which it had been pegged for some time.

A Textbook on Foreign Exchange

DEVALUATION-PRONE. A currency which is widely expected to be devalued.

"DIRECT" QUOTATION, also called "FIXED" or "CERTAIN" QUOTATION. Method of quoting fixed units of foreign exchanges in variable numbers of the local currency unit.

DISCOUNT. Spot exchange inferior to parity is at a discount. Forward exchange that is cheaper for future delivery than for immediate delivery is at a discount.

EQUILIBRIUM LINE. The series of interest parities for various maturities, towards which forward margins for the corresponding maturities tend to adjust themselves.

EQUILIBRIUM RATES. Rates at which supply and demand of foreign exchanges or Euro-currencies balance through the attraction of adequate counterparts. In respect of forward exchanges equilibrium rates are usually deemed to be the rates which conform to interest parities.

EURO-CURRENCIES. Time deposits in terms of a foreign currency lent and borrowed in a market other than that of the currency concerned.

EURO-DOLLARS. Time deposits in terms of dollars lent and borrowed in financial centres outside the U.S.

EXCHANGE ARBITRAGE. See SPACE ARBITRAGE.

EXCHANGE CLEARING. Agreement between two Governments by which exporters are paid out of the proceeds of imports by their own countries, paid into clearing accounts for that purpose.

EXCHANGE CONTRACTS. Documents issued by foreign exchange brokers to both parties, confirming foreign exchange transactions.

EXCHANGE CONTROL or EXCHANGE RESTRICTIONS. Limitation of free dealings in exchanges or of free transfers of funds into other currencies and other countries.

EXCHANGE CONTROL RISK. The possibility of defaults on obligations through imposition or reinforcement of exchange control.

EXCHANGE RATES. Unless otherwise stated, the middle rates for telegraphic transfers quoted for spot exchanges in inter-bank dealing.

FIRM EXCHANGE. Appreciating exchange.

FIRM QUOTATION. Rate quoted definitely which is binding, if immediately accepted, to the extent of the amount for which it is quoted or, if no amount is stated, for the customary minimum of transactions between banks.

FIXED EXCHANGES. Exchanges with fixed parities whose fluctuations are confined to the spread between support points.

"FIXED" QUOTATION. See "DIRECT" QUOTATION.

FLEXIBLE EXCHANGES. System under which exchange parities are liable to relatively frequent changes.

FLOATING EXCHANGES. System under which there are no parities and exchange rates fluctuate freely, subject to occasional or systematic official intervention to influence their trend.

FLUCTUATIONS OF EXCHANGES. Movements of exchange rates either within their support points or in the absence of official limits.

FOREIGN BALANCES. Credit balances of non-residents on current accounts. In a broader economic sense all foreign liquid assets.

FOREIGN BILLS. Bills of exchange drawn on a foreign centre in terms of a foreign currency.

FOREIGN CURRENCY ACCOUNTS. Current or deposit accounts in terms of a currency other than that of the country in which the accounts are kept.

FOREIGN EXCHANGE (in singular). The system or process of converting one national currency into another and of transferring the ownership of money from one country to another.

FOREIGN EXCHANGES (in plural). The means of payment in which currencies are converted into each other and by which international transfers are made, also the activity of transacting business in such means.

FOREIGN EXCHANGE BROKERS. Firms acting as intermediaries between banks for foreign exchange or Euro-currency transactions within local markets.

FOREIGN EXCHANGE BROKERS' ASSOCIATION, or F.E.B.A. Association of London foreign exchange brokers representing their professional interests.

FOREIGN EXCHANGE MARKET. Meetings, or systematic communications by telephone or telex between foreign exchange dealers and brokers for the purpose of transacting wholesale business in foreign exchanges and in Euro-currencies.

FOREIGN EXCHANGE RETURNS. Monthly or weekly returns submitted by banks to the monetary authorities, giving a record of their foreign exchange transactions during the period concerned, or their open positions and covered commitments outstanding on the day for which the return is made.

FOREIGN NOTES. Bank notes bought, sold and held by banks in countries other than their countries of issue.

FOREX CLUB. Association of foreign exchange dealers to promote their professional and social interests.

FORWARD EXCHANGE (in singular). The system or process of operating in foreign currencies for future delivery.

FORWARD EXCHANGES (in plural). Foreign currencies bought and sold for future delivery against payment on delivery at a pre-arranged date.

FORWARD-FORWARD. Forward purchase for shorter maturities against sale for longer maturity, or vice versa.

FORWARD MARGIN, also called SWAP MARGIN or SWAP RATE. The premium or discount on forward exchanges against spot exchanges.

FORWARD RATES. The actual rates at which foreign exchanges for future delivery are quoted, bought and sold.

GOLD ARBITRAGE. Transactions before the War to take advantage of discrepancies between the cost of international payments through gold shipments and through foreign exchange transactions. Since the War it is limited to transactions in gold bought in the free markets.

GOLD BULLION STANDARD. System under Central Banks are under obligation to convert their currencies into gold bars for the purpose of shipment abroad, but not into coins for domestic circulation, or into bars for domestic holders.

GOLD EXCHANGE STANDARD. System under which the international stability of a currency is maintained by its convertibility at a fixed rate into another currency based on gold or stabilised in terms of gold.

GOLD POINTS. Limits of fluctuations of currencies under the gold standard and gold bullion standard, determined by the cost of gold imports and exports.

GOLD PRICE. The official American buying and selling price of gold fixed since 1934 at $35 an ounce.

GOLD RUSH. Strong demand for gold in the free markets by private buyers for purposes of speculation or hoarding, or by Central Banks for strengthening their reserves.

GOLD STANDARD. System under which the international value of a currency is kept stable in terms of gold and in terms of other currencies based on gold by means of its free convertibility into gold.

GOLD WITHDRAWALS. Conversions of official holdings of dollars into gold through purchases from the U.S. authorities at the official price.

HEDGING. Foreign exchange or foreign borrowing operations to safeguard against indefinite and indirect exchange risk arising from assets or liabilities whose value is apt to be affected by changes in exchange rates. According to an alternative definition, hedging is taking a speculative risk in order to offset a bigger speculative risk in the opposite sense.

"HOT MONEY". Foreign funds temporarily transferred to a financial centre and liable to be withdrawn at any moment.

I.M.F. PARITIES. Parities approved by the International Monetary Fund, fixing the gold and dollar value of currencies of countries associated with the I.M.F.

INCONVERTIBLE CURRENCIES. Currencies not transferable by non-resident holders.

"INDIRECT" QUOTATION. Quotation of a fixed unit of the local currency in variable numbers of units of foreign currencies.

INTER-BANK STERLING. Money lent in large round amounts in London between banks without security.

INTEREST ARBITRAGE. Operations to benefit by higher yield obtainable on the short-term employment of liquid funds in a foreign currency with or without covering the exchange risk.

INTEREST ARBITRAGE, COVERED. Transfer of short-term funds into a foreign currency for the sake of higher yield, with the exchange risk covered.

INTEREST ARBITRAGE, INWARD. Transfer of short-term funds into local currency for the sake of higher yield.

INTEREST ARBITRAGE, OUTWARD. Transfer of short-term funds into a foreign currency for the sake of higher yield.

INTEREST ARBITRAGE, UNCOVERED. Transfer of short-term funds into a foreign currency for the sake of higher yield, without covering the exchange risk.

INTEREST, NEGATIVE. Commission charged on foreign deposits on which no interest is allowed.

INTEREST PARITIES. Differences at a given moment between interest rates charged or allowed in two centres on short-term credits or investments or time deposits of identical maturity.

INTERMEDIARY MARKET. Foreign exchange centre whose banks and whose currency are used systematically by non-resident banks for operations between two foreign currencies.

INTERNATIONAL BROKERS. Firms engaged in acting as inter-mediaries for Euro-currency and similar transactions between banks and non-banking clients in different countries.

INTERNATIONAL FOREIGN EXCHANGE MARKET. Regular exchange transactions between banks situated in different countries through long-distance telephone and telex.

INTERVENTION, or OFFICIAL INTERVENTION. Foreign exchange operations by the monetary authorities with the object of preventing or causing movements of exchange rates in accordance with the aims of the policy or tactics they pursue.

INTERVENTION, ACTIVE. Official foreign exchange operations by which the authorities take the initiative for the purpose of bringing about changes in exchange rates.

INTERVENTION, PASSIVE. Official foreign exchange operations by which the authorities provide the counterpart for excess supply or demand in the market in order to prevent them from affecting the exchange rate.

INVESTMENT CURRENCIES. Foreign currency proceeds of foreign securities realised by U.K. holders, usable for purchases of foreign securities by U.K. holders.

INVESTMENT DOLLARS. Dollar proceeds of dollar securities realised by U.K. holders, available for purchases of dollar securities, or other foreign securities by U.K. holders.

INVISIBLE EXPORTS AND IMPORTS. Services bought or sold abroad, or on account of non-residents, and other current payments not appearing in Customs returns.

LEADS AND LAGS. Timing of payments or of covering arrangements connected with foreign trade transactions, adjusted for the purpose of avoiding losses or securing profits through an anticipated change in the exchange rate.

LIMITS. Maximum amounts for which names of banks are taken by other banks in the foreign exchange market (*a*) for forward exchange transactions, (*b*) for Euro-currency transactions, and (*c*) for payments arising from foreign exchange transactions on the same day.

LIQUID FUNDS. Balances on current account, sight deposits, short time deposits, long time deposits with escape clauses, money at call or at short notice, bills which have a good market.

LOCAL MARKET. Systematic contact between banks through private telephone lines for transactions in foreign exchange through the intermediary of brokers. In some Continental centres meeting places of foreign exchange dealers.

LONG FORWARD EXCHANGES. A relative term, usually applied to maturities of over three months.

LONG POSITION. An excess of short-term balances or forward

claims in a foreign currency over short-term liabilities in the same currency.

Loro Accounts. Current accounts of banks with foreign banks in terms of a foreign currency held on behalf their clients.

Mail Transfers. Foreign exchange transactions executed by instructions sent by air mail.

Market, Official. Meeting places of banks in Continental centres, for the purpose of dealings, or of fixing daily official exchange rates to be applied for certain limited purposes.

"Marrying" Foreign Exchange Transactions. Covering a foreign exchange position or commitment resulting from an operation with a client by an operation with another client in the opposite sense, of identical amount and maturity in the same currency.

Maturities, Graded. Long and short positions maintained by a bank for many different dates, while aiming at balancing the overall position.

Maturities, Odd. Maturities for dates other than the standard dates for which most forward exchange and Euro-currency business is transacted.

Maturities, Standard. Maturities for 1 day, 2 days, 7 days, 1, 2, 3, 6 and 12 months.

Maximum Support Points. The present-day equivalents of gold import points.

Minimum Amounts. The smallest amount of individual transactions customary in foreign exchange dealing in the market.

Minimum Support Points. The present-day equivalents of gold export points.

Non-Resident Accounts. Current and deposit accounts owned by residents outside the country or monetary area concerned.

Nostro Accounts. Current accounts of banks with their correspondents in foreign centres in terms of the latter's currencies, for current requirements of their foreign exchange operations in those currencies.

One-Way Market. The overwhelming majority of inquiries are either buyers only or sellers only. In the case of Euro-currencies they are either borrowers only or lenders only.

Open Position. The difference between long positions and short positions in a particular foreign currency, or between the grand total of long and short positions in all foreign currencies.

Optional Forward Contracts. Forward exchange transactions in which one of the parties has the choice between various delivery dates.

OUTRIGHT. Forward exchanges bought and sold unconnected with a simultaneous sale or purchase of spot exchanges.

OVERLENDING. Lending abroad in excess of the supply of foreign exchange available through an export surplus or through long-term borrowing.

OVER-VALUATION. Appreciation of spot exchanges above their purchasing power parities, so that the goods which enter into foreign trade are dearer than in other countries. In relation to forward exchanges it means that forward premiums are wider or forward discounts lower than the interest parities between the two centres concerned.

PEGGING. Maintenance of the exchange at a rigidly fixed rate by means of unlimited official buying or selling at that rate.

POSITION SHEET or POSITION BOOK. List of all foreign exchange transactions creating a position, to enable the senior dealer to follow closely the open position in particular currencies and the overall open position in all currencies, also the position for various dates.

PREMIUM. Value of spot exchange in excess of parity. In relation to forward exchange it means that the currency is dearer for future delivery than for immediate delivery.

PREMIUM DOLLARS. See INVESTMENT DOLLARS.

QUOTATIONS. Exchange rates or Euro-currency rates quoted by banks or brokers, at which they are prepared to deal.

RENEWING COMMITMENTS. Carrying forward covered commitments on maturity by means of a swap transaction.

RENEWING POSITIONS. Maintaining open positions on maturity by means of a swap transaction.

RESIDENT ACCOUNTS. Current or deposit accounts owned by residents of the country concerned.

REVALUATION. Upward change in the official parity or in the exchange rate at which an exchange was pegged for some considerable time.

RISK, CREDIT. Possibility that the buyer or seller of foreign exchange may be unable to meet his obligation on maturity.

RISK, DELIVERY. Possibility that a seller of foreign exchange, having collected the payment in local currency may fail to deliver in the foreign centre the foreign currency sold.

RISK, EXCHANGE. Possibility of loss suffered on an open position as a result of an appreciation or depreciation of the exchange.

Appendix

RISK, FORWARD EXCHANGE. Possibility of loss on a covered position as a result of a change in the swap margin.

SCHEDULED TERRITORIES. See STERLING AREA.

SEASONAL EXCHANGE MOVEMENTS. Fluctuations of exchanges resulting from crop movements or other regularly recurrent seasonal influences.

SECURITY DOLLARS. See INVESTMENT DOLLARS.

SECURITY STERLING. Proceeds of realised foreign holdings of sterling securities, usable only for investment in sterling securities before it was abolished in 1967.

SELF-AGGRAVATING TENDENCY. Exchange depreciation which, instead of attracting demand that halts or reverses the movement, accentuates pessimism leading to an increase of supply and to further depreciation, or exchange appreciation which, instead of attracting supplies that would halt or reverse the movement, accentuates optimism leading to an increase of demand and to further appreciation.

SELLING RATE. Exchange rate at which dealers are prepared to sell foreign exchanges in the market and at which potential buyers are therefore able to buy foreign exchanges from those dealers.

SHORT FORWARD RATE. A relative term, usually applied to maturities under one month.

SHORT POSITION. An excess of short-term liabilities over short-term assets and claims in a foreign currency.

SPECIFIED CURRENCIES. Non-Sterling Area exchanges which U.K. residents have to sell to authorised banks within six months.

SPECULATION. Creation and maintenance of uncovered positions in foreign currencies for the sake of making a profit through a change in the exchange rate.

SPOT EXCHANGES. Foreign exchanges bought and sold for immediate delivery — in practice almost invariably for delivery two clear days after the conclusion of the deal — and paid for on the day of the delivery.

SPREAD. Discrepancy between buying and selling rates, also between support points or between arbitrage support points.

STANDARD AMOUNTS. Large round amounts in which foreign exchange transactions or Euro-currency transactions are usually concluded between banks in the market.

STANDARD EURO-CURRENCY RATES. Interest rates at which Euro-currency deposits are lent to first-rate names.

STEADY EXCHANGE. Stable exchange with a slight bias towards firmness.

243

STERLING AREA or SCHEDULED TERRITORIES. Countries of the Commonwealth (except Canada and the New Hebrides), Ireland, Burma, S. Africa, Iceland, Kuwait, Persian Gulf and Trucial Sheikhdoms, Jordan, Libya and W. Samoa.

SUPPORT POINTS. Exchange rates at which Central Banks of I.M.F. member countries must intervene to prevent the dollar rate from appreciating or depreciating beyond them.

SWAP. Purchase of spot exchanges against sale of forward exchanges or sale of spot exchanges against purchase of forward exchanges. In a broader sense, also purchase or sale of short forward exchanges against long forward exchanges.

SWAP ARRANGEMENT, RECIPROCAL. Bilateral agreement between Central Banks enabling each party to initiate swap transactions up to an agreed limit for the purpose of gaining temporary possession of the other party's currency.

SWAP AND DEPOSIT. Combination of swap transactions with the borrowing of the amount involved by one of the parties from the other, so that the former has the use of both currencies for the duration of the transaction.

SWAP MARGINS. See FORWARD MARGIN.

SWAP RATE. See FORWARD RATE.

SWITCH DOLLARS. See INVESTMENT DOLLARS.

TELEGRAPHIC TRANSFERS, or T.T. Foreign exchange transactions executed by instructions sent by cable.

TERMS OF TRADE. Relative price level of goods exported and imported by a country.

TIME ARBITRAGE. Transactions to take advantage of discrepancies between forward margins for various maturities.

TRADE BALANCE. The difference between the value of exports and that of imports. (See also BALANCE OF PAYMENTS.)

TWO-WAY QUOTATIONS. Simultaneous quotation of buying and selling rates (in the case of Euro-currency transactions borrowing and lending rates) implying the willingness of the bank in question to deal either way.

ULTIMO. Continental practice of timing transactions to mature on the last business day of the calendar month.

"UNCERTAIN" QUOTATION. See INDIRECT QUOTATION.

UNDER-VALUATION. Decline of the spot rate below purchasing power parities, so that goods of two countries entering into foreign trade are cheaper than in other countries. In relation to forward exchange it means that forward premiums are narrower, or forward discounts are wider, than the interest parities between the two centres concerned.

UNDOING COVER or HEDGE. Creating an open position through reversing an earlier transaction that had covered it.

VALEUR COMPENSÉ or "HERE AND THERE". Practice under which payment arising from a foreign exchange contract is to be made on the same day in the two centres concerned.

VALUE DATE. The date on which foreign exchanges bought and sold have to be delivered and the price payable for them in local currency has to be paid.

VALUE TODAY. Arrangement by which spot exchanges have to be delivered and paid for on the day of the transactions instead of two clear days after.

VALUE TOMORROW. Arrangement by which spot exchanges have to be delivered and paid for on the clear day following the transaction instead of two clear days after.

VERY LONG FORWARD EXCHANGES. A relative term which is usually applied to forward contracts maturing beyond twelve months.

VOSTRO ACCOUNTS. Current accounts of banks abroad with their correspondents abroad in the latter's currency. The *nostro* account of one bank is the *vostro* account of the other bank.

WEAK EXCHANGE. Depreciating exchange.

WEEK-END INFLUENCES. Technical influences affecting exchange rates on the eve of week-ends as a result of temporary re-arrangements of positions.

WINDOW-DRESSING OPERATIONS. Temporary repatriations of funds held abroad, for the purpose of increasing the proportion of liquid assets in balance sheets or in quarterly or monthly returns.

BIBLIOGRAPHY

A GREAT deal of material on recent developments in the sphere of foreign exchange is now easily obtainable in official publications, such as the Annual Reports of the International Monetary Fund, of the Bank for International Settlements and of the principal Central Banks. The *Quarterly Bulletin* of the Bank of England and the monthly *Federal Reserve Bulletin* of the Federal Reserve Board, the *Monthly Review* of the Federal Reserve Bank of New York, and the *Monthly Report* of the Deutsche Bundesbank — to mention only these — contain a wealth of relevant factual and statistical material and disclose much hitherto closely guarded information about official intervention in foreign exchanges. The *Annual Report on Exchange Restrictions*, issued by the I.M.F., deals with recent changes in exchange control measures of member countries. The I.M.F. also publishes much relevant material in a monthly survey of *International Financial Statistics*.

Owing to the intervening changes and the need for an essentially post-War approach I confined myself in the following list to post-War publications.

CRUMP, NORMAN, *The A.B.C. of the Foreign Exchanges.* 13th ed. London, 1963.

District Bank, *Digest of U.K. Exchange Regulations.* 15th ed. Manchester, 1963.

DUDLER, H.-J., *Diskont- und Terminkurs-Politik.* Frankfurt, 1961.

EINZIG, PAUL, *A Dynamic Theory of Forward Exchange.* 2nd ed. London, 1967.

— *The History of Foreign Exchange.* London, 1962.

— *The Euro-Dollar System.* 3rd ed. London, 1967.

— "What Bankers know, or ought to know, about Foreign Exchange Theory", *Banca Nazionale del Lavoro Quarterly Review*, September 1964.

— "The Support Points Mechanism", *Banca Nazionale del Lavoro Quarterly Review*, September 1965.

— *Foreign Dollar Loans in Europe.* London, 1965.

— *Foreign Exchange Crises.* London, 1968.

A Textbook on Foreign Exchange

EINZIG, PAUL, *Leads and Lags*. London, 1968.
— *The Euro-Bond Market*. London, 1969.
EVITT, H. E., *Manual of Foreign Exchanges*. 5th ed. London, 1962. 6th ed. by W. W. Syrett, 1967.
— *Exchange and Trade Control*. 4th ed. London, 1960.
GRANT, A. T. K., *The Machinery of Finance and the Management of Sterling*. London, 1967.
HIRSCH, FRED., *Money International*. London, 1967.
HOLGATE, H. C. F., *Exchange Arithmetic*. 4th ed. Revised by H. E. Evitt, London, 1961.
HOLMES, ALAN R., and SCHOTT, FRANCIS H., *Foreign Exchange Market*. Federal Reserve Bank of New York, 1965.
LIPFERT, HELMUT, *Devisenhandel*. Frankfurt, 1959.
MIKESELL, RAYMOND F., *Foreign Exchanges in the Post-War World*. Toronto, 1961.
Neue Zürcher Zeitung, Finanzzentern der Welt. Zürich, 1959.
RODGERS, DAVID, *Exchange Control*. 9th ed. Edinburgh, 1962.
SHEPHERD, SIDNEY A., *Foreign Exchange in Canada*. Toronto, 1961.
STEIN, JEROME L., *The Nature and Efficiency of the Foreign Exchange Market*. Princeton, 1962.
Swiss Bank Corporation, *Foreign Exchange*. Basle, 1964.
SYRETT, W. W., *Finance of Overseas Trade*. 4th ed. London, 1964.
WALTON, L. E., *Foreign Trade and Foreign Exchange*. 2nd ed. London, 1958.
YEAGER, LELAND B., *International Monetary Relations*. New York, 1966.

INDEX

Index